THE BODIES OF OTHERS

# TRIANGULATIONS
## Lesbian/Gay/Queer ▲ Theater/Drama/Performance

**Series Editors**
Jill Dolan, Princeton University
David Román, University of Southern California

**Associate Editors**
Ramón H. Rivera-Servera, Northwestern University
Sara Warner, Cornell University

# THE BODIES OF OTHERS

*Drag Dances and Their Afterlives*

Selby Wynn Schwartz

UNIVERSITY OF MICHIGAN PRESS

*Ann Arbor*

Published in the United States of America by
the University of Michigan Press

Printed on acid-free paper

First published April 2019

A CIP catalog record for this book is available from the British Library.

ISBN 978-0-472-07409-9 (hardcover : alk. paper)
ISBN 978-0-472-05409-1 (paper : alk. paper)
ISBN 978-0-472-12502-9 (ebook)

Cover: A photo of the five male ballerinas of Les Ballets Trockadero de Monte Carlo is framed by a black background. The title of the book appears at the top of the cover, and the author's name at the bottom. The ballerinas are gathered in a park, looking at the camera and posing on a green lawn. They are dressed in bright blue and orange tutus with gold details and wearing tiaras and tights. One ballerina holds his pointe shoes up by the ribbons.

For Tory Dobrin
*Non si sa mai*

# Acknowledgments

I have learned about dance mostly from dancers, and I am indebted to them, especially the ones who let me sit in on rehearsals, the ones who shared bottles of wine with me, and the ones who taught me to see from backstage. In particular, this book would not exist if it were not for the generosity of Tory Dobrin, who perhaps didn't know what he was getting into but said yes anyway.

I would first like to thank the artists in this book for sharing such beautiful and strange things with me. Conversations with Richard Move, Robert Carter, Paul Ghiselin, Raffaele Morra, Tory Dobrin, Monique Jenkinson, John Kelly, Chi Chi Valenti, Catherine Cabeen, Katy Pyle, Miguel Gutierrez, Jane Comfort, Takao Kawaguchi, and Trajal Harrell have only made things stranger and more beautiful. I am also grateful to many choreographers, dancers, and transformative thinkers/movers whose names are not in this book, but whose spirits were often hovering over the writing: Amie Dowling, Kat Galasso, Katie Faulkner, Erika Chong Shuch, Hope Mohr, Faye Driscoll, Sean Dorsey, Joe Goode, Melecio Estrella, Keith Hennessy, Eric Beauchesne, Christine Bonansea, Marina Fukushima, Alonzo King, Arturo Fernandez, Meredith Webster, David Harvey, Michael Montgomery, Keelan Whitmore, Caroline Rocher, Ricky Zayas, Kara Wilkes, Courtney Henry, Ben Wardell, Aesha Ash, Maurya Kerr, Laurel Keen, Tiersa Nureyev, Sebastian Alvarez, and Emile DeWeaver. And special thanks to Robert Rosenwasser, who was always telling me to write something beautiful about dances, but not *what*.

To the people who made me feel welcome in dance studies, even though I was often wearing the wrong shoes, thank you for the theory without chairs: Julian Carter, Megan Nicely, Claudia La Rocco, Kate Elswit, Michelle LaVigne, Chris Nagler, Kate Mattingly, the late Doran George, Ann Murphy, Joanna Dee Das, Kyle Bukhari, Phoebe Rumsey, Lisa Wymore, Carrie Gaiser Casey, Wayne Hazzard, Lynn Garafola, Jeff Friedman, Jill Nunes Jensen, Rachel Carrico, Anthea Kraut, Molly Rogers, and most of all Sima Belmar, for everything that is fiercely human in dance writing. Paul Scolieri and André Lepecki have been kind to me for years. My archival research has been supported by Elena Cervellati at Università di Bologna; by Tory Dobrin, Liz Harler, and Isabel Martinez Rivera of Les Ballet Trockadero; and by Yoko Shioya and Lara Mones at the Japan Society. At UC Berkeley, David Hult, the late Steven Botterill, and the late Joe Duggan might not have known that they helped create this book, but in fact they read the very first drafts. The somewhat magical process of transmutation from manuscript to book has been graciously guided by LeAnn Fields, Sarah Dougherty, and Marcia LaBrenz at University of Michigan Press, my thoughtful anonymous readers, and the editors of the Triangulations series. Initial drafts of various chapters benefited from the insights of Corinne Jola, Vicki Thoms, Lisa Manter, Judy Halebsky, Megan Nicely, Maxe Crandall, Sam England, and Mark Franko.

This book came into being over the course of a peripatetic decade; a little circle of people lived through years of this project with me. I could not have done it without my marvelous family—my mother, my father, and my sister Marna—who went from the dress-up trunk into countless other unforeseen adventures with love, generosity, and openness. And my heartfelt thanks to that little circle who held me in the many years of *non si sa mai*: Masha Gutkin, John Hill, Lucile Raux, Amanda Jo Goldstein, Tom McEnaney, Claudio Rosati, Siavash Karimzadegan, Sima Belmar, Carlo Bodini, Sabrina Sanità, Amie Dowling, Amanda Davidson, Stacey Cobalt, Frank Mauro, Marisa Mandile, Ida Dominijanni, Donna Hunter, Meg Formato, and Reggie Daniels. Maxe Crandall has been one long poem alive in my heart since the day we met. Jesús Rodríguez-Velasco taught me patiently how to write a book, and then how to end one.

And to Michael, who first showed me how to close the door to the writing room: thank you, *tesoro*, for the many voyages out.

An early version of chapter one was published as "Bad Language: Transpositions in Mark Morris' *Dido and Aeneas*" in *Dance Research Journal* 44.2 (Fall 2012): 71-94, and is reprinted with permission from Cambridge University Press. A version of chapter two appeared as "*Martha@Martha*: A Séance with Richard Move" in *Women and Performance: A Journal of Feminist Theory* 20.1 (2010): 61-87 (© Women & Performance Project Inc), and is reprinted by permission of Taylor & Francis Ltd, www.tandfonline. A section of chapter four was published in *Ballet-Dance Magazine* (May

2012) as "*The Dying Swan*: How Les Ballets Trockadero de Monte Carlo Solve the Problem of the Aging Ballerinas," and is reprinted with permission from CriticalDance. Brief excerpts from chapters two, four, and five appeared in the article "Dance History According to Drag," in *In Dance* (June 2007), and are reprinted with permission from Dancers' Group.

# Contents

Digital materials related to this title can be found on the
Fulcrum platform via the following citable URL:
http://doi.org/10.3998/mpub.8783686

THE BODIES OF OTHERS

# Introduction

## To Work the Body

To be real, in this sense, is to hold one's body and one's self open to
the possibilities of what one *cannot* know or anticipate in advance.
  —Gayle Salamon, *Assuming a Body*

I very much like the idea of the body as "a turbulent performative
occasion."
  —Judith Butler, *Dispossession: The Performative in the Political*

## Repertoires of Gender

In the opening scene of *S/He* (1995), choreographer Jane Comfort appears
in a wretchedly scraggly goatee with a blue baseball cap jammed backward on her head, lounging moodily on a couch. With a possessive sweep
of her arm, she takes up the space that separates her from dancer Andre
Shoals—in peep-toe heels, a black evening dress, and an upswept wig—
who clings to one arm of the sofa with demure resistance. As Comfort set-
tles her arm around Shoals's shoulders, crowding him nearly off the couch,
Shoals gives a prim little shudder and fends her off with an indignant wave
of his hand, rippling his fingers. When Shoals stalks off downstage, he
sways his hips so pointedly that you can almost hear the roll and snap of
each step. Facing the audience, he crosses his arms tightly in front of his
chest, wrapping the fingers of one hand around the other bicep, and then
mimes with irritated alacrity a phone call that should have been made and
obviously never was; he is moving his head loosely and laterally on his
neck, gesturing through the ends of his fingertips, swiveling his torso away
from his hips. But Comfort swaggers right up to him, undaunted, jerking her chin upward to emphasize that she is well within her rights here.

Figure 1. Jane Comfort and Andre Shoals in *S/He*. Photo by Arthur Elgort, courtesy of Arthur Elgort.

Her shoulders are thrown broadly open under an oversize gray hoodie. When she jabs a finger in the air, she leans her weight back on a heel, self-satisfied, centering the force and amplitude of her gestures. Each step she takes forward also dominates the space behind and sideways.

What is it that these dancers are doing, exactly, under the auspices of that ambivalent and very '90s mid-word slash? They are enacting a familiar scene of gendered movement, for one thing: the one in the slinky dress is the one who perches, pouts, and shrinks away; the one in slacks strides around the stage, grabbing and pursuing with arrogant impunity. It's a staging of masculinity and femininity in the stagiest possible terms. And because it's so theatrical and yet so familiar—so denaturalized—scenes from drag dances like this one are excellent places to begin exploring how bodies appear to make meaning when they move, how identities are read from bodies as they move, and what happens when there is something unsettled, like that "/" in *S/He*, which starts to pry apart some of the stuck-together bits of expressive movement and significance and identity. Dance, after all, is predicated on the capacity of the body to produce movement that we find meaningful, in the broadest sense of that word. And drag is a way of confounding the surface markers of gender identity—of resignifying its meaning by enveloping the body in the semblance of a different gender. Drag dances, then, take gender from the surface of the body (what the body looks like) and embed it in the kinetic and kinesthetic experience of dance (what the body can do).

Whether on the street or on the stage, bodies are wrapped in signifiers all the time: for much of the twentieth century, social theorists have been trying to get us to see the theatricality of "presenting" our bodily identities to others, in the words of Erving Goffman (1956). Instead of bodies whose identities are soldered right into them—as if everyone were naturally seared at birth with what they would be—or bodies whose identities somehow float free of any cultural constraints, we now have an idea that, as Judith Butler wrote in an essay on Simone de Beauvoir's *The Second Sex* (1949), each body offers something like "a *field of interpretative possibilities*" (1986, 45). As soon as we start watching bodies, in other words, we perceive a network of intersecting codes—not just gender, but also race, sexuality, age, ability, size, and class—that hover around those bodies, clinging to them and making their identities 'apparent.'[1] It is as if we believe that legible identities could be seen sitting on the surfaces of bodies, and this idea in itself—that people wear identities like layers of clothing draped over some private, visceral interiority—already hints at the potential of drag as a framework.

Butler called these identities "styles of the flesh" but was careful to note that they are "never fully self-styled"; rather, they are, very much like dancing, "a practice of improvisation within a scene of constraint" (1986, 48; 1999, 177; 2004a, 1). Based on visual judgments of these "styles," meanings are assigned, assumptions are solidified, and actions are undertaken. So it matters what a body's uprightness means, or the rigidity of certain joints, or an indolence in gesturing, or a body's proximity to other particular bodies. In this scene of *S/He*, the pair of legs possessing the uncontested right to loll apart on the couch gets gendered as masculine, and the hand that trills its little wave, breaking the line of the arm at the wrist and fanning out through the fingertips, gets gendered as feminine. This gendering of gesture determines who gets to demand and dominate, and who has to cross their legs and put up with it. More specifically, seeing these bodily codes through Kimberlé Crenshaw's concept of intersectionality (1991)—linking gender with race, class, and ability—helps to explain why audiences of *S/He* could well read Jane Comfort's role not just as generically 'male' but as that of a low-class straight white guy who has never learned to keep his hands to himself, while Andre Shoals is likely to be seen as a high-maintenance, long-suffering, strong black woman with attitude.

Moreover, any bend at the wrist reminds us how frequently gender and sexuality are read together from the ways that bodies move and hold themselves.[2] Often, queerness is attributed to bodies when gendered *style* (the affect a moving body seems to effuse) and gendered *morphology* (the anatomy this moving body appears to have) don't seem to 'match' each other. If an apparently male-bodied person moves in masculine ways, it is hardly worth noticing: that's just cisgender heteronormativity, humming along as usual. But as soon as any discrepancy is perceived between body, movement, and clothing, questions arise about the identities of those bodies and, consequently, about our ability to conclusively 'read' and categorize those bodies at all. As Juana María Rodríguez writes in *Sexual Futures, Queer Gestures, and Other Latina Longings*, "Queers make the sexual and social meanings that surround bodies and gestures appear" (2014, 136). Bodies that do not fit neatly into the equation *x matches y*, and bodies that are not clearly x *or* y, challenge the decidability of bodily identity itself. In the 1980s, when feminist—and especially lesbian feminist—theater scholars were looking at performances whose chromosomes were more WOW (Women's One World) than XY, they were interested in the political effects of restaging gender;[3] Marianne Goldberg, for example, asked in 1987 if it were possible to "assert gender nonsequiturs that might allow different meanings to arise" (1997, 313).[4] Following this logic, if Comfort's open-legged lounging might just as well be 'butch,' or if Shoals's exasperated flicks of the wrist could also be effeminately 'gay,' or if one or both of them might be transgender, then the effect of *S/He* is not only to restage and denaturalize existing gender codes. It is also to suggest how we might broaden the repertoire for embodying identity.

This means that drag dances like *S/He* aren't just about a mid-'90s fascination with subversion, gender play, parody, and unfortunate facial hair. One thing that *S/He* proposes, for example, is that the right to enact a certain kind of gender isn't determined by the anatomy or genetic material of Jane Comfort and Andre Shoals's bodies. They are dancing what their *costumes* imply, not moving from some morphological essence. Like all of us, they have been trained in normative gender codes, but they have also been trained as dancers. It is their job, literally, to have a broad repertoire of styles of moving, a strong kinesthetic sense, and the agency to improvise. In this framework, then, there is a creative space between the generalized structures that dance scholar Susan Foster called "choreographies of gender" (1998) and the individual bodies that are supposed to enact them.[5] Within this space, other reconfigurations of bodily signifiers can be explored, including material prosthesis: in another scene of *S/He*, a male dancer named Joseph Ritsch indicates his gender by patting his burgeoning, 'pregnant' belly. As Ritsch points to this unmistakable anatomical evidence of identity, he invokes gender codes that don't hold for his body. In other words, even though he is doing the choreography with his own body—those are his real lower-back muscles hoisting the weight of that prosthetic belly—the choreography was not made for his body, and therefore Ritsch must draw on a broader repertoire of gendered styles of moving in order to do the dance.

We could dismiss Ritch's drag gesture and costume as fake, parodic, theatrical, or inauthentic: *Anyway, a guy can't be pregnant. He's just a dancer doing a part, so what? It's a joke, not a gender revolution.* Or, instead, we could think about how Ritsch's expanded repertoire is linked to other gestures that matter, in the sense that philosopher Gayle Salamon summons gendered gestures to answer the urgent trans and queer call "to strive to create and transform the lived meanings" of "the materiality of our own bodies" (2010, 42). Within this political framework for queer gesture, Rodríguez emphasizes that the sentence "*The butch grabs his cock*" is a very real statement of gendered and sexual meaning in a scene of performance and spectatorship (2014, 123). It is a crucial moment of improvisation within the heteronormative choreography that might otherwise relentlessly restage itself in everyone's bedrooms. To declare that a guy cannot be pregnant or that a butch cannot have a cock is to make the same dangerous assumption: to arrogate to oneself the right to limit someone's identity to a perceived morphology, despite their lived experience of embodiment. If drag dances show up the grave wrongness of that assumption in viscerally theatrical ways, they are doing the work of queer and trans politics.

In the space between given choreography and individual embodiment, then, drag dances investigate *what can be done with the bodies we have.* Jane Comfort is a lithe white woman, and Andre Shoals is a muscular black man who stands six feet tall—without heels—and they are onstage in a country with a terrifying history of viewing and interpreting physical relations between the bodies of white women and black men. So what meanings are entailed when they dance together along the borders of gender and sexuality, given centuries of antiblack racism, misogyny, homophobia, and transphobia? What does it do when dances stage intersectional experiments in the domain of deliberate cultural spectacle, enacting simultaneous challenges to normative models of gender, race, and sexuality? For mid-'90s dance audiences in the cities where Jane Comfort and Company performed,[6] the shock or revelation of interracial duets (like Arthur Mitchell and Diana Adams's pas de deux in George Balanchine's 1957 ballet *Agon,* for New York City Ballet) would have been a distant history. But our historical imaginations are very much alive: they reverberate, they underpin and overlay the way that we continue to interpret bodies.[7] And drag dances act on these inherited imaginations, rattling the frames of interpretations that enclose bodies.

Specifically, drag dances work against tropes of the 'wrong' body—of not having the right to inhabit a space or claim a name because of the body you bring.[8] In terms of race in the United States, this touches some of the most troubled histories of boundaries separating bodies from rights. It is not an accident, for example, that old anxieties about racial passing are resurfacing in new hysterics about gender passing.[9] The question of whose body is allowed to claim whiteness or maleness, or kinship or intimacy, or simply the right to appear in a quotidian public sphere, is still being contested. If this were not the case, there would be no need for separate *#whileblack* hashtags for walking, driving, swimming, shopping, renting flats, studying in university libraries, delivering mail, unlocking your own front door, and so forth. No one would be massacred in clubs because they were queer, Latinx, and dancing together. It would be perfectly safe to walk down any street in this country, as a transwoman of color, in whatever outfit you felt like wearing that day. But clearly this is not yet true. Still, now, creatively, in as many public spheres as possible, it is necessary to militate against the phobic violence that tries to mark off some bodies as 'wrong,' thereby denying them access to acts, clothes, names, rights, spaces—and to life itself. And because, as Butler writes of bodily politics, "The claim of equality is not only spoken or written, but is made precisely when bodies appear together or, rather, when, through their action, they bring the space of appearance into being" (2011a), dance stages can be spaces where bodies gather together, declaring their right to appear in nonnormative ways, improvising within the choreography, and acting against historical constraints on embodiment.

## To Work the Body

Quite literally, drag dancing is not a superficial phenomenon. If drag is taken to be a subversion of gender codes that happens only on the surface, we lose the layeredness of embodiment itself, including the ways race works within and through gender and sexuality. Rather, it is *within* the strata of bodies moving in drag—in the intercalations of subjectivities, skin, costumes, movements, muscles, histories, perceptions, stances, voices, feelings, and touch—that a corporeal potential for politics is harbored. As queer-of-color scholars in particular have insisted, drag performance can do more than flip a binary or mock a gender stereotype. To see drag as a light romp through the daisy fields of camp,[10] or to accuse of it of being "casual and cynical mockery" (Frye 1983, 137), is to forget what live drag performance has meant to communities like the one Marlon M. Bailey describes in his ethnographies of Detroit ballroom culture (2011; 2013), where queer people of color "must draw upon their creative resources to survive homophobic and transphobic violence" (2011, 366). For similar reasons, when Madison Moore describes his childhood experience as "a black gay boy" dancing in Tina Turner drag, he attributes to one fierce fringe dress the potential to "crystallize a solid identity for people who might otherwise be overlooked" (2012a, 71, 84). The labor that ball participants undertake, Bailey notes, is both for themselves and for others, and it is not simply about increasing visibility. It is about the creative work—or *werk*[11]—that can be done, with the body you've got, to make a little space where queerness and nonnormative embodiment can be *real.*

From this perspective, getting stuck on the question of whether drag queens are "more gender-conservatives than gender-revolutionaries" is somewhat beside the point (Taylor and Rupp 2004, 115). Performance scholars like Bailey and Moore attest that seeing drag, doing drag, and being in communities where drag is valued are experiences of affirming diverse embodiments and sharing strategies of resistance to oppression. In drag, despite its inevitable tensions and complexities, they find glamour, humor, histories, kinship, recognition, and a creative repertoire of dressing and moving. Their experiences underscore Salamon's insistence that by now we should have learned from the lived experience of queer and trans people that "how we embody gender *is* how we theorize gender and to suggest otherwise is to misunderstand both theorization and embodiment" (2010, 71–72).[12] For that reason, as Bailey demonstrates, a "Butch Queen Up in Pumps" can be both a shirtless person wearing shorts with "fishnet backsides" *and* "a form of communal performance labor whereby the community creates, recognizes, and confers legitimacy on particular performances of gender and sexuality" (2013, 126, 45). Treating drag as frivolous simply because it involves the theatricality of dressed-up bodies comes from an old and pernicious bias. Dismissing the work produced by bodies as less intellectual, less critical, and inherently less *serious* than work done in writing underpins a historical marginalization of live performance[13]—as well as a prejudice against femininity as artifice. Writing about drag means acknowledging bodily performance as live theorizing in public: those fishnet backsides, fringe dresses, spirit gum, duct tape, pancake, packers, binders, and heels are supports for thinking.

The objection could be made that Bailey chronicles a very close-knit community, and Moore was dancing in a house with his cousins; does this mean that only drag done in semiprivate spaces offers this sanctuary? Scholarship on club drag suggests that drag stages, like invitation-only spaces, provide a place for experiments in embodiment—and these experiments result in work that sounds more like postcolonial critique than like an entertaining frolic in a fright wig. For example, José Muñoz has argued that what he calls the "terrorist drag" of Vaginal Creme Davis not only produces "newly imagined notions of the self and the social," but also, specifically because it is a *stage* performance, acts as "a survival strategy on a more symbolic register than that of everyday practice" (1997, 85, 83, 92). In a similar vein, Kareem Khubchandani, who doubles as self-described "subaltern drag queen" LaWhore Vagistan ("because I see the subcontinent as one big, beautiful Vag . . . istan," she explains), proposes that onstage club drag actually works as pedagogy, as well as a forceful reclaiming of queer-of-color histories and spaces (2015, 285–86). And it's not only drag queens: an article on Haitian American club drag king Dréd ends with a vision of how "queer utopias" could be pursued if only we would think about race, gender, and performativity more like Dréd does (Braziel 2005, 185). Across these varied venues, drag performances are asking us to see how interrelated constructions of gender, sexuality, and race can be done differently by a diverse array of bodies—thus providing a crucial sense of hope for *undoing* what is restrictive and violent about bodily normativity.[14]

"To 'work the body'" in drag, Bailey explains, is a strategy that directly confronts the dangerous daily experience of having your body "read as a text" (2011, 366, 367). This form of queer bodily labor starts to reconfigure the language of realness—and of fauxness. For example, by the end of this scene in *S/He*, Jane Comfort has unbound her breasts, fluffed her auburn hair, daubed her lipstick, and gotten into a long flame-red gown. Now she perches on the couch, crossing her legs just above the knee, and trails one pale arm languidly along its back. Andre Shoals finishes donning his suspenders and crisp white shirt, and then, seated side by side, they both slowly cross their hands behind their heads and lean back, comfortably stretching their legs wide apart, like men who've done a hard day's work together. You might say that these two dancers are now no longer in drag—but they are still onstage, performing recognizable gender codes marked by race and class. They are still, in fact, deliberately staging identities for their bodies, calling upon audiences to interpret their expressive gestures and postures in relation to their clothing and morphologies.

Directly facing their spectators, Comfort and Shoals blur the line between the safe space of roles on a dance stage—in which they are just 'in character' or 'in costume'—and the offstage world in which their bodies also move. So are these final costumes and gestures *also* drag? Or are they even more queer, because you can't tell that they're in drag? Or is Andre Shoals not in drag anymore, because he now looks like a man moving in masculine ways, while Jane Comfort, stretching her legs out with that nonchalant ease, is instead performing some kind of trans-occupation of gendered space? Is Andre Shoals doing less work because male privilege gives him an automatic and unmarked access to masculinity, or does he have to do *more* work, because black masculinity doesn't confer that same privilege? Is Jane Comfort really that femme, or is she just playing the *role* of a highly feminine woman who would conversely play a man playing a drag queen? These kinds of questions demonstrate the conjoined problems of limiting the definition of drag, assuming that realness has some biological basis, and valuing virtuosic legibility over kinesthetic experience.

The dance stage is a place where the gestures, postures, movements, physical qualities, and bodily affects we are constantly interpreting in our quotidian cultural lives are deliberately intensified and aestheticized: concert dance is culturally metonymic.[15] Just as the impact of Vaginal Creme Davis's performance wasn't determined by the square footage of Don Hill's bar in downtown Manhattan or the number of audience members who could be crammed into its Friday night Squeezebox! party, it's not the size of your Marley that limits what you can do with dance.[16] So why shouldn't dance—a theatrical art that is done by bodies and for bodies, that is housed in bodies and comes coursing out through bodies, and that makes its meaning primarily through the different qualities and styles of bodies—be one model for inclusive corporeal politics? Perhaps it is for this reason that Muñoz urges us to value not only the political potential of the drag performances we might attend, but also queer dance itself as an experience of performing identities otherwise. If drag can be tactical, and if queer dance, according to Muñoz, "rematerializes" (2001, 441) possibilities that would be shut out by categorical divisions between bodies, identities, and claims of realness, then drag dances can 'rechoreograph' a set of claims about realness and relationality between bodies.[17]

The work of this rematerializing, like the work of dancers who take class together and rehearse as a company, depends upon individual bodily discipline as well as collective labor. And rematerializing is a generally sweaty and time-consuming process. For this reason, two years before the premiere of *S/He*, when Jane Comfort became interested in drag, she went to a workshop run by Diane Torr, a modern dancer whose explorations of gender as a set of physical styles had led her to drag-kinging and then to teaching other women how to be a "Man for a Day." King culture was still young then: when Torr first began her workshops in 1990, collaborating with transman Johnny Science, the term "drag king" was "so unfamiliar that people sometimes misheard us, thinking we'd said we were conducting 'dry cleaning workshops,'" she recalls (Torr and Bottoms 2010, 98–99).[18] Torr and Science showed Jane Comfort how to craft her body, in movement and in stillness, until she could enact the identity of her drag king persona, a "weeny little guy" named Jack Daniels (Zimmer 1994).

As a dancer, Diane Torr taught gender as a kind of choreography that required rehearsal, not as an expression of biology or anatomy: "Gradually, through repetition, the gestures become more real; they appear 'natural,'" she explained (Torr and Bottoms 2010, 109). And as a dancer and choreographer, Jane Comfort got the new work into her body just as she would with any dance piece, picking it up phrase by phrase, rehearsing the unfamiliar movement vocabulary: the *"guy* way" to take up a subway seat ("legs-apart, crotch-presenting," as dance critic Deborah Jowitt put it), the shouldery swagger, the hetero-consumerist roving eye, the gimme-that grabbiness (2010, 241). As it turns out, the idea that gender and sexuality can be practiced as an arbitrary set of gestures is not that surprising for people who spend their professional lives learning artificially constructed, complex series of gestures and performing them under blazing lights for critical audiences.

'Movement vocabulary' implies that gestures are like words, and it is, after all, a kind of declaration to appropriate codes that have not been designated for your body. There is a natural line of inquiry into whether 'body language' means that movement is somehow linguistic: do dances speak?[19] But although bodies are constantly swaddled in signifiers, they are not metaphors. Internally, the proprioceptive feeling of being in a body and the kinesthetic sense of moving your body—or of being moved by something within your body—are quite different from language, with all of its abstractions and insistence on fixed definitions. It is true that interesting questions arise from framing bodily performance and performativity in linguistic terms, especially inquiries into 'infelicitous' performances and gestures as performative utterances; the first chapter of this book looks at one dance that identifies its gestures with words. But I would argue that drag dances are doing more than just standing in for language; they are not lip-synching or, as dancers might say, 'mickey-mousing' to speech-act theory. Bodily theorizing happens in its own material, kinesthetic, and phenomenological ways, departing from the premise that bodies have depth and weight, techniques and histories, tenacity and mutability. Dancing bodies demonstrate how certain kinds of agency, although inextricable from structures of vulnerability and exclusion, work out interdependencies that support them. In *Precarious Life* (2004b) Butler calls this arrangement "livable lives," but you could also call it the possibility of dancing 'full-out' in the body you have.

Diane Torr's workshop lasted only one day—culminating in a night at Billy's Topless, where the amateur kings tried out their new routines amid the regular patrons—but restyling the body requires ongoing practice and discipline, so Jane Comfort turned to an expert in her own company: Andre Shoals, who also performed drag as Afrodite. In the studio, Comfort took her cues on masculine codes for *S/He* from Shoals, because his experience of performing femininity had heightened his kinesthetic awareness of the range of gender affects.[20] On the one hand, Comfort found Afrodite to be "so perfect as a woman" that Shoals's drag gave her a critical distance from her own femininity; on the other, Shoals could also direct her in rehearsing *S/He*'s boxing-derived, masculine phrases (Zimmer 1994). And why shouldn't the person with the most practice in gender restyling get to teach the "bio" person both parts? Furthermore, why shouldn't the dancer make work on the choreographer every once in a while, affirming the knowledge that dancers' bodies hold, instead of assuming that all creative visions arise in the brain of the choreographer and are thereafter bestowed on the selected dancers who most faithfully carry on the lineage of genius? In apprenticing herself to a Scottish female dancer-turned-DIY-drag-king, a white transman whose expertise extended from makeup to phalloplasty (and who would later identify exclusively as a gay man), and a gay black man who both danced professionally with the Bill T. Jones/Arnie Zane Company and performed frequently as a drag queen, Jane Comfort shows why drag dance illuminates how gender and sexual identities are adopted, instilled, ingrained, experienced, articulated, altered, reiterated, and transmitted on kinesthetic and kinetic levels. This practice is not about erasing difference: Jane Comfort was never going to virtuosically achieve either a 'perfect' imitation of masculinity or a 'pure' reception of the bodily knowledge transmitted to her. What she was doing instead was *werking*.

Because they are queer forms, drag dances do not require compliance with bodily normativity in the way that dance forms like traditional ballet would. But they do rely upon dancers' willingness to alter the bodies they have, to practice other modes of moving, and to present themselves in public as somehow both 'real' and 'not really.' Jane Ward, who writes on feminist, queer, and trans issues, describes acts of "gender labor" that involve "giving gender to others" as well as self-fashioning (2010, 237). Clearly, drag dancers are working hard while they learn the choreography and as they shape it to their own bodies through rehearsal; the case of Jane Comfort demonstrates why this work happens in collective and queer ways. But in conceiving of performances of *S/He* and other drag dances as public acts of gender labor that are also *for others*, we can begin to think of the ways in which repertoires of gender are shared, refused, transferred, recognized, diverted, and adapted between performers and audiences. Drag dances are reflective and reflexive practices, in the sense that David Román proposes in *Performance in America*: "the performing arts might be understood as embodied theories that help audiences restructure, or at the very least, reimagine their social selves" (2005, 4). In changing the repertoire of gender, drag dancers gain kinesthetic knowledge: Comfort was astonished to find that Jack Daniels could spend a whole night in a club without once being harassed, as long as he kept his arms folded impassively and leaned up against the wall (Zimmer 1994). Then, in transmitting that knowledge to audiences, these dancers demonstrate how we might reimagine embodiment ourselves.

## Action Histories

On most days, dancers in concert dance companies like Jane Comfort's put on a motley array of baggy and stretchy things, go into a studio somewhere with other dancers, and take class. This gives them the chance to warm up, stretch their muscles safely, build strength and agility, feel out their bodies' particularities, and practice movements they already know, often in new combinations that have been devised by a teacher or director to challenge them. Judith Jamison, a renowned dancer and choreographer with the Alvin Ailey American Dance Theater, who later became the company's artistic director, advises dancers to take "class, every day, modern class, ballet class, whatever kind of class you can take, lie down on the floor class. To keep the body tuned" (n.d.). In other words, the exact type of class isn't important (Ailey dancers start with a ballet barre, for the record), but the ongoing discipline, the repetition and the practice, the warming and the opening: these are essential.

When drag dancers take class, they're doing all of the things that non-drag dancers do, but with an extra layer. This is because, while their bodies are their own, these dancers are also preparing to embody someone else as they cross the line that is normatively drawn between genders. For this reason, drag dancers tend to characterize their long-term practices not only as stretching and strengthening but also as an attention to opening, making space, listening, welcoming, even channeling—forms of tuning, as Jamison says, but more specifically, of attuning your body to other bodies that are not there with you and that are not yours. This might sound like a sweet, fuzzy kind of mindfulness, but it is actually a determined claiming of kinship within and through difference. For example, Catherine Cabeen, a former dancer with the Bill T. Jones/Arnie Zane Dance Company (and the Martha Graham Dance Company), made a drag piece called *Into the Void* (2011), in which she danced as the male painter Yves Klein. Reflecting on how it was that she had somehow come to be a choreographer of drag dances, Cabeen explained that she thought of her body as holding its own "action history," a kind of imaginative kinesthetic capacity that had been enriched by the experience of inheriting roles that were supposed to be 'wrong' for her body (2011). Her ability to envision herself dancing as Yves Klein, she thought, had grown out of "the honor of being cast in roles that Bill T. Jones created for himself, initiating interesting conversations about what it meant for a white woman to take on the testosterone-driven roles originated and performed by a black man in the 1980's." In making her body a haven for the roles she was inheriting, Cabeen necessarily confronted the difference of bodily identities—notably, she mentions not only race, gender, and gendered affect, but also the historical context for masculinities—but these differences enhanced her kinetic repertoire to the point that they began to generate new dances.

For dancers and choreographers like Cabeen, drag dance can be a form of embodied historiography, an "action history" that allows for kinships beyond those sanctioned by similarity. That is why in this book drag dance is simultaneously about self-performance and about performing someone else. At its most extreme, this claim is conceived as mystically, inexorably "becoming as one" with another, as Japanese butoh dancer Kazuo Ohno described the process of creating his 1977 piece *Admiring La Argentina* (Ohno and Ohno 2004, 116). In conceiving of drag dance as a way to commune with his beloved La Argentina, a Spanish flamenco and gypsy dancer who had been dead for many years, Ohno creates a space in his body, preparing it for an "action history" radically different from his own. This unexpected understanding of drag as embodied coexistence derives in part from Ohno's belief that his own flesh is a kind of costume—in other words, that the experience of being wrapped in your own body is drag. Multiple layers of identity are simultaneously present, Ohno suggests, as the drag dancer's body generously makes space at its center for lost dances, collective memories, and haunting images. Over and over, entering the studio and taking the stage, there is this gesture of opening, this willingness to be inhabited again.

And so drag dances are based on a special practice of repetition, of continually moving the singularity and certainty of selfhood off to one side. In order to do these kinds of dances, you must not only make space where the self usually presides in its wholeness and unity, but also suspend the idea of the body as 'bio' as it gets used in phrases like "bio queen" or "biologically male" and, more generally, in terms of "biological life" as the basis for distinguishing what is real and present from what must be dead or forgotten. 'Bio' would limit bodies to a state proclaimed when they were born, and we have already learned from trans studies that this is unhelpful at best; so the practice of drag dance does not depend on the exact type of 'biological' body that you have but rather on the commitment you make to harboring others within you. Some of these others are other genders, and some are other races, ages, techniques, and morphologies—and many of the others are no longer alive, creating a bodily practice of moving from and with the afterlives of other dancers. When dance critic Deborah Jowitt praised drag ballet company Les Ballets Trockadero de Monte Carlo, for example, it was not only for the impressive quantity of their fouettés but also for their embodied feats of simultaneous multiplicity: "The delights of watching them perform have to do with layered transformations" (2006). Superficially, Jowitt's comment could be taken to mean that the Trocks are serious professional ballerinas with prodigious chest hair (and many of them are), but it also hints at the Trockadero's willing imbrication of histories of mortality, of the aging *étoiles* of the Ballets Russes and of artists lost to the AIDS epidemic. Instead of policing the boundaries of the body, insisting on its singularity and coherence, artists like Ohno and the Trockadero dancers actively invite other bodies—foreign bodies, estranged bodies, bodies that cross not only the borders of gender and race but often also those of life itself—to dance within them. Moving in these layered transformations, drag dancers can perform both 'otherwise' and "as one." Their dances are embodied histories of past dances and dancers, afterlives that are not archived but channeled.

It is for this reason that instead of prizing feats of virtuosic performance—the demonstrably perfected replication of some original form—above all else, drag dances emphasize the discipline, willingness, and relationality it takes to prepare the body to be inhabited. Like other queer modes of opening the body, this process often entails the risk of involvement with others who cannot be fully known in advance of the act, whose edges and effects are not entirely discerned or contained.[21] Unsurprisingly, then, these drag practices also engage with queer understandings of mortality, care, kinship, and nonlineal temporalities. This acceptance of multiple action histories, this practice of layering your own body with striations of muscle memory that belong to other bodies, is not as simple as subversion. Its valence as movement is not the flip or the reveal,[22] but rather an opening and a broadening. Ultimately, drag dancing entails a reconfiguration of what is held at the center of a body: what makes a body real, unified, identifiable, indexable, itself? And what would happen if we recentered our definitions of what bodies can do by taking embodied theorizing seriously—by acknowledging that performances are ways of thinking, and by listening to the verbal and corporeal articulations of artists who spend their whole lives working with moving bodies? By paying attention to drag dances in particular, we get to see bodies in the act of rethinking their boundaries.

When Butler's *Gender Trouble* (1990) was taken by many to champion the power of drag to dismantle gender normativity, she took pains in *Bodies That Matter* to "underscore that there is no necessary relation between drag and subversion" (1993a, 125). But, in *Undoing Gender* she does allow that

> when one performance of gender is considered real and another false . . . then we can conclude that a certain ontology of gender is conditioning these judgments. . . .
>
> And what drag can point out is that (1) this set of ontological presuppositions is at work, and (2) that it is open to rearticulation. (2004a, 214)

This formulation of "rearticulation" seems to put drag's power back into the realm of language, as if drag should *say* something different about gender and thereby change its terms. But this is a problem only if we understand "articulation" in a very narrow way, as strictly linguistic. Dancers understand that articulation is also bodily: it is just as much a way of bending certain joints, thereby extending a range of motion, as it is about language. Rearticulating gender and sexuality allows us to experiment with the limits of normativity through a practice of movement. And if drag and other queer forms of dance have some chance of improving flexibility and alignment in our cultural norms, it will happen through kinesthetic discipline; they will work the joint differently, and open the body.

*Fictional Archiving*

In 2015, the New York–based choreographer Trajal Harrell was being interviewed in a glossy art magazine about his recent work, which involves, among other things, the legacy of Judson Church postmodernism, the cofounders of butoh, the uptown vogue scene, the revered *nouvelle danse* figure Dominque Bagouet, dances made for museums, and all-night chance meetings in bars (Howe 2015). A point was made about "artists in New York . . . appropriating the minority vogueing community in their work," and Harrell, who might have established his credentials by remarking that he is African American and attended his first ball in 1999 (Moore 2014, 7), instead responded that not only had he deliberately not cast trained voguers, but he also hadn't cast African American dancers, or, for that matter, any American dancers at all (Howe 2015, 77–78). Why not? "If there had been five African American dancers, it would be so easy to label that a kind of strategic representation," Harrell explained (Howe 78). And although his choreography explicitly and continually engages dance histories—the series of dances in question was titled *Twenty Looks or Paris Is Burning at the Judson Church* (2009–2013), after which he created *The Ghost of Montpellier Meets the Samurai* (2015)—Harrell categorically refuses historiography based on representation. Instead, he proposes the principle of "fictional archiving," a practice of hosting disparate historical moments and subjectivities in the body through dance.

Harrell doesn't characterize his oeuvre as drag dancing, but much of his choreography is quite literally about incorporating histories different from his own. Channeling past dances instead of 'reenacting' them, his work regularly crosses the boundaries that are supposed to distinguish gender, race, age, technique, nationality, historical context, and the singularity of names. In other words, Harrell and his dancers are doing the work of opening the body through costume, being moved by the resurgences of historical figures that both are and are not 'themselves'—and this is exactly the work that drag dancers do. Moreover, Harrell is theorizing this practice as a kind of *realness*: claiming the truth-value of archival historicity for the shifting live repertoire of performance.[23] "This realness turns out to reveal the artificiality being performed at the root of all social identities," Harrell explains in his artist statement for New York Live Arts. When Harrell and his dancers come out onstage, "oscillating between voguing's 'realness' and early postmodernism's 'authenticity,'" wearing weird bathrobes and knotted scarves and scanty underwear, looking nothing like Dominque Bagouet or Tatsumi Hijikata or anyone from the Judson Church years, they dance their right to remember and inherit from these histories. They do the labor of dance historiography in the bodies they have.

Linking this concept of "fictional archiving" to philosopher Henri Bergson's vision of a past that constantly attends our present (and to Gilles Deleuze's reinterpretation of this idea in his book *Bergsonism*), performance studies scholar Tavia Nyong'o calls Harrell "an afrofabulist: an artist who summons shards from the virtual past and ritualistically reintroduces them into the present" (n.d., 1). As an archive, a drag dancer's body often connects to a ghostly inheritance that would otherwise be lost, embedding an "afterlife" into its own flesh—a metaphor that is almost spookily consistent for scholars writing on drag dance.[24] In emphasizing the permeability and multiplicity of the body, drag dance approaches historiography not as a project of 'accurate representation' but rather as a kinesthetic practice of memory and reanimation. The dance being performed may not look anything like the dance it draws upon, and the body doing the dancing may bear little resemblance to the body it is channeling, but the claims to realness that drag dances make do not rest upon resemblance, representation, similarity, or verisimilitude. In Deleuze's terms, drag dances operate through repetition, a practice that incorporates difference. What, then, is produced by these repetitions with differences, these stagings of live pastness, these warm homes for wandering histories?

By incarnating past dances and dancers, even though their bodies are often classified as 'wrong' for those roles, these dancers help us to reimagine what is possible for both bodily styles and historical narratives. For example, it is regularly noted in reviews of drag artist Richard Move that he is 'too tall' to embody Martha Graham. This charge of bodily wrongness is countered by performance theorist André Lepecki, who sees Move's drag as a Deleuzian displacement of the past that has metamorphic potential in the present: it is a form of repetition, not representation or resemblance. In fact, Lepecki characterizes Move's performances as "affective historiography," a way of doing history by being touched and being moved (2010, 43). So it is perhaps surprising that Lepecki has a story about what *was* wrong with Move's body when he channeled Graham. The problem, Lepecki relates, was not that he was too tall, or too male, or not divinely pelvic enough to embody Martha; the real issue was pointed out by former Graham dancer Bertram Ross, who told Move, "You need to change your lipstick. Martha would use a much darker tone." This is not to say that gender presentation is a question of individual agency, selective alterations, and getting the lipstick right. But it is to value what *can* be done with the bodies we have over what cannot be changed about bodies, which can always be deemed as evidence of what is 'wrong' or 'not really' or 'not a real—'.[25]

In the early days of his Martha performances, Richard Move actually received cease and desist orders. People doing these drag dances are generally not authorized to inherit: the patrimony is not supposed to be theirs. When choreographers Bill T. Jones and Arnie Zane took up elements of George Balanchine's *Serenade* (1934) in their 1985 dance *How to Walk an Elephant*, created for the Alvin Ailey American Dance Theater, they cast men in all the women's parts, prompting Anna Kisselgoff, the venerable *New York Times* dance critic, to write peevishly that they had thereby ruined *Serenade*'s "most celebrated and beautiful moments" and disrespected the choreographer whose credo, "ballet is woman," ought to govern the rest of the century of American ballet in uncontested glory (Boyce et al. 1988, 83).[26] Unsurprisingly, Jones saw his own work not as despoiling the history of ballet but rather, he explained, as a productive way of "tackling our problem of gender identification and its boundaries" through dance (95). Then he added, "And, hopefully, if you agree with me, you will reexamine what led Balanchine to do what he did in the first place," highlighting an important facet of the politics of drag dance. It wasn't that without Jones and Zane to channel *Serenade*, Balanchine's legacy would be lost—far from it. The whole edifice of the Balanchine Foundation exists to buttress the choreography against impurities, disappearances, and infidelities. What Jones was pointing out, and what the drag of *How to Walk an Elephant* was doing, was to reveal the otherwise invisible histories that undergird those "beautiful moments"—to see the strains of gender, race, and sexuality in dance history, especially when they have not been seen, and even more especially when their invisibility is the condition upon which a legacy rests. In channeling a past, drag dances bring a history into a present moment, embodying it again, but differently. But they also ask us to look back again at that history, to consider why it was made that way, what it presumed and what it excluded.

So if the right of drag dances to inherit is not sanctioned, what is the basis for this claim of "archiving" or incorporating? It consists in a fierce generosity, a persistent and implacable caring for histories that might otherwise be lost, flattened out, written over. It really is a kind of love. And this stubborn, creative, nostalgic love, this queer and tender attachment, drives the practice of inviting others to enter your body and dwell there,

Figure 2. Robert Carter (Olga Supphozova) and other Trockadero dancers backstage. Photo by Zoran Jelenic (zoranjelenic.com), courtesy of Les Ballets Trockadero de Monte Carlo.

to permit them to attach like colonies of barnacles to your own private interiority, to feel their dispositions and styles taking shape within your own. Drag dance often meets its subjects by picking them up when the straight dance world won't touch them: Les Ballets Trockadero de Monte Carlo embrace the rouged-up, grande-dame style of ballet that went out with Maya Plisetskaya; performance artist and faux queen Monique Jenkinson brings amplified campiness to modern dance (her artist statement reads, "Yvonne Rainer said 'no to spectacle' so that I could say yes to sequins"). These drag dancers signify the difference of their bodies from the gender roles they are performing and at the same time insist on the absolute 'rightness' of their bodies to inherit, hold, and perform the afterlives of the dances and figures they cannot help but feel as real and present. When drag dancers open themselves corporeally in this way, they forge a strange and generous kinship; their relations to the past are necessarily queer, nonlineal, wrought from discipline rather than descent, marked by mourning for what has been lost, and given over to a temporality that embeds the past in the present.

In emphasizing the permeability and multiplicity of the body, then, drag dances approach historiography not as a project of 'accurate representation' but rather as a kinesthetic practice of collective politics. Like Butler's idea of "plural performativity," this means using your articulate body to make statements on public stages, in ghostly conjunction with those whose bodies seem most precarious and most different from your own (Butler and Athanasiou 2013, 175). In order to do this, you must first be willing to be "dispossessed" of an absolute and sovereign sense of selfhood, so that there is space inside you for others to dwell. And this willingness is not passive: it takes discipline, like all dancing does, and a radical kind of generosity. In their eerie, mystical sense of being inhabited—of being both dispossessed and multiply possessed—drag dancers make their bodies into archives that contest the separation between living and dead, between pasts and presents, between what deserves to be forgotten and what might be remembered, between the 'wrong' bodies and the 'right' ones for dancing. In this way they propose not only a genealogy of dance that runs in layered transformations rather than straight lines, but also a different way of embodying the archive: dancing with the others inside of you.

## Four Decades of Dances

This book is not a comprehensive history of drag dances.[27] It is a close reading of five bodies of work in drag dance created over the last forty years or so, performed on established US proscenium or black-box stages, and presented as dance for paying audiences. In the course of those roughly forty years of American concert dance, cultural norms around gender and sexuality have been shifting dramatically—even theatrically. In 1974, when Les Ballets Trockadero de Monte Carlo first performed in Manhattan, urban drag theater was emerging from a history of female impersonators, travesty roles, and floor shows into a volatile, uneven moment of gay liberation. The "pansy craze" was over and the psychedelic pandemic of the Cockettes was raging. STAR (Street Transvestite Action Revolutionaries) had been founded by Sylvia Rivera and Marsha P. Johnson in 1970; Esther Newton had published *Mother Camp* in 1972. Amid the cross-currents of queer culture, both Tatsumi Hijikata and Lindsay Kemp were reading Jean Genet, while both Kazuo Ohno and Charles Ludlam admired Norma Desmond in *Sunset Boulevard*. In the 1980s—as AIDS began to decimate the queer communities so central to dance, theater, drag, and nightlife—politics and performance became more urgently inseparable. Mark Morris's *Dido and Aeneas* was made as the '80s turned into the '90s, in an era of queer landmarks including Judith Butler's *Bodies That Matter* (1993), Jennie Livingston's *Paris Is Burning* (1990), and the Five Lesbian Brothers' first official production, *Voyage to Lesbos* (1990), at the WOW Café. In 1996 Richard Move began channeling Martha Graham; these were the years of Vaginal Creme Davis founding a band called Black Fag, of Carmelita Tropicana starring in a film subtitled "Your Kunst Is Your Waffen," of Kiki and Herb at Gay Shame. But the strident calls for subversion came alongside laments (like Dido's) for the precarity of bodies (like Venus Xtravaganza's) lost to pervasive misogyny, racism, homophobia, femmephobia, and transphobia.

In the last twenty years, drag has expanded its borders and become more self-reflective; artists and theorists are intertwined, intersectionality is recentering perspectives, and enriched vocabularies of gender and sexuality mean rethinking the terms of drag. The late '90s brought Del LaGrace Volcano and Jack Halberstam's *The Drag King Book* (1999), José Muñoz's *Disidentifications* (1999), and Monique Jenkinson's victory in the Miss Trannyshack Pageant (1998), a first for a faux queen. Postmillennial drag has been a dazzling proliferation of the possibilities of earlier histories, exploring what might be done with "undoing gender" (as Butler titled her 2004 book). Even as drag's pop visibility has increased with the rise of *Hedwig and the Angry Inch*, *RuPaul's Drag Race*, and other mainstream media representations, artists like Kalup Linzy and Ryan Trecartin are working to unsettle the digital spheres of drag, encroaching on the territories of art museums and viral video. Trans artists like boychild and Charlene carry on the spectacular live club drag tradition of the Pyramid Club, Mother, and Squeezebox!, while questioning the category of 'drag' itself.

The artists in this book theorize their practices eloquently; I take at least half of my understanding of drag dance from the people who create and perform it. For this reason, I have shaped my readings of dances around concepts like "realness," as it is theorized by Trajal Harrell and Monique Jenkinson, drawing on a shared vocabulary of queer labor (*werk* or *werq*) related to Diane Torr's and Jane Comfort's accounts of "rehearsing" gendered gestures. Central to the realness of drag dance is an imaginative, inclusive model of historiography that Trajal Harrell often calls "fictional archiving" and Katy Pyle describes as the "heart-opening practice" of gathering lost queer and activist histories into new dances (2016). In particular, from Kazuo Ohno's insistence that the impetus of dance is a dense population by the dead, and from Richard Move's characterization of haunting and channeling as fundamental to drag, I have come to see embodiment across gender as inextricable from the movement of bodies across other slashes: past/present, live/dead, real/fictional. This emphasis on drag as an afterlife of dances helped me to understand the fierce, tender nostalgia that the Trockadero evince for ballet history and its most melodramatic ballerinas, which in turn led me to see drag dance as mounting a queer challenge to dance historiography as a genealogy of rightful inheritance. The queer kinship that drag dancers were extending to past bodies, in other words, was also a way of thinking about how we remember dances and dancers—and of resisting the delineations that would keep people's bodies from the names they choose, the other bodies they love or desire, and the histories they claim.

When I began this project, roughly ten years ago, I started with the conviction that drag was parody (which is where many people start with drag, undoubtedly to the ongoing dismay of Judith Butler), gender was an inscription, and dance was an embodied speech-act. In the end, this became a book about generosity, ghostliness, kinship, mourning, histories, queer politics, and how we might get to realness. I had thought that I was writing about the brave agency of drag dancers who throw off the restrictions of gender norms on the body, but I hadn't known that I was writing about how drag dances invite other bodies in, how our corporealities are interdependent, how the temporality of dances is not exactly ephemeral but rather striated, like muscles are, with bundled strands of the past. Accordingly, this book is structured so that the first chapter begins with a dance that proclaims itself to be a speech-act—Mark Morris's *Dido and Aeneas* (1989)—and ends with a dance by Monique Jenkinson/Fauxnique that reexamines fauxness, realness, and collective 'autobiochoreography.' Beginning with what happens when gender is inscribed on bodies, the chapters move through a series of strategies for 'undoing': channeling another body, mystically dancing "as one," expanding beyond the solo to the collective, and finally returning to the question of 'faux' and 'real' drag from a feminist perspective. By concluding with an inquiry into what drag dances might show us about reworking normative 'bio' forms, this book also opens questions about the potential for a shared queer and trans politics of embodiment. Each chapter also includes a little ghost of its own—at least one other artist who speaks to the work, elucidating a theme that haunts or reanimates it. For example, the chapter on Kazuo Ohno is not only about Ohno's theory of dancing La Argentina "as one," but also about Trajal Harrell's refraction of this genealogy as he is "voguing Ohno" (2015). In this way, I am trying to honor the openness and intercalations, the haunting and queer kinship, that I have learned from the artists themselves.

The archive of this book is thus constrained in some ways and open in others: it reflects the dynamics that have historically determined who could pay for studio space, find supportive presenters, convince dancers to take the risk of appearing in gender-nonconforming roles, fill houses, garner reviews, receive grants, and book tours. In 1989, for example, the funding that white, gay choreographer Mark Morris received from the Belgian government allowed him to make *Dido and Aeneas*, an evening-length dance set to live opera. But if African American "drag superstar" (Muñoz 1997, 82) and genderqueer club icon Dr. Vaginal Creme Davis had wanted to set an elaborate operatic performance to live music at that time, would she have been granted access to that kind of support?[28] While there are many venues for drag performance in the United States that are adamant about their status as havens for trans and queer-of-color communities, there have historically been very few commercial dance theaters that present drag dances *as concert dance*. Thus, while this archive of forty years of drag dances skews white, cisgender, male, and gay, it also indicates where stages are being made open to more bodies, and when dancers with nonnormative bodies are making creative and political uses of drag. In 1974 the fledging Les Ballets Trockadero company practiced a remarkably inclusive politics of casting for ballet, but they only did shows at midnight, because all of their dancers necessarily had other jobs. In 2014, L. N. Hafezi reported firsthand that Katy Pyle's Ballez company, which features mainly lesbian and trans performers, "has an unusually large cast of minoritarian bodies in downtown dance" *and* "really excellent, fair labor practices"; it helps that Ballez is presented at places like Danspace Project at St. Mark's Church and BAX/Brooklyn Arts Exchange (and that Pyle has raised thousands of dollars on Kickstarter to pay dancers' wages). The work of prying apart terms like "*S/He*" continues, in other words, but a more diverse array of people is getting the chance to do that work on concert dance stages. This book is about what they have been doing for the last four decades, and the work that artists continue to do, as Harrell says, to "collectively reimagine the impossibilities of history and thus make room for new possibilities in the world."

The first chapter looks at a drag dance, Mark Morris's *Dido and Aeneas*, that makes a statement about the limits of inscribing gender on bodies.

Not unlike Jane Comfort's *S/He*, Morris's work was created in part as a righteously angry response to being 'read' through the toxic stereotypes of gender, sexuality, and race that the choreographers and dancers were encountering in their offstage lives. Like Shoals's and Comfort's roles, therefore, *Dido* establishes its own kinetic vocabulary to communicate gender identity and then deliberately sets this language at odds with the body performing it. But its drag tactics depart from *S/He* in key ways: instead of reversing gender portrayals across two bodies over time, Dido transposes two sets of drag gestures over the same body, intermittently. (Morris danced both the queen Dido and the Sorceress himself.) In Morris's stylized late-'80s staging, the inscription of a fate determined by gender, sexuality, and the choreography of others is fatal: at the end of the dance the queen is dead. By following Morris's choreographic logic in making a dance about inscriptions and forcible transpositions, we encounter the conceptual limits of gender as a scene of constraint *without* improvisation. But over time, other bodies inhabit the roles and perform them otherwise: a female dancer cast as the Sorceress draws on drag to expand her repertoire of female masculinity; the ensemble, a collective of varied bodies, is foregrounded over the virtuosic solo. Half-hidden queer dance histories emerge, as *Dido* is haunted by Ted Shawn and the 'problem' of double-bodied queens. This chapter traces the performance history of *Dido and Aeneas* as part of the historical shift from gay rights toward a more inclusive queer politics.

*Dido and Aeneas* could be seen as a dark duet between two mythic queens forced to dwell together in one body. In the second chapter, it is the drag practice of creating space inside one body that animates Richard Move's drag portrayal of the aging Martha Graham. "A dancer, more than any other human being, dies two deaths," Graham proclaimed; in her proud, self-conscious mortality, she herself invoked the possibility of eerie reincarnations (1991, 238).[29] But Richard Move does not conduct the drag séance he calls *Martha @* through virtuosic dancing or physical resemblance. Instead, Move shifts embodiment into other registers, ventriloquizing Martha's voice and stretching underneath her costume. By hollowing the center of his body as well as the structure of his *Martha @* show, Move generously offers his own body as a ghostly archive for Graham's imperiled legacy. And just as Move is haunted by Martha, *Martha @* is animated by dancers from Graham's company—one of whom is Catherine Cabeen, a choreographer in her own right, whose experience with both male and female drag challenges the paradigm that privileges male access to theatrical femininity. When 'straight' dance genealogies fail, how can queer claims on inheritance give us models for preserving dances in a way that acknowledges bodily difference, loss, aging, and mortality?

The third chapter continues to investigate how drag dances harbor the dead and their histories, but shifts away from Move's channeling of a separate body toward a mode of dancing 'as one.' In this case the Japanese butoh dancer Kazuo Ohno finds himself animated by La Argentina (1888–1936)—a Spanish dancer famous for her flamenco, bolero, and 'Gypsy' styles—decades after her death, compelling him to create *Admiring La Argentina* (1977) after he had already retired from the stage.[30] Expanding the capacity of the body beyond the séance, Ohno conceives of hosting the dead as unborn, theorizing his dancing as a work of repetition, difference, gestation, and embryonic movement. With a poetic intensity that invokes Bergson and Deleuze, Ohno interprets the concept of the bodily archive as a teeming, animate, imbricated space. Although *Admiring La Argentina* is not often treated as drag, it is only through dresses—with ever more flounces, fichus, and bedraggled bits of lace—that Ohno is able to invite La Argentina to inhabit his aging body. Drag emerges as Ohno's methodology for the radical attachment between bodies that would otherwise remain separated by identity categories, as well as by mortality and temporality. Two artists who have taken up the legacy of *Admiring*, Takao Kawaguchi and Trajal Harrell, demonstrate a twenty-first-century split in drag dance strategy: either drag dances can pursue the surfaces of synchronicity, like a lip sync in concert dance form, or they can follow Ohno's reincarnation beyond re-performance into "fictional archiving," as Harrell calls it.

The fourth chapter turns from the mystical solo toward the political collective, exploring an explicitly queer and hopeful politics of embodiment. Since 1974 the dancers of Les Ballets Trockadero de Monte Carlo have been 'undoing' normativity in ballet by doing ballet in the bodies they have, including all the best ballerina parts. By claiming their right to incorporate histories of Western classical dance, the Trockadero dancers challenge ballet's ossified prescriptions for bodies beyond their own, especially in terms of gender, sexuality, age, race, and size. Continuing Ohno's focus on process, repetition, and the durational, this chapter explores how drag dance practices open and layer the body, but across a collective of diverse bodies. Against ballet as a pale and feathery poetry of pure line, these dancers take the precarious materiality of bodies as a basis for channeling lost histories and mourning the dead. In this way, the Trockadero not only create new genealogies for ballet; they also reimagine 'discipline' as a form of queer work that makes room for failure and reconfiguration. Tracing a tangle of lineages from Charles Ludlam to Maya Plisetskaya, this chapter spotlights the role of Trockadero cofounder Antony Bassae in envisioning the potential for queer, antiracist ballet. That legacy is carried on by Katy Pyle's Ballez company, the ghost in this chapter, which proclaims cross-temporal queer inclusivity—specifically for trans and lesbian dancers—as a core value of ballet.

Fauxnique/Monique Jenkinson, who proudly counts the Trockadero among her drag foremothers, takes up the queer framework of 'realness' from a distinctly feminist perspective in her semiautobiographical dance theater piece, *Faux Real* (2009). To be faux real is to undertake, in public, the process of assuming a body that people generally assume you should already have; as a faux queen, Jenkinson illuminates Gayle Salamon's insistence that "the perceptual truth of the body is not necessarily what we see" (2010, 62). Returning to questions raised by *Dido*'s casting changes—how can gender be performed as if it were not self-identical?—this chapter analyzes the faux drag reclaiming of makeup, costume, gesture, and collage. Following Les Ballets Trockadero—and drag king and modern dancer Diane Torr, the ghost in this chapter—Jenkinson employs drag as an embodied mode of mourning and persistence linked to AIDS history. If the Trockadero unit of collective embodied politics is the company, Jenkinson works at the level of the house: in *Faux Real* the audience literally holds the show together. In this process of incorporating histories and dancing them differently, Monique Jenkinson shows us how drag genealogies can be layered into an 'autobiochoreography' that challenges biotic and epistemological categories. *Faux Real*'s challenge to the fixity of 'bio' forms like biography and biology moves toward a trans politics, using live performance to explore how—as philosopher Alva Noë proposes—we might move the category of 'real' closer to the bodies that reach toward it.

## CHAPTER ONE

## "Remember Me! But Ah . . ."
### *Mark Morris's* Dido and Aeneas

I am not as interested in what the queer gesture means so much as I am interested in what such gestures perform.
—José Muñoz, *Cruising Utopia*

But the drag queen does not give up his drag just because he has cracked its code.
—Wayne Koestenbaum, *The Queen's Throat*

*The Fate of Bodies*

At the very end of Mark Morris's *Dido and Aeneas* (1989), set to the Henry Purcell opera of the same title, the queen Dido is dancing toward her death.[1] With regal, resigned sorrow, she signals her acceptance of the fate that has been meted out to her—the doom that attends a queen who loves, especially if she loves a man whose destiny is to depart, bare-chested and brave, on his next heroic conquest. If she has not only loved but also desired, also lain her body down with his, then she has felt tragedy shadowing her from the moment her back touched the earth. When Aeneas sails off into the distance, then, Dido puts an anguished hand to her forehead and prepares to follow the script to the end: as she knows, when a body accedes to the codes of gender and sexuality that have been inscribed upon it, the fate of that body is already determined. All you can do is perform the rest of the choreography that has been given to you. This fate is fatal, and Dido is dancing it.

In *Dido and Aeneas* the sung text of the libretto is echoed and amplified by the gestures of the dancers, creating a movement vocabulary of "dance words," as dance scholar Stephanie Jordan calls them (2015,

Figure 3. Dancers perform the "fate" gesture in *Dido and Aeneas*. Photo by Costas, courtesy of Mark Morris Dance Group.

229), that stretches over the whole piece.[2] To make the gesture for "fate," a dancer fans her arms open overhead and then sideways, outstretched to their full extent but twisted backward so that the wrists are wrenched in reverse, with the fingers spread apart like the arms of a spiny starfish.[3] This gesture is eventually performed by everyone in the cast: sometimes one-handed, sometimes with both hands; at times facing the audience, at other times while walking offstage; sometimes starkly against the air, sometimes pressed knowingly into the body of the dancer.[4] In the end of the piece, when "fate" returns like a bird of prey that has been circling Dido's body watchfully since the curtain went up, the gesture looks as if it were being pried out of her wrist sockets. But Dido herself remains noble, austere, stylized. Her steps under her black sarong are deliberate and composed, kept tightly to narrow lines of movement. Now she shows her concern for the others she is leaving behind in her court; she doesn't want them to suffer the "trouble" that presses down like a hand on her heart. She will bear the tragedy herself, on her own body. She turns the gesture backward and forward, and finally she just holds it there, wrists wrenched and fingers splayed, while her court of dancers—facing upstage, each with one hand also raised in the "fate" gesture—walk her inexorably toward her death.

The line that ends in "fate," during which Dido dances her last phrase, contains a strange contradiction: "Remember me! But ah! forget my fate." The gesture for "remember" is adapted from the American Sign Language word for "learning" (Jordan 2011, 202). It looks like one hand pulling a thread of thought out of the other open palm, and continuing to pull as the wrist curls past the face and spirals open until the whole body is arched backward, almost falling, with the top arm and the upper spine parallel to the ground. Its complementary gesture, "forget," is shared, curiously, with words in the libretto like "known" (Preston 2000, 348), "guessed," and "thought" (Duerden and Rowell 2013, 150). To "forget," you bend your arm at the elbow and wrist, then touch the inner wrist to your temple, while stepping forward diagonally with the opposite foot. Forgetting has a stylized crookedness to it, with the jagged line of the arm and the step across the body: an $X$ that simultaneously tells you something is there and bars you from seeing exactly what it is. Just underneath forgetting, there is a palimpsest of what is known or guessed—it's a coded gesture, an open secret. Remembering, on the other hand, demands that you open the whole front of your chest, that you lean far back into empty space with your hand outstretched behind you. In the choreography, this vulnerability at the center of the body as it arches backward is related to the gesture for a certain kind of death: the kind you see coming inexorably toward you, so that you have a long time to live with the certainty of its arrival.

But what does it mean to remember Dido if we are told to forget her fate? To begin we might remember that *Dido and Aeneas* was made in 1989, during a three-year residency at the Théâtre Royal de la Monnaie in Brussels, Belgium. This was the same year that choreographer Alvin Ailey died of AIDS-related causes, although officially the cause of death was given as "blood dyscrasia." The year before, World AIDS Day had been inaugurated. And the year before that, when Arnie Zane became the first major American choreographer to make his HIV-positive status public (Gere 2004, 123), *Vanity Fair* reported that AIDS was the primary cause of death for men in New York between twenty-five and forty years of age (Shnayerson 2013). "Simply put," David Gere writes in *How to Make Dances in an Epidemic*, "for bodies and bodiliness in the age of AIDS, dancing is ground zero" (2004, 40).[5] In 1989, the year after he moved from New York to Brussels, Mark Morris was thirty-two years old and openly gay; it is not surprising that he made a dance culminating with the idea that the fate of certain bodies is unavoidable death.

Originally, Morris had conceived *Dido and Aeneas* as a ballet in which he would dance all of the parts himself. When he was feeling mischievous, he explained this decision nonchalantly: "Why not? I'm a fabulous dancer" (Morris and Acocella 2009). In more pensive moods, though, he acknowledged that his deep, brooding fear of AIDS had spurred him to choreograph *Dido* as if it were the last piece he would ever make, because it seemed inevitable to him that he, too, would fall sick and die. Dido's role expresses this private, bitter foreknowledge: no matter how you try to hold your body apart from what is expected of it, somehow you end up following a script that leads to your death. In public, Morris was out and proud, and habitually let everyone know that he was, as he was wont to say, "fabulous"; he was infuriated by the homophobia he regularly encountered, with its stereotypes and paranoid secrecy. Brussels, a place he perceived as tolerating homosexuals only "if you wear a suit and have a firm handshake and don't give any trouble," intensified his desire to declare, "I'm not like that" (Montgomery 1989). Feeling "dramatic, frightened and histrionic" (Palmer 2016), as waves of friends, fellow dancers, and a former lover fell ill (Acocella 2015), Mark Morris took his fears and theatrical intensity and resentment of the ways bodies got forced into codes, along with substantial funding from the state-sponsored Théâtre Royal de la Monnaie, and made a drag dance.

## Codes

Although he ultimately choreographed for his full company—and gave the role of Aeneas to Guillermo Resto, whose nickname happened to be "Didi" (Dalva 2003)—Morris kept the two lead female roles for himself: one was Dido, and the other was the maleficent Sorceress who orchestrates Dido's tragic fate. In order to communicate to the audience, without relying on elaborate costumes,[6] that a male-bodied person should be read as a queen and a sorceress, *Dido and Aeneas* had to establish a vocabulary of overt signifiers that communicate heteronormative gender. When Dido is described as "fair," the dancer's palm makes a flat, regal circle over the side of the face, like a painter positioning a model's head in profile or someone applying blush to a cheekbone; Aeneas's heroism is conveyed in a strong lunge with the legs planted firmly apart, torso tilted sideways, and arms stretched upward like tree branches.[7] In hyper-literalizing bodily signifiers like gender style, Morris shows them up as a series of codes, a system of signs. And because Morris danced the two main roles in drag, *Dido* took a recognizably gendered movement vocabulary and set it at odds with the gender of the body most often onstage performing it—an embodied critique of the ways in which gendered signifiers are so often conflated with the gender and sexuality of bodies.

When the piece premiered, predictably, the fact that both of the lead female roles were cross-gender cast outraged the conservative Belgian press; *Le Soir*, Brussels' main newspaper, deemed it not only "debased" and "tasteless" but also a demonstration of Morris's "lack of respect for Woman" (Acocella 1993, 214). Within a month, a homophobic encapsulation appeared in *Le Drapeau Rouge*, another Belgian paper: "Obviously, Morris's choreographic inspiration is to be found up his butt—which is not worth going far to see" (215). Despite the long tradition of male performers playing female roles in Western and Asian theater, Morris's piece was understood as 'gay' and scandalous. This was because Morris refused, onstage and offstage, to subsume his body to what Susan Foster calls the "closets full of dances" that kept homosexuality suppressed, implicit, sublimated, and as discreetly coded as possible during a century of modern dance (2001, 149). Maurice Béjart, the French-born choreographer who had been in residence for decades at Théâtre de la Monnaie before Morris arrived, was gay, too, and many people knew it, but he didn't, as is so often said, 'throw it' in people's faces—a formulation in which, Gayle Salamon points out, someone's embodiment of gender or sexuality is bizarrely "figured as a potential projectile" (2015, 194). In interviews Morris made it a point to announce his sexual orientation, in case anyone might still be unclear on that point; he often added something snide about Béjart, who had been something of a paragon of Belgian culture in his time. In *Dido and Aeneas* Morris didn't merely invert gender roles for laughs, and he didn't allow the audience to relax into a conventionally theatrical, classical understanding of cross-gender casting.[8] Instead, he used his own almost monumentally masculine body, dancing doubly in drag, to make explicit how the toxic normative codes of gender and sexuality work on bodies.[9]

Taken together, in fact, Dido and the Sorceress are chiasmic counterparts of coded and explicit bodies. As Dido, Morris is anguished and queenly, deliberately evoking a stylized femininity. Dancers who learn this role describe its "formality" and "restraint," emphasizing how "challenging" it is to "maintain" a posture that is so "twisted, archaic, and flat" (MMDG

2016a); to dance Dido, you more or less hold your body open on one plane and carve gestures across it. "To try to get your body to fit between two panes of glass and to find the absolute profile without just being a little bit this way or a little bit that way," dancer Amber Star Merkens explained (Kourlas and Merkens 2012), "requires a specific musculature" (Wenzel 2012). Dido's court mirrors her tensed two-dimensionality: Tina Fehlandt, a dancer in the original cast, recalls that "sitting still on the bench in a hieroglyphic pose was more rigorous than any of our other dancing," to the extent that dancers who did the court scenes began to complain of "*Dido* neck" (2015, 190). That hieratic flatness, derived partly from Indonesian and Indian classical dance traditions, is often interpreted as 'Eastern,' in contrast to the Sorceress's loosely expressive, heavily grounded movement style.[10] Another way to read this posture, though, is to see that the body held in two dimensions makes a kind of screen, a space for images to be projected upon or words to scroll across. Dido's body and the arrayed bodies of her court are stretched open for audiences to read, their shoulders pinned back. A gesture like "Remember me" happens across that body as if it were a film being shown to us—a film about how the effort of remembering not only means unspooling the taut thread of memory across your torso, but also means holding your body in that place, letting yourself be projected upon, letting your body be read.

To the phrase "press'd with torment," in Dido's first aria, Morris faces the audience, places one palm flat on his chest and one palm on his stomach, with the fingertips pointing downward, and then—maintaining the tension of the gesture by tightly pressing his fingers together—slides both hands down his body toward his pelvis while slowly opening his legs.[11] This gesture, traversing Dido's body from heart to crotch, is one version of what it looks like to be inscribed with the codes for heteronormative feminine sexuality. Once she gives her heart, it's a short downward slide until she opens her legs—and once she opens her legs, it's only a matter of time until "fate" bears down on her whole body. The narrative might look pretty at first—when Dido is watching her court dance its communal reassurance that Aeneas will return her love, she gets girlishly carried away by the sprightly dancing and the polyphonic energy of the "dotty canon for two soprano voices" (Jordan 2011, 186) and begins to shift her torso coyly from side to side—but in the end, Dido's death is the consequence for a body without agency in the "scene of constraint" that gender entails (Butler 2004a, 1). Like the gesture for "remember," "press'd with torment" opens the body toward the audience almost painfully, with visceral tension. But if remembering presents Dido in profile for public commemoration, this frontal opening, this splitting apart of the legs as the hand slides down, is a physical, personal, and markedly gendered transmission. In the last scene, Dido presses her arrowed palm down on the chest of her sister, Belinda; the line being sung is about Dido's wish not to cause any "trouble in thy breast," but Belinda still opens her legs. So much power is carried in that gesture that when Dido removes her hand, Belinda remains immobilized for a moment by its imprint, with her legs rent asunder and her head thrown back.

As the Sorceress, Morris seizes on the phrase "conjure up a storm" and conveys it by shimmying vigorously. He tosses his long curls with a flick of his wrist, taps his witchy fingernails in bored little trills, makes faces when his coven goes too far, rolls his eyes dramatically for emphasis, and generally "lounges about in parodies of *femme fatale* poses," as Gay Morris puts it (1996, 148). Femininity, for the Sorceress, is a performance of high camp; her movement vocabulary plays on many of the stereotypes of 'flamboyant' gay gestures. In fact, as Gay Morris points out, Morris's Sorceress is the parodic drag role of the ballet, overloading the codes that make men who gesture 'too much' sexually suspect.[12] If Morris was under pressure offstage to conform to the firm-handshake, no-trouble model of masculinity, onstage he would find a way to demonstrate exactly how much 'trouble' he could be. The Sorceress therefore takes the assumptions of unspoken homophobia and performs them as explicitly as possible: she is bitchy, campy, catty, and crass; she is into unspeakable, titillating, anonymous, loveless, debased forms of rough sex; and, behind the scenes, she controls all kinds of things that nice people don't know about, bending them to suit her perverse tastes. She is also the one in the ballet who sees the codes for what they are—forms of domination and constraint—and she likes to manipulate them on other people's bodies.

When the Sorceress is in charge, in fact, she directs her coven in a series of short mime sequences that imagine Dido's death at Aeneas's hands. In the 1995 film version of the first charade, the witch acting as Dido is female, and the one acting as Aeneas is male; they kiss, and then "Aeneas" slits "Dido's" throat with one savage gesture. In the second, "Dido" is male and "Aeneas" is female; they kiss, and then the hero slices the queen's throat open. Any witch may signal that he is "Dido" by making the "fair" gesture of sweeping his hand in a semicircle across his profile, and any another witch may signal that she is "Aeneas" by holding her arms out in a strong, definite triangle that lays claim to a swath of air. Eventually this gets to the point where entirely random pairs of witches are mashing into each other and then jerking apart, falling to the floor, scrambling up again, throwing their bodies together and then springing apart again. It is not the gender of the witches' bodies that determines whether they are "Dido" or "Aeneas," but rather the signifying gesture that temporarily defines their identities as either "fair" or "hero"—and, in fact, the more quickly they switch roles, the more the Sorceress seems to enjoy it. It appears that the Sorceress is pleased by any gender combination of her coven, as long as their gestures of killing and dying fulfill two requirements: first, they must be legible; second, they must be repeated. This high-speed reiteration of arbitrary codes of gender identity ends up looking like Butler's idea of drag, but in free fall. It envisions gender codes to be so contingent, and so based on imitation, that bodies can signify an identity in almost no time at all, simply by making a mimetic gesture. That identity is almost immediately exploded: the body falls to the floor, and when it rebounds, it is ready to enact a different but equally legible gender identity. In other words, the codes hold while the bodies slip freely in and out of them.

If gestures in this dance had simply indicated the identities of the bodies dancing them, Morris would have created a kind of musical pantomime. The Queen would make noble, feminine, queenly gestures, and the Sorceress would make witchy, hag-like, cackling gestures; the heroes would stride with bold manliness toward their destinies, and the sailors would strut around, jauntily hoisting the sails. It would be like 'mickey-mousing' applied to the realm of character, with each gesture keyed invariably to its proper identity. But "thinking about queerness through gesture animates how bodies move in the world, and how we assign meaning in ways that are already infused with cultural modes of knowing," as Juana María Rodríguez writes (2014, 2). In *Dido and Aeneas* the gestures are movements made by dancers, but they are also movements made to reveal how meaning is assigned to those gestures. To make the artificiality of gendered gestures more visible by dancing them in drag is a queer attempt to render those gestures less available to a hegemonic system that will otherwise simply go on generating compulsorily firm masculine handshakes and inevitably noble female suicides. With its late-'80s gay politics, then, *Dido* does not represent the bodies underneath the gendered codes as 'wrong' for their roles; rather, it theatricalizes the violence and power that these codes wield when they are relentlessly applied to bodies. By making a dance that first inscribes meanings on bodies through gestures, and then points out the tragedy of that process of inscription, Morris asks us to consider how bodies encounter and bear the "fates" that are prescribed for them.

## Explicit Acts

While Mark Morris was making *Dido*, he was living in a place he described as "highly racist, highly sexist, highly homophobic"—a city in which both Morris, who kept wearing pink triangles to press conferences, and his Aeneas, Guillermo Resto, who had dreadlocks and read as nonwhite, were regularly stopped by the police and asked for their papers (Acocella 1993, 227–28). The female dancers in the company were constantly being told by dance critics and costumers that their breasts were too small, their butts were too big, they needed to go on diets and wear makeup: "over and over," dancer Clarice Marshall remembers, "they kept saying to us . . . 'You look like a man'" (234). It is no wonder that, "almost unanimously," as the company's managing director reported, "people were miserable" while *Dido and Aeneas* was being created and premiered in Brussels (233). Their bodies were being inspected and found lacking, suspected of criminal and degenerate acts, patrolled for indiscretions and illicit foreignness, critiqued and condemned as 'wrong' for the parts that they, as dancers and temporary citizens of this culture, were supposed to perform.

Negotiating these attempts to police the bodies of his company in their offstage and backstage lives, Morris brought them onstage in *Dido and Aeneas*, restaging the accusations on his own terms. So the women in the company looked like men, did they? Then Morris would perform in drag, using his own body to ironize and exceed gendered expectations. Countering the racist suspicions of Resto as a foreigner, Morris would make him "the hero" Aeneas, icon of European cultural history. And as for the homophobia (and attendant femmephobia), Morris would stage scenes of explicit sexuality with a frankness that countered expectations about what dancers' bodies were expected to sublimate, aestheticize, or disavow. Notably, he made these explicit scenes for himself—one for Dido and one for the Sorceress, both danced in drag—thereby confronting assumptions conflating what the body looks like with what the body can do. At the center of the ballet, for example, Morris put in a brief, wordless, heterosexual coupling: Dido lies down on her back on the floor and opens her arms to Aeneas, who lies down on top of her. Eleven seconds later he is standing upright again, staring off into the distance, contemplating his heroic destiny. If you're looking at Dido as a tragically romantic female figure, this is not a very flattering view of heterosexual love. Moreover, if someone in the theater has squeamish homophobic feelings about men who have sex with men, there is Mark Morris, lying down in the middle of the stage during a nice *ritornelle* and pretending to have sex with Guillermo Resto.[13] Depending upon a viewer's perspective, this scene either asserts that there is no problem with an apparent 'inconsistency' between a gendered gesture and the gendered body performing it, or else it affirms gay sex in public.

Moreover, the choreography for the role of the Sorceress includes a scene in which she lies prone, downstage center, walks the fingers of one hand down her body to her crotch, caresses her breast with the other hand, closes her eyes and opens her mouth, shudders, arches her back, and unmistakably mimes female masturbation to orgasm. After she comes, the Sorceress wipes her finger clean on her dress, as if the gestural force of her body were so real that it had produced messy material consequences. The Sorceress's masturbation scene is a limit case of gender and movement, in which a gesture appears to visually contradict the gendered body producing it. If prudish spectators are horrified that Morris is *miming* female masturbation onstage, they've succumbed to a basic logic of drag: seeing gender as something that can be performed as a series of gestures, not as an inherent essence assigned to a body at birth. If they're horrified by the *act* of female masturbation onstage, it means that Morris has successfully embodied an identity that gender normativity would prohibit to him, thereby demonstrating that those spectators have underestimated his body's range, capacity, and repertoire.

In responding to its contemporary context for bodily codes, this scene delved into half-hidden queer dance histories—particularly, as Gay Morris points out, that of the "ghost" of Vaslav Nijinsky, which "hovers over *Dido and Aeneas*" (1996, 148).[14] In Nijinsky's *L'après-midi d'un faune* (1912), the Faun, choreographed and performed by Nijinsky himself, masturbates into a scarf abandoned by a fleeing nymph. The day after the premiere, Bronislava Nijinksa reported, the newspaper *Le Figaro* published a front-page polemic decrying Nijinsky's "vile movements of erotic bestiality and gestures of heavy shamelessness," an accusation very like those leveled at Morris for the masturbation scene in *Dido* (1981, 436). Nijinsky, who did not make his sexual interest in men public knowledge, did nevertheless choreograph ballets with explicitly sexual, 'deviant' premises—besides *Faune*, there were the implications of homoeroticism in *Jeux* (1913)—and Lynn Garafola characterizes these two ballets as part of Nijinsky's "erotic autobiography" (1989, 57). Both ballets were choreographed and danced by queer men who used the same device: the masturbation scenes were mimed as if the bodies were not those of men (one was a hybrid creature and the other was a witch) so that the sexual act was explicit but also displaced.

In the history of American modern concert dance, this seems to be the first time that female masturbation was explicitly portrayed onstage (Acocella 1993, 100; G. Morris 1996). But Morris was not the first major white American male choreographer whose homosexuality visibly inflected his work; that title probably belongs to Ted Shawn (1891–1972), who remained closeted while marrying Ruth St. Denis and using the dance stage to publicly perform his untarnished heteromasculinity. Susan Manning called this "the blatant double-coding of Ted Shawn's choreography," a contradiction that conveyed how visibly queer his dances were, for an audience attuned to the significance of that gestural vocabulary (2004, 92). As Paul Scolieri demonstrates, Shawn was drawn to the pseudo-science of eugenics partly because of his anxiety about his own "glaring sexual unfitness (his childlessness, his adulterous marriage, his homosexuality)" (2013).[15] Shawn managed his homosexuality with a mixture of phobic suppression, sublimated longing, and discreet codes that might attract "comrades" without arousing too much suspicion; he was romantically involved for many years with one of his dancers, Barton Mumaw, who was not allowed to call him by his first name in public. By contrast, what Morris "hated in the dance world was that so much of it was fake—fake sentiment, fake sexuality, fake love," as one of his longtime friends and dancers put it (Acocella 1993, 85). In this case the evident and theatrical fakeness of the act of masturbation called out the careful staging of the dance world as an artistic milieu where elevated choreographic visions of romantic love and sublimated desire were enacted by healthy heterosexual bodies. Onstage and off, Morris was working against gestures of stylized forgetting that foreclosed the possibilities for sexuality and love.

Like Shawn, Morris alludes onstage to his own sexuality by exaggerating the codes of gendered and sexual performance. Both Shawn's marriage to St. Denis and the scene in which Dido and Aeneas have sex could be seen as performances of heterosexuality choreographed by gay men. But drag allows Morris to simultaneously perform his own sexuality in a way that Shawn never could, so that what looks most heterosexual in *Dido* is actually quite queer and autobiographical. Morris really is someone who has sex with men—moreover, Acocella reports, he was mostly falling in love "with heterosexual men" in that period, one of whom had been Guillermo Resto (1993, 115, 110). In Brussels they lived together. In *Dido* they danced the lead roles, partnered each other, lay down on stage on top of each other: Dido and Didi, dancing together for so long that eventually Mark Morris would say to a journalist, "Guillermo and I are the two ancientest people in my company" (Conrad 2000). With this scene, then, Morris puts the offstage queer history of twentieth-century dance right into the middle of his ballet. In drag as Dido, Morris takes the stage as a place where heterosexual acts only make his queerness—and the queerness of dance history in this century—more explicit. And by refusing to continue the histories of bodily censure, he makes a gesture that is much more like remembering than forgetting, a movement that opens the body and arches it backward toward center stage.

### Queens and Greeks

In addition to choreographic history, Dido has an unstable duality, also tinged with queerness, that comes from her relation as a character to the categories 'queen' and 'Greek.' First, Dido's double body reflects the traditional 'paradox' of queens: correlating the power of monarchy with the body of a woman. The idea that the queen's royal body is publicly male (unemotional, rational, aggressive) and privately female (physically weak, sexually feminine, subject to variable emotions) underlies Dido's history as a character. In book 4 of the *Aeneid*, Virgil emphasizes pointedly that the Queen's love for Aeneas has caused her to turn her attention away from the prosperous, industrious civic life of Carthage, absorbing her instead in the idle luxuries of romance. The implication is that Dido, as a queen, is split between a robust, imperial, masculine body and a love-struck, idle, intimately feminine one. Morris reverses the performance—instead of being privately female and publicly male, he spends his offstage life as a man and occasionally plays female roles in the theater—but he maintains the concept of Dido as a queen who inhabits both a masculine and a feminine body, and whose body is thus double-coded in terms of gender.

Doubly gendered royal bodies in classical literature lead not only to queens, but also to Greek narratives of the dangerous power of drag. In fact, if there were a character that illuminated Morris's conception of the Queen Dido, it would be Pentheus, the protagonist of Euripides's tragic drama *The Bacchae*. Pentheus, a prince of Thebes who is overcome by Dionysian madness, spends a significant amount of the play cross-dressed, toying with his wig of girlish curls and admiring his pretty dress.[16] In *The Bacchae* the moment when Pentheus cross-dresses is the moment when he splits from himself; he sees double suns in the sky, and Dionysus arranges the prince's long hair to resemble his own exotically feminine curls. When Morris changes costume between the role of Dido and that of the Sorceress, he simply pulls out the hair clip that has been holding back Dido's hair, and the long, curly locks of the Sorceress twine down around his shoulders. The echo in *Dido* is that the Queen, like Pentheus, embodies an internal split: she looses her curls and becomes her opposite, the Sorceress. In the context of American dance history, moreover, 'Greek' has been tantamount to male homoerotic code. For example, Ted Shawn's 1923 *Death of Adonis*, as Julia L. Foulkes explains, "drew on Greek ideals," which is to say that Shawn "powdered his body white, and wore only a fig leaf G-string" (2001, 127). Shawn's asserted faithfulness to Greek aesthetics gave his sculptural poses a defensible classical pedigree, but this only thinly veiled their queer implications.

Strictly speaking, of course, Dido is not Greek but Carthaginian, and Aeneas is Trojan; their love story is told in Latin in Virgil's *Aeneid*. But because Aeneas had been a hero in Homer's Greek epic *The Iliad* before Virgil had adopted him, his adventures were associated with idealized Greek heroism—with companies of men, banding boldly together to undertake epic quests, always sailing off to found new empires or slay something. To begin with, then, there is always a little question around the identification with 'Greek' masculinity: just how closely are those men banding together? Then there is the historical problem of whether European or Euro-sympathetic audiences should "weep for Dido"—a pagan North African queen standing in the way of Aeneas's grandly imperial project to found Rome, which will become the seat of Western Christianity (Dolven 2015, 187).[17] The complicated navigation of alliances around issues of race, nationality, gender, sexuality, and colonial history is mitigated if everything is the Sorceress's fault, as Jeff Dolven notes (2015), but Dido remains a shifting signifier: 'Greek' by association, but not quite Greek enough to escape suspicion; queenly in bearing, but not impervious to sexual implications.

In terms of casting, the role of Dido was originated (and made iconic) by Morris, a white dancer, while Aeneas was first performed by Guillermo Resto, whose heritage was Puerto Rican; Resto danced the role with great dignity until 2000, despite receiving such press mentions as "Dido had

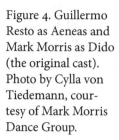

Figure 4. Guillermo Resto as Aeneas and Mark Morris as Dido (the original cast). Photo by Cylla von Tiedemann, courtesy of Mark Morris Dance Group.

alfresco sex with the swarthy Aeneas" (Conrad 2000). In terms of costume, though, Dido wore the same modest sarong as everyone else, while Aeneas appeared bare-chested, "drawing attention to his performance of masculinity," Ramsay Burt proposed, "as if putting it in quotation marks," and framing him as an object of the audience's gaze (2007, 166). Morris justified this costume decision as if he were actually the civilized Queen Dido regarding a barbaric proto-European—seeing Aeneas as an exotic foreigner "from somewhere else, more vulgar," as he put it (Morris and Acocella 2009)—continuing the uneasy conflation of actual bodies, theatrical roles, gender presentations, and racialized histories that haunt Dido as a classical character. As Charles Nero pointed out in his introduction to Essex Hemphill's *Ceremonies* (1999), Purcell's Dido can be read as "a highly stylized ideal of Africa before the horrors of the transatlantic slave trade," an image "of a majestic African woman's nobility in the midst of great suffering" that, Nero argues, "has been important for diasporic black people" (2000, xviii). Should we weep for Dido?[18] Who are 'we,' and who is Dido? How much do we see the bodies dancing the roles as bringing their own identities into the work, and how much do we see roles, histories, and codes overlaid upon those bodies?

These questions were amplified when *Dido and Aeneas* premiered; Dido's performance of double-bodied queenliness, with its uncomfortable implications for the offstage identities of bodies and the lingering imprints of colonial histories, would now be watched by another queen. When Queen Fabiola of Belgium, royal patron of the Théâtre de la Monnaie, had attended a performance during Morris's first season in Brussels, the Belgian audience called out, "*Vive la reine!*" With mock innocence,

Morris commented to a journalist that he had supposed the shouts were for him (Acocella 1993, 6). What was worse, when he was granted an audience with Queen Fabiola after the show, he summarized it with the nonchalant remark "Best blow job I ever had" (86). There was a reporter at his elbow when he said it. This very camp version of queeniness—the outrageous, trashy, explicitly sexual, larger-than-life performance of feminine power—featured Morris's somewhat tactless impulses to be fabulous against the atmosphere of conservative gentility surrounding Queen Fabiola. By declaring himself *la reine,* Morris deliberately switches his grammatical gender and confuses the proper referent with its queer meaning. Then, when he asserts that he has been enjoying sexual favors from Queen Fabiola, he makes a claim of hypermasculine virility that strictly adheres to hetero codes but outrageously overloads them. It's like temporarily blowing the fuses in the heteronormative sex-gender circuit—too many things are plugged into too many different sockets. With his offstage behavior, his insistent performance of outré queerness, he was making a joke about the kind of queen Dido would never be: a drag queen.

The character in the ballet that does, of course, closely resemble a drag queen is Dido's opposite—the campy, theatrical, vulgar, entertainingly wicked Sorceress. As Esther Newton attests, there is an "overwhelming emphasis upon the queen" in camp contexts generally (1996, 173),[19] so Queen Dido and the Sorceress-as-drag-queen neatly interlocked as characters. By exaggerating what femininity looks like in explicitly sexual terms, the Sorceress takes the performance of gender to its breaking point. Her queeniness is meant to weigh heavily on the brittle certainties that men's bodies are never women's bodies, that women's sexual pleasure should be modestly effaced, and that female desire is not aroused by visual porn. In addition, the gestural vocabulary of the Sorceress is often more pantomimed than danced; there are more facial expressions, for one thing, like the slow cruel smile she gives when devising Dido's doom. She is full of the base feelings and visceral impulses that Dido can't have, and she scrambles the codes from which Dido cannot deviate. When Newton writes about the figure of the camp queen, she emphasizes that drag can become "a performance in relation to what is subjectively experienced and socially accepted as an authentic self, defined by more or less coherent gay gender positions" like butch, femme, or queen (189). This idea of performing identity not against 'biological' gender but rather against one's "gay gender" leads to the possibility that Newton calls "compound drag": an effeminate gay man—a "queen"—could use drag to inhabit conventional or butch masculinity.[20] As soon as Morris claimed the position of queen for himself—he was a queenly Dido, he was a big queeny drag Sorceress, and he was the direct object of the patriotic salute to the Queen's health—he queered it in the direction of compound drag, pretending to be the kind of straight man whose unbridled sexual prowess brought queens to their knees before him.

Wayne Koestenbaum, writing on opera divas and homosexuality, noted the fact that "only one mark, one letter, separates queen and queer: n/r, the 'r' an incomplete 'n'" (1993, 107). Similarly, the Sorceress, a queer camp 'queen,' is only one mark away from Dido, a queen embodied by a queer man. The Sorceress might be dismissed as a parody, in the tradition of the pantomime dame and a long-standing view of drag as light misogyny, but it is difficult to ignore her power—even the hero Aeneas obeys her dictates. Moreover, it is unsettling to see the Sorceress as a body within Dido's body, a double that sometimes shadows her gestures and sometimes animates her actions. Like Dionysus in *The Bacchae*, the Sorceress is a figure of untamed femininity, holding sway over a ruler whose half-feminine body must be kept under control for the good of the state. And even Dido is not wholly immune to the allure of camp. In an otherwise moralizing, reproachful scene about the fate of the hunter Actaeon—another deadly "fate" ascribed to a body that can't control how its identity is interpreted—Aeneas announces, "Behold, upon my bending spear / A monster's head stands bleeding." Obediently, Dido looks. Aeneas, facing upstage, is holding the flaps of his sarong apart, presumably impressing the whole court with the sight of his "bending spear." This is a low, low joke—a cheap sight gag whose camp humor belongs to the realm of the Sorceress. But Dido looks.

When Queen Fabiola is in the audience at Théâtre de la Monnaie, she is watching Morris's choreography: she looks too. This suggests an impolitic question: could Queen Fabiola, with her impeccably stiff coiffure, ever be *that* kind of queen, ever let down her hair, ever—perhaps watching an opera about a queen, in a theatrical mise en abyme like Hamlet's "Mousetrap"— pull back the modest, solid appearance of the queen's "n" and show the bare slip of an "r"? If Morris could occupy at least three different positions relative to queenliness, whose queenly status could remain unassailable in its fixity? In *Dido* Morris imported not only backstage knowledge into the narrative of the piece but offstage knowledge as well: the dancer is a man, the man is queer, the queer man is the choreographer who is making off-color jokes about the queen of Belgium. From her velvet seat in the royal box *côté cour*, the European queen—a devout Roman Catholic—watches as the African queen, a paragon of morality imbued with the sanctity of self-sacrifice, dismisses her faithless beloved, the future founder of Rome. The choreographer becomes a supernatural creature, like the Sorceress, who can move between worlds by shape-shifting—onstage he becomes a queen, then a witch, then a queen again. The double drag casting of Queen and Sorceress is played off the double casting of Sorceress and choreographer, and off the antagonistic double appearance of two Queens in the lobby of the Théâtre de la Monnaie in Brussels, in the postmodern late '80s , where, as Mark Morris pointed out, when the crowd shouts *Vive la reine!*, its referent is actually subject to interpretation.

*Transpositions*

In this ballet the two lead roles are female, but both are danced by a man; that man is the choreographer, but he is also the dancer who must perform the movements dictated to him by the choreographer. From this perspective, *Dido and Aeneas* is an elaborate experiment in transposing gestures from one body to another. It shows up how certain bodies have to bear the consequences of what is inscribed upon them while other, more powerful bodies get to choreograph the movements that convey that fate. When Morris split his body into two roles (choreographer and dancer) and then split his dancing into two roles (Dido and Sorceress), he was reflecting this hierarchy of creation and performance, but he was also attempting to layer all of the roles in his own body.

The most zealous choreographer in the ballet is the Sorceress, who amuses herself by devising gestures and imparting them to her coven. When the Sorceress and her witches are gleefully envisioning the results of the plan to destroy Dido, they dance several repetitions of the lines, "Destruction's our delight / Delight our greatest sorrow." The first of these lines gets the Sorceress, who is downstage center, clapping like she's at a hoedown, and then on the word "sorrow," she makes a big 'boo-hoo' gesture by pretending to rub her fists in her eyes, with her lower lip stuck out in a pout. It's a five-year-old's idea of conveying a grown-up word like "sorrow."[21] In the "Delight our greatest sorrow" scene, the Sorceress takes great satisfaction in making gestures to the lines "Elissa bleeds tonight" and "Elissa dies tonight." ("Elissa" is another name for Dido.) The acting out of Dido's imminent death is done, first by the Sorceress and subsequently by her whole twitchy coven, by making two similar gestures. The line "Elissa bleeds tonight" is taken up by a two-handed gesture in which the Sorceress stabs an imaginary dagger into each of two witches' bellies and then slices their bodies open to the throat in three shuddering zig-zags. With each motion, the two witches mime their death agonies, their eyes rolling back and their mouths open; then they collapse to the ground. To the line "Elissa dies tonight," the Sorceress gestures as if gutting herself with one quick, decisive, ripping motion. It is graphic, and it is accompanied by the coven's interpretative demonstration of other improvised death gestures, which range from shooting themselves in the head to slitting each other's throats. It is during this scene, watching the violent antics of her coven, that the Sorceress masturbates.

This scene occupies an interesting place in the structure of the ballet: it shows the Sorceress creating and directing the narrative of the piece, 'setting' movement phrases on her company of witches. Following a real-world model of dance-making, the Sorceress generates movements on her own body and joins them together to make phrases; then the dancers pick up the movement sequences through imitation, and everyone rehearses the section together. In the rehearsal period there is even some improvisation, in which the coven dancers create related movements based on what they have already learned from their choreographer.[22] In the final stages, the choreographer has the pleasure of sitting off to one side, watching the company perform her new dance; this is, more or less, what the Sorceress does when she masturbates. The fact that Morris is both the choreographer of *Dido and Aeneas* and the Sorceress who 'choreographs' this scene makes it a self-ironizing joke about what choreographers are doing when they make dances.

The Sorceress's choreographic pedagogy is the index of success for the gestural vocabulary of the ballet as a whole: she teaches everyone what the gestures mean, how to use them, and that their transmission is powerful enough to incite bodies to action. Combining gestures that convey meaning to a naïve audience (the 'boo-hoo' gesture means she's crying) and to sophisticated readers of gender dynamics in dance (Morris, a queer choreographer, is ironizing the perverse egotistical pleasure of the choreographer through camp gesture), the Sorceress amplifies and reinforces the movement phrases by having her witches perform them again and again. Because the "dance words" in Dido are so dedicated to communication, Morris gains the freedom to unsettle less literal bodily meanings. In this scene, for example, *Dido and Aeneas* sets out to 'mickey-mouse' to the words of the libretto, setting up a deliberately heavy-handed synchrony of movement and language in order to mickey-mouse with heightened irony to gender codes.[23] The Sorceress, however, is not just choreographing these movements for her witches to rehearse in private. She has created this scene to be performed by Dido—the one person who can't be onstage learning movement phrases from the Sorceress, because they share the same body. This configuration is familiar in dance history from the Odette/Odile casting in *Swan Lake*. There is an Odette/Odile paradigm in *Dido* too—the principal female role is an embodiment of the split self: one part flashy and wicked and dark, and the other part noble and loving and self-sacrificing—but because Morris is also the piece's choreographer and doing both roles in drag, his performance has a vertiginous queer edge. That the Sorceress is both the high-camp drag role of the ballet and the choreographer of its essential narrative action (Dido's suicide) does affirm drag dance as a mode of rechoreographing codes. But the Sorceress, who has no interest in making the world a better place for other people's bodies, uses this power only to scramble and reimpose the codes in pernicious variations, getting off on how bad they can be.

The first time the audience sees the Sorceress onstage, at the beginning of the second scene, her face is hidden: she is lying facedown over the middle of the bench, with her hair and hands dangling to the floor. Her shoulders are hunched, her curls are a riotous mass, and her wrists are twisted inward so that her knuckles lie on the ground while her long, gleaming fingernails curl up slightly. It's a creepy posture; it looks like she could wake up at any minute and slither off the bench toward the audience. She lies there for some time, though, draped over the bench with her wrists twisted backward—long enough that the image impresses itself in everyone's mind—and then, in slow deliberate movements, she starts to knuckle-walk her way down the bench, rippling her long, snaky fingers but still keeping her face hidden.

This movement phrase represents a puzzling choreographic choice, because it means that Morris, who has just spent the whole opening scene establishing himself as a credibly queenly Dido, must now communicate without changing costume that he has become her nemesis, the Sorceress. A significant portion of the audience is likely either to be unfamiliar with the plot entirely or to be unaware of the fact that Purcell's opera differs from Virgil's text by including the Sorceress figure. And, most crucially, Morris has very limited modes of conveying that he is now playing an entirely new character who is the opposite of the character he has been until now. Because only the back of his neck is exposed in this position, the audience can't see yet that the hair clasp is gone. Moreover, he can't use any facial expressions—his only modes of signification are the way he holds and maneuvers his body. At the beginning of the Sorceress's first scene, Morris *looks* like Dido to the audience, just as he probably *looked* like a man to some spectators when he initially appeared onstage as Dido. But what Morris is performing to the audience at this moment is that this mode of reading bodily identity is a mistake, because it assumes a legibility and a fixity to identities that may in fact be fluid, indiscernible, or transforming. Before the Sorceress begins to choreograph for her coven or for Dido, she choreographs this opening posture for the audience, signaling that we should be wary of those moments when identities are visually assigned to bodies.

At the end of the piece, when Dido's final lament unfolds, those splayed-apart fingers signifying "fate" retract themselves from the clear air and start pressing grimly into her chest, heralding her suicide.[24] Dido's death seems to demonstrate that the Sorceress has successfully transposed her brutal choreography first from her own body to the bodies of her witches—who have improvised even more guttings and slittings and stabbings—and finally to the regal body of the Queen. Of course, because the first and final bodies are really the same body, which is also the body of the choreographer, the effort of all this movement-making and rehearsing and refining starts to seem pointedly ironic, a way of stacking frames of reference inside other frames. The Sorceress is Dido's choreographer, but they are also dancing each other; Morris is the Sorceress's choreographer, and yet he still has to dance the death that the Sorceress has made up for Dido. And when Dido commits suicide, it seems that she does stab herself, just as the Sorceress's choreography has mandated.[25] But it is a brief and modest little movement, a quick, sad slip of the hand toward the abdomen, and then Dido collapses forward—she just falls, before anyone from her court can catch her, and her body is lying there draped over the bench, her long hair spilling onto the floor, the back of her pale neck exposed and vulnerable. Her shoulders are drawn in a little, and her arms are twisted at the wrists so that the backs of her hands rest on the floor, with her fingers curling slightly inward like a sleeping child's might. Dido ends her life in the exact same position as the one in which the Sorceress appeared the first time she was seen onstage.

This is the most ambiguous moment of transposition in *Dido and Aeneas*, because it brings together the opening and closing gestures of the Sorceress and Dido. Even *after* Dido has performed the Sorceress's choreography for her suicide, faithfully completing the phrase she has been assigned, she is still bound to the Sorceress's gestural vocabulary. The signature pose of the Sorceress—the one Morris works so hard to imbue with coiled, witchy spitefulness—is now unmoored from its frame of reference, and stands as Dido's noble, self-sacrificing gesture of doomed pride. The two characters can't be onstage together, and yet they are superimposed, as if the live ghost of the Sorceress were inhabiting Dido's body after her death. Dido's body remains in this position for the lengthy dénouement of the piece while her court dances its sorrow and then exits the stage in a slow procession of stately mourning, until there is no one left onstage except the still, spilled-over shape we had learned to recognize as the Sorceress. Dido has sought to express the grave and mournful meaning of her life; shouldn't she have her own singular vocabulary with which to express it? And yet, as her body makes its final statement, as she performs the movement that seals her identity as a tragic queen, she appears to be overwritten by someone else's toxic gestures—a dark view of the insidious inscription of codes upon the body.

It might be possible to interpret Dido's final gesture as one more transposition in an unfinished series of gestures that extend beyond their frame, a last "dance word" to the audience. She has been given a choreographic phrase by the Sorceress, which is full of demands and prohibitions: fall halfway over this bench, stretch your arms out like you're inverting the "fate" gesture, curl your wrists backward, drape your hair away from your neck, lie perfectly still. But because choreography is subject to the particularity of performance, a gesture will change as different bodies take it up and enact its significance. Articulating a "dance word" means inflecting it with accent, tone, cadence, pitch, and emphasis; the antiphrastic performances of Dido and the Sorceress demonstrate that the same vocabulary can be made ironic or imperative, maleficent or mournful. Does Dido's agency lie, then, in giving her last breath to ground the lethal charge of the choreography she inherits? Perhaps when Dido dances her last phrase— "Remember me, but ah! forget my fate"—we should memorialize this tiny, brave improvisation on a bitter theme and forget that it leads to her death all the same. But what would it mean to remember Dido without the gestures that communicate her death?

Forgetting Dido's fate would be like forgetting that it is not just in theaters that some gestures, for certain bodies, are fatal.[26]

## To Be in the Dance

From the perspective of fatal gestures, *Dido and Aeneas* is a duet-to-the-death between Dido and the Sorceress alone. No one else really matters—Aeneas leaves, the court mourns ineffectually, the coven is a chaotic riot of evil children at play. But there is one group of characters in *Dido* whose dancing is not about darkly enforced hierarchies of power and inscription, and they make an interlude in the tragedy that is like the cozy little light of a village in the midst of a tangled, brambly path toward desolation. In a rare moment when neither Dido nor the Sorceress are onstage, the audience is given this respite, this scene of the good-humored collaborative coexistence of people, where everybody works and everybody plays. In this idealistic scene, gender is not marked except as a position you could take up if you wanted to, and everybody dances together.

Joan Acocella has emphasized how thoroughly Morris's choreography is a product of his early training in Balkan folk dance with the Koleda Folk Ensemble—how "the democratic look of his dances" emerged from the collectivism and geometric patterning of this folk tradition, which in time "made his company too look like a village" (1993, 22).[27] "If I want a big number with everybody in it," Morris affirms, "you don't get to decide which sex you get to be, you just get to be in the dance" (Carman et al. 2005). This vision of a gender-inclusive folk-dancing "village" emerges in a scene called "The Ships," in which Aeneas gives the order for the Trojan ships to be made ready to sail, and his sailors—the same dancers who perform in Dido's court and in the Sorceress's coven—exuberantly set about hauling in ropes, hoisting up sails, and taking "a boozy short leave / of your nymphs on the shore." To do this, they hike up the skirts of their costumes just above the knees and tuck them in so that they are wearing something like short, loose, blousy trousers. It's an even more unisex look than the sarongs they wear in the other scenes. The sailors' *gaillarde* includes elements of Irish step dancing (the arms held straight at the sides; quick, light kick steps with the knees kept together), general folk-dance formations like the two lines of dancers who face each other, and, in keeping with the rest of *Dido*, gestures keyed to words in the libretto. Among these are the pantomime of tossing back the rest of one's drink, to signify the "boozy short leave," and a finger to the lips that wags back and forth to the line "and silence their mourning." The sailors do look happy that they get to be in the dance; they clap, they play tug-of-war with a rope, and at one point they put their thumbs in their armpits and flap their elbows like chicken wings, which is an exceedingly goofy gesture but one they do cheerfully.

Another salient aspect of the sailors' dance is that it is pointedly not virtuosic. When Morris described the gender dynamic among the early members of his company by saying "They can all do everything," he perhaps meant something more like 'They're all up for anything' (Acocella 1993, 91). The sailors' ensemble dance is a little good-naturedly ragged around the edges (especially in the 1995 film version). They are sometimes cast against gender and body type,[28] and just as often not, which gives the impression that Morris hasn't even really noticed which of his dancers are male and which are female.[29] The dancers attest to the kinesthetic effects of this communal, non-gender-based casting: dancer Joe Bowie described the experience of joining MMDG after two years of dancing with Paul Taylor, a company for which "I was always squatting and jumping, always picking people up, because with Paul, men are men and women are women. But after a few months with Mark, I noticed I could wear jeans again. My thighs were no longer too big. . . . Oh. And I finally had a neck" (Senior 2002). In addition to resisting normative gender roles for his dancers, Morris is stalwart in his opposition to what he sees as the youth-beauty-virtuosity algorithm that dismisses dancers after wearing them out.[30] Twenty years after joining the company, Guillermo Resto was nearly fifty, and his dreadlocks were going gray; instead of pushing him to retire, Morris made a piece in which the two of them could dance together again (Dalva 2003).

At the end of the sailors' dance—after the very last boozy leave has been taken from the nymphs on the shore—two dancers remain onstage. One is a man and the other is woman, and the man throws the woman over his shoulder like a sack of potatoes and saunters offstage. It's one of the very few lifts in the entire ballet, and since, traditionally, men are both the ones lifting women in dances and the ones known for throwing women over their shoulders and carrying them off, it seems that this interaction should signal something nefariously normative about the gender relations between these two dancers. It completely refuses to do this. Instead, it's clear that they're both sailors, and if one of them is too drunk to walk, the other one will pick her up and helpfully carry his shipmate back to her berth to sleep it off.[31] "I want men and women to be able to do everything the other can do, because I need that in my work," Morris explained (2003,

235). "And I think it makes everybody better." Even this trivial moment, the movement phrase for the last dancers' exit, is choreographed to exude it-takes-a-village goodwill rather than gender-bound roles.

There are two other notable lifts in *Dido and Aeneas*. One happens during Dido and Aeneas's duet; this is the citation from *The Sound of Music*, which includes Dido running up on a bench while holding Aeneas's hand. The lifts in this scene are possible only because Dido whirls the mass of her body around, and the momentum this creates allows Aeneas to lift her briefly from the floor, in the midst of her turn. When Dido runs along the bench, Aeneas merely holds her hand; she jumps down to the floor by herself, and then *he* runs along the bench in the same way, while she politely holds *his* hand. The romance of the power imbalance between two gendered bodies—a dynamic that underlies classical ballet and that is far from absent from modern dance—is subverted by three things in this scene. One is a citation of a popular musical (with a camp connotation in queer culture); the second is the equality of movement that Morris has taken on as a principle; and the third is the fact that by bringing in a prosthetic support, Morris has figured out how to accommodate the gendered body he has *and* the gendered role he is playing. This duet is as close to a romantic pas de deux as *Dido and Aeneas* comes, but it is full of queer solutions to problems of power, weight, and heteronormative sentimentality.

The other significant lift in *Dido and Aeneas* is an unusual one, involving three people. When the Sorceress has planned Dido's ruin, she squats down slightly and holds out her arms to her two witchy minions—the same ones who have just been jumping up on each other's backs—and they hop right up onto her big thighs, one perched on each meaty leg, and she holds them there, looking back and forth between them with an evil half-smile. One of those witches is female and the other is male, but their choreography is absolutely equal. In the first cast, those witches were Morris's longtime dancers and good friends Ruth Davidson and Jon Mensinger. The backstage history of this lift is woven into the origin story of the piece: Morris had first created Dido's part on Davidson while choreographing the Sorceress on Mensinger; he then learned the roles back from them—something he often does with his own solos (Morris and Acocella 2009; Jordan 2011, 207). From the beginning, then, Dido and the Sorceress had double bodies, bodies that embedded other gestural histories under their roles, bodies inflected with their own specific configurations of gender and sexuality. At the same time, according to dancers who learned Dido's part later, the steps were premised on a challenge specific to Morris's own body: "he wanted to make them impossible for himself," Amber Star Merkens reported, by "giving himself things that could trip him up" (Kourlas and Merkens 2012). This layering of bodies, so central to drag dances, meant that Morris was both dancing full-out in his own body, to the very limits of his impressive technical capacity, while also dancing the particularities of other bodies that inhered in the roles from the moment of their creation. At the premiere of *Dido and Aeneas*, when Davidson and Mensinger hopped up on Morris's thighs and he held them there, he was a Sorceress who had his arms around other versions of Dido and the Sorceress, as if he were embracing the ghostly imprints of their bodies in his roles.

It was only a few months after the premiere of the piece, in the summer of 1989, when Jon Mensinger learned that he was HIV-positive (Acocella 1993, 113). He was determined to dance as long as he could, and Morris continued to make work on him as long as he could dance. In 1991 Mensinger was too sick to rehearse (115). In 1994, when he was thirty-seven years old, he died in a hospital in Manhattan. The *New York Times* obituary described him as "a dancer of special delicacy." Other dancers took on his roles, and Morris kept performing the Sorceress for years afterward, settling himself squarely into the squat that could support two other dancers. When the witches scrambled up on his thighs, after the summer of 1989, Morris was holding something besides the substantial weight of two bodies and the insubstantial, transposed origins of his own roles in other dancers. Morris was also holding a dancer who was holding the place where Jon Mensinger had been—remembering him through the body of someone else, and remembering with his own body what it had been to hold the body of this person he loved, this dancer, this gay man, this other Sorceress, this death, this friend, this fate: this delicate balance of bodies and ghosts.

## The Afterlife of Drag in Dido

The combination of a double female lead role in drag and non-gender-based ensemble casting established a dynamic that lasted until 2006, when Morris decided to bring the piece back into repertoire, after he had stopped dancing both Dido and the Sorceress. (At that point, he was forty-nine years old; his last performance in *Dido* had been in 2000.) This brought up a new question: what statement would a drag dance like *Dido and Aeneas* ultimately make about the identity politics of gender and sexuality? Morris seems to have had some problems settling this question himself, because he first proposed splitting the roles apart. Acocella reported in the *New Yorker*, just before the company opened its twenty-fifth anniversary season at the Brooklyn Academy of Music, that "the grand-legged Amber Darragh [Star Merkens] will be Dido; the maenadic Bradon McDonald, the Sorceress" (2006). However, in 2007 Morris decided that the role would belong to a single dancer during each performance, and the casting would alternate from evening to evening between Merkens (female, lanky, broad-shouldered) and McDonald (male, lithe, muscular, in cat-eye makeup). Then, in 2013, he gave both roles to Laurel Lynch, who was 5'9", ballet-trained, and promptly anointed by *Dance Magazine* as "Morris' Golden Girl" (Harss 2015). This has meant that sometimes the love story between Dido and Aeneas would be acted out by a woman and a man, and at other times by a man and a man; sometimes the Sorceress would be a drag role, sometimes more like a faux drag role.

This casting choice shifted the performance away from some of the most marked aspects of Morris's performance, and toward a balance of gender inclusivity like the one already present in the ensemble dances. The ballet that had originally scandalized the Belgian press with its anti-gender-based casting now seemed to be unconcerned with gender altogether. But one interesting thing about the backstage life of the Dido/Sorceress role is that it continues to draw upon drag as a form of bodily knowledge, even when a woman is dancing the dual female roles. Both Merkens and McDonald felt that the experience of performing in drag for a burlesque show was "important preparation," as they stated, for the Sorceress role (Jordan 2011, 207). In fact, when "Merkens began her explorations of the Sorceress role and felt that it was not working for her, Morris suggested that she 'play it as a man,'" Jordan relates (171). Merkens described this strategy to Jordan as "an interesting twist on the gender reversal": she could thereby deploy a set of masculinities and femininities, including a female masculinity that would help her to inhabit a role already imprinted with male femininity.

When McDonald played the Sorceress, he tended to hike up his costume and flash his gold nails, simultaneously emphasizing what was viciously femme and what was full of rough power—not only did we see his strong calves and big feet, but we heard the slaps of palms and soles as he slammed them down. He shoved his witches around with real force and irritation, but when he was dancing with them, he kept his shoulders

Figure 5. Bradon McDonald as Dido (with Craig Biesecker as Aeneas).
Photo by Costas, courtesy of Mark Morris Dance Group.

Figure 6. Amber Star Merkens as Dido (with Domingo Estrada Jr. as
Aeneas). Photo by Susana Millman, courtesy of Mark Morris Dance
Group.

breathy and mobile, rising and falling like shivers, trembly, thrilled. When Amber Star Merkens played the Sorceress, she sat on the bench like a basketball player, slouching, her knees apart, propping her elbows, hunching her sizeable shoulders, pushing her jaw out sulkily. She used her height and the length of her torso; she moved abruptly and decisively, handling the space of the stage like something she'd already owned for a long time.

But when Merkens played Dido, a surprising element of 'gay' male camp crept in. Her courtship scene with Aeneas ended in sassy, triumphant hip-swaying and a loose-wristed, flippantly dismissive wave to the side. Somewhere in her explorations of how to dance a drag role that wasn't, strictly speaking, a drag role for her, she had expanded her range of movement styles in more than one direction. She took up these styles selectively; Dido is a tragic queen, and when Merkens danced the injunction "remember me," her first movements were long, elegant, performed with straight arms and an elegiac reaching of her spine. As she danced toward her death, Merkens tightened her gestures to mirror the constraints of "fate," almost jerking the thread from her palm, the legs snailed into a curl. In her final moments she appeared almost genderless and infinitely aged, posed behind the bench with a bowed head and hunched shoulders, like a standing stone. For the recent casts of *Dido*, drag has become less stridently a statement of political visibility; in the first quarter of the twenty-first century, you can't shock the American concert dance world by exclaiming, *We're here, we're queer, get used to it*. What drag retains, though, is its kinesthetic power: if you need access to more gender styles than normativity has given you, drag continues to be a strategy for finding and exploring those styles.

Like Amber Star Merkens, Laurel Lynch uses her height to convey Dido's imperious pride and her lean, loose-jointed muscularity to get down into the Sorceress's casual malevolence. She describes the Sorceress as "crasser, more masculine," all "looser" movements and "lower impulses" (MMDG 2016a; Palmer 2016). Whenever the Sorceress sits on the bench, Lynch's knees lounge apart and her shoulders slump up toward her ears; she nods to her witches by jerking her chin up at them, and her mouth tends to yaw open nastily, like a rabid fan jeering his team on to ever more violent victories. She throws like someone with a Molotov cocktail, heaving from her shoulder. Ballet might have helped her with Dido's restraint and formality, but in order to dance the Sorceress, Lynch was forced to counter the kinesthetic gender training a young ballerina receives: she had to get weightier, wider, lower, looser, rougher, ruder. It is perhaps not coincidental, therefore, that Lynch thinks of the Sorceress as "undoing" Dido (MMDG 2016b). In working out how to route Morris's drag-queeniness into her own body through a masculinity she had never been given, she *was* thinking about "undoing" gender.

And what would Morris himself do, now that he wasn't onstage dancing both female leads? He has chosen to do two things, and both of these bespeak his roots in folk dance traditions. (The third option, he quipped to Joan Acocella in 2009, was to sit in the back of the theater and be a sniper.) As *Boston Globe* critic Thea Singer wrote in 2008, "In this production, both female leads have shrunk; they now fit neatly into the frame of the work as a whole. Morris has, as if casting a bas-relief in reverse, brought the chorus—10 members of the Mark Morris Dance Group—to the fore." Meanwhile, Morris himself is down in the orchestra pit, out of sight, conducting the musicians and singers who are performing the score live. From the pit, he sees not only a new cast; he sees a new idea of casting. He watches Dido danced by people who are not living with the certainty that they will die from AIDS. Moreover, those roles are doubled differently from his perspective as a conductor, because Dido, like the Sorceress, is now equally a singer and a dancer. Morris is still leading, but he is not starring; he assumes responsibility for the harmony of the piece as a whole.

As the emphasis on singular lead roles has diminished, there has been a privileging of the group—the chorus of voices, the company of dancers, the ensemble, the village—whose intermingled patterns idealize a democratic harmony. It is telling that the current Aeneas, Domingo Estrada Jr., describes himself ardently as "a 3rd generation Mexican-American [who has] strived my entire life to immerse my every being in the melting cultural pot that is America" (2014). Like Guillermo Resto before him, Estrada dances the role of Aeneas bare-chested; the problem of who is seen as "foreign," "swarthy," or "barbarian" is unresolved, and troubling questions of assimilation and representation persist in the uneasy cliché of the "melting pot." The racial politics of casting are still as unsettled as the lived experiences of dancers of color in this country; what has shifted is gender equity in casting—even for drag roles. If at first it was important to shock audiences by casting a man in the female lead roles, and then it seemed right to share those roles between a man and a woman, now it is time for them to be done by a woman. After all, it's only fair that people with different genders should be able to dance Dido and the Sorceress; the roles aren't a constative description of the gender or sexuality of the body performing them. Someday, maybe, the lead roles will be open to even more genders, and the people who dance Aeneas won't have to constantly defend their citizenship, their heritage, their right to belong.

This vision is admittedly utopian, like Koleda, and it doesn't erase the fact that in every performance, Dido dies from the choreography she is made to bear. But as José Muñoz points out, "Queerness is utopian" (2009, 26). And drag dances, like other queer artistic practices, investigate some possible, partial, imperfect, troubled, and hopeful answers to Muñoz's question: "How does one stage utopia?" (97). *Dido and Aeneas* asks its dancers as well as its audiences to consider the histories of reading bodies and constraining identities, but also to think about potential futures. What can these bodies do, and what will happen if they do that? What must be remembered under the injunction to forget? What imprints certain bodies with certain fates, and how can we interrupt that toxic transposition of bodily codes? Mark Morris, having made his provocative declaration that queerness should be visible in dance and that gestural codes for gender should be scrutinized critically, finally decided it wasn't 1989 anymore. Drag wasn't only about flinging open the closets of the dance world; it was also a way to broaden repertoire, both for individual dancers and for the whole company, and that meant more roles were open to more people— and that those people could perform the genders and sexualities of those roles differently, and still be applauded. In *Dido and Aeneas*, at least, the afterlife of cross-gender casting is the communal, utopian, slightly bewildering world of the sailors, where if everyone lends a hand, they all get to be in the dance.

## CHAPTER TWO

## Martha @ Martha

### A Séance with Richard Move

Just think of yourself as dancing towards your death.
  —Martha Graham, *Blood Memory*

When you do the work, you do feel the people—the spirits—come
in sometimes. It keeps you connected.
  —Chi Chi Valenti, 2016

Keep the channel open.
  —Martha Graham to Agnes de Mille, in *Martha*

### Blood Memory

"A dancer, more than any other human being, dies two deaths," Martha
Graham proclaimed in her autobiography,[1] but the one she brooded over
was the first one: the knowledge that as she aged, her body could no longer respond to the demands of dancing (1991, 238). Still, she continued to
perform until she was well into her seventies, adapting the steps of the
roles she had choreographed for herself decades earlier so that she could
still get through them.[2] "But I knew," she said bitterly. "And it haunted
me." Fiercely attached to the act of performing live, Graham resisted being
filmed while she danced until she was in her sixties, when she suddenly
took to the camera with a driven, harrowed sort of determination that
suggested, as dance scholar Victoria Thoms writes, cinematic representation "as an almost necessary punishment" for the knowledge of her aging
body (2013, 114).[3] When someone asked her how it felt to see a film of
herself dancing in her late sixties, Graham replied, with acrid wit, "I have
faced death before" (Thoms 2013, 103).[4]

Graham wanted to fill up the stage with the dramatic intensity that emanated from her own body. She was consistently drawn over the years to female characters who underwent anguished, heroic, soul-searing struggles; sometimes she would dance them as Joan of Arc, sometimes as Emily Dickinson, sometimes as Medea. She took the divine calling of dance seriously, and whenever she was performing—as the heretic or the heroine, the priestess or the pioneer—she burned with that proud, lonely singularity.[5] Later in her life, she could barely stand to watch her own dancers take on the roles she had originated. In a rehearsal for *Appalachian Spring* (1944), when Ethel Winter would dance the Bride—a role Graham had choreographed for herself, casting her lover Erick Hawkins as the Husbandman—for the first time, fellow dancer Phyllis Gutelius recalled, "The agony of Martha's bitterness almost cut the air as she watched another dancer rehearse a role in which she had been so happy" (Horosko 2002, 114). Even though she had chosen to create a company comprised entirely of women until the arrival of Erick Hawkins in 1938, Graham guarded her own roles jealously, keeping her acolytes and understudies out of the spotlight.[6] The character she performed, over and over, was choreographed as a self-proclamation, and when Martha Graham poured herself into a role, it brimmed with her.

By the time she died, at the age of ninety-six, she had decided to call her autobiography *Blood Memory*, because she believed that a dancer's body bore its own unspoken, aeonic way of knowing, and that in a dancer's veins ran "a blood memory that can speak to us" (1991, 9).[7] But *Blood Memory* itself is a fragmented and reluctant autobiography, undertaken by a woman who wanted still to be dancing instead of writing down her memories of dancing. When choreographer Antony Tudor asked her whether she would rather be remembered as a dancer or a choreographer, she replied immediately, "As a dancer" (Graham 1991, 236). Tudor regarded her for a moment. "'I pity you,'" he said, and that was that: choreography might be preserved, pieces could be kept in repertoire, but what memory of a dancer could really be held, fixed, communicated? For this reason, *Blood Memory* was doomed never to illuminate its central conceit, because to explain exactly what animated Martha Graham—to write down in words what was coursing through her body—was antithetical both to her fervent belief in dance as an expressive art and to the unique ferocity of her dancing.[8] This is probably why, when "Graham was prodded with the question, 'How do you describe blood memory to your class?' she retorted with a single sentence, 'I say blood memory'" (Phillips 2013, 71). But in fact Graham did give a more specific definition to her dancers: she stood in front of them, wordlessly, and acted out "the slitting of her wrists and bleeding onto the planks of Studio One's wood floor" (71). For Graham, blood memory could be felt by dancers, and it could be evoked through gesture—but you couldn't parse it out for people who needed words to understand what moves bodies.

"The main thing, of course," she said in a National Public Radio broadcast in 1953, "always is there is only one of you in the world, just one, and if that is not fulfilled then something has been lost." On the surface, this sounds like an encouraging Modernist affirmation that the artist is unique and essential, but its emphasis—"of course, always . . . only one of you in the world, just one"—goes beyond that, hinting at something defensive and perilous. It stipulates a fantastically satisfying and self-contained narrative for the artist: you are born, you create, your art expresses the essence of you, you become entire and replete within yourself, and so nothing is lost. However, Western concert dance does not allow for this continuous fullness of a dancer's bodily presence, nor does it offer the reassurance that works will endure.[9] There are two hard, historical kinds of disappearance: choreography is forgotten and dancers stop dancing. These are interrelated; the reason that dances are lost is, fundamentally, because dancers are lost, and this happens at an incredible rate relative to any other art form.[10] Canvases do not forget the paint that has been laid upon them two decades ago, and poems, sitting on their pages, are not shattered by the deaths of their poets. But there is a third, uneasy question about dance's impermanence: Does dance disappear in the very moment it is being performed? Is it ephemeral, fleeting, borne away in the instant of its arrival, burnt up just as it flames into being? Or, as dance theorist André Lepecki suggests, might dance be instead "a dynamic, transhistorical, and intersubjective system of incorporations and excorporations"—and dancing, therefore, could be seen "not only as that which *passes away* (in time and across space) but also as that which passes around (between and across bodies of dancers, viewers, choreographers) and as that which also, always, *comes back around*" (2010, 39)? This "coming back around" is not quite the same as Graham's idea of a transcendent blood memory, although they both hold out hope for a dance whose ontology isn't lostness, for a genealogy of dance that isn't simply deaths and inheritances. "Blood memory," in its mythopoetic resonances, was like an underground river or a transcendent spirit that welled up in you—and its abstract universality could run close to essentialism, especially in terms of gender and race.[11]

Lepecki's insistence on the strange, cyclical touching of dances and dancers across time is, by contrast, like queer and elliptical forms of kinship, like shivering when a shadow passes over your skin.

It is like haunting.


## A First Death

"What Becomes a Legend Most?" the 1976 Blackgama advertisement for mink coats asked provocatively, proffering an image of Martha Graham swathed in fur. What was becoming *to* the legend and what was becoming *of* the legend were, at that time, uncomfortably similar questions. The Martha Graham who had ruled her own body with such Puritan zeal that her dancers, by proxy, ought to be the kind of "wholesome American girls who carried their own luggage to hotels in support of a cab drivers' strike" in Chicago in the 1930s, was now having facelifts, being seen at Studio 54, and posing for photographs with the wives of rock stars (Thoms 2013, 83; Croce 2000, 680; Phillips 2013, 68). If, as dance critic Alastair Macaulay would write in the *New York Times* in 2011, "it should go without saying that Martha Graham is one of the greatest of all American artists," what did it mean that she was becoming a proliferation of images, a character framed by fawning captions?[12] What would be lost now that the dancer had stopped dancing?

From the perspective of the archivist, there is a safety, however partial, in materials that can be copied and filed. For the choreographer, the issue of duration is more delicate, because if you have made a piece on dancers' bodies, you then depend on the capacity of those bodies to preserve an intensified physical memory—a memory that has also been designated as your work of art. And for a dancer, what remains of the choreography depends on the uncertain duration of the kinesthetic memory of dancing it, like a soft and dusty precipitate in the body.[13] Martha Graham, perhaps perversely, gave the impression that she didn't much care what happened to her choreography: she left dancer Helen McGehee to her own devices in 1965 when McGehee was to perform the lead role of Medea in *Cave of the Heart*, and there was a general sense, as Emiko Tokunaga reported, that "Martha offered little help in the reconstruction of her dances" (Franko 2012, 180). But she cared terribly—viscerally—about her dancing.

For Martha Graham, aging was not a gradual and abstract decline; it was the specific foreknowledge that dancing could be erased from her body. "Until the mid-1950s her age was difficult to determine on stage," Mark Franko observes in *Martha Graham in Love and War*, but this age-less stage creature was a performance in itself, a brave show against the on-coming years (2012, 176). In fact, she was haunted by the ruthless brevity of a dancer's career, and by the way her aging body would, hollowly, echo back memories of how she had once danced. To live in a body that could only *see* dances, she felt, was an infernal agony:

> It wasn't until years after I had relinquished a ballet that I could bear to watch someone else dance it. . . . I believe in never looking back. . . . Yet how can you avoid it when you look on stage and see a dancer made up to look as you did thirty years ago, dancing a ballet you created with someone you were then deeply in love with, your husband? I think that is a circle of hell Dante omitted. (1991, 200)

This is her vision of the dancer's 'first death,' and it is not only an experience of death but also one of ghostliness, of being present in the afterlife of one's own body. If the dancer undergoes a first, early death of the body, when it no longer succeeds in expressing choreographed movement, then what remains for the dancer afterward?

The perceived first death of the body must leave a dancer with a second body: a non-dancer's body. Haunted by the memories of her first body—which are amplified by the harrowing visual experience of watching another body express her 'self'—Graham sees her second body as empty of dance (200). Instead, this space is filled by an enlargement of character, an exaggeration of the insistent signs of selfhood. This is why she begins *Blood Memory* with the line "I am a dancer"; the tense is wrong, but this is exactly what conveys the most autobiographical information possible (3). The first body was capacious, filled by the dances it held and could hold, and aligned with a dancer's spirit and memory, while the second body is evacuated of dance but still *there*, sitting uneasily in the audience, watching someone perform its role. This is a displacement that allows for eerie doubling, which is the opposite of the aphorism of singularity and fulfill-ment that Graham offered on national radio in 1953.

Graham's sense of the dancer's two deaths insinuates that perhaps there is not only one of you, and perhaps, as a dancer, you are destined to leave yourself empty in this morbid, keenly particular way. Perhaps your truest knowledge of the temporality of dance occurs when the first body slips away, and the second body acquires its double consciousness of loss and presence. In the idealized circle of artistic fulfillment, you might say that your dancing is an offering, poured out lavishly before audiences, burnt up in honor of the presiding deities: this act of giving is enough for you. But when your body cannot give its dancing anymore, the circuit of fulfillment is broken. The gift does not come back to you. The second body, which cannot merely dance its self-expression—which is forced to insist, "I am a dancer!" instead of dancing—has to fill itself with a different kind of performance of identity.

By the time *Blood Memory* was being assembled, Martha Graham's first body had been dead for a long time. In the "thirty years" she counts of living in her second body, she struggles with the vision of younger dancers, made up to look like she used to, moving in her place onstage, scything their legs through the air, and sweeping into the arms of their partners. The dancers in her company cannot help but see this bodily disjunction— "Martha danced too long, you know," said Betty MacDonald, one of Graham's original trio of dancers, as if you *did* know, and so did everyone else (Tracy 1996, 8). Martha Graham is haunted by the visible knowledge that she, as a dancer and choreographer, has not simply created and been fulfilled, and thus left no room in the world for imitation. Instead, there are ghosts everywhere, and none of them will ever be the original dancer in her first body, and she is like a shell of herself, hardened and empty of its meat. And because Martha Graham's idea of hell was to be in the audience, she developed in her second body a relentless self-performance of character, with all of its trappings: the watchful dark eyes in a face caked with makeup, the bony little gestures of the hands, the brittle low voice of a deposed queen.

## Mothers

Martha Graham, often hailed as the "Mother of Modern Dance," died on April 1, 1991. On September 10, 1996, in the Meatpacking District of Manhattan, Chi Chi Valenti, known as the "New York Nightclub Empress," and her husband, the DJ Johnny Dynell, threw open the golden doors of a club called Mother, on Washington Street at W. Fourteenth. Mother boasted a gilded vestibule of pornographic frescoes, an eight-by-fourteen-foot stage, and sixty folding chairs, with standing room for twenty-five more people, if they stood very close together. Since March 1991, Valenti and Dynell had been running a party called Jackie 60—a Tuesday-night "scathing cabaret" of experimental club performance on themes ranging from "Fear of a Blond Pussy" to "Jackie the Ripper" (Reardon 2001)—in the same space, but now it was *theirs*, transformed from "raw space" into a red velvet dream factory (Valenti 2016). Five nights a week, Mother joined fine establishments like the Toilet, Crisco Disco, and the Mineshaft in making the Meatpacking District a better place for everything. "We have wigs, we have Guido drag, we have lorgnettes," Valenti said, enumerating the many treasures kept backstage, and "we have gigantic cage dresses" (Trebay 1996, 20). Down the block, Lee's Mardi Gras Boutique—run by Lee Brewster, the drag activist who founded the Queens Liberation Front and published *Drag* magazine—kept Mother's patrons in "size-12 fetish shoes" (Valenti 2016). As long as you didn't step into a pile of offal upon leaving the club at dawn, it was a convivial neighborhood.

The dream of Mother had first come into being one night during an ice storm, when Dynell and Valenti, drinking their way through the worst of winter in New York, had gotten the idea that the thing to do was to get into a yellow cab and go look at a decrepit space that had been occupied first by the lesbian Clit Club, which opened in July 1990, and then by the gay club Meat (Valenti 2016). Before they even walked through the door, Chi Chi Valenti remembers, they just knew. It was as if they had heard a voice, and the voice had said, "The hacienda must be built!" just as the Situationist Ivan Chtcheglov had written in his 1953 essay "Formulary for a New Urbanism." They loved it. Eventually, they put the Situationist quote on the invitation to Mother's opening-night party—"You'll never see the hacienda. It does not exist. The hacienda must be built"—and so many people came to build the hacienda that all the decorations had to be hung from the ceiling; nothing else could fit on the floor.

Jackie 60 was the heart of parties at Mother: its ethos of mash-up collective punk drag outré queer go-go art madness had been inspired by theme nights at the Mudd Club, where Valenti and Dynell had first met, by the Situationists, and by Valenti's work as a window-dresser. "That's where I learned that if you want something to look real, you don't use the real thing," Valenti explained (Trebay 1996, 20). In the beginning, Jackie 60 had been a lark, something to take up the deadness of Tuesday nights at Nell's, which was generally a "very posh, celebrity velvet-rope place" but was owned by the open-minded Nell Campbell of *Rocky Horror* fame (Valenti 2016). It was late 1990; "AIDS had just decimated three-quarters of the creative people in our generation," Valenti noted; they thought Jackie 60 might brighten the scene for a few months. Instead, Jackie 60 became a steady beacon of midweek revelry, a disco ball in the wilderness, "a louche little house on the prairie," as Guy Trebay wrote fondly in the *Village Voice* (1996, 20). It provided a home and a family for people who thought het-eronormative, cisgender structures like "home" and "family" ought to be fodder for queer window-dressing; when Dynell went off to gigs as a DJ, he would say, "Daddy has to turn a trick to pay for Mother!" Madame Ekaterina Sobechanskaya, the grande dame of the Original Trockadero Gloxinia Ballet (who was also known as Larry Ree), wafted in weekly for Jackie 60, even deigning to dance once or twice for her admirers (Valenti 2016). The theater critic Hilton Als declared, "When I die, scatter my ashes over Jackie 60!" Until the very last Tuesday of the twentieth century, Jackie 60 held court.[14]

In those years, downtown club drag performance was polarized: there was the East Village avant-garde aesthetic of the Pyramid Club (which Valenti describes as "finding your dress in the garbage and putting it on and pouring blood all over yourself, and all the stuff we loved"), set against the more genteel style of Boy Bar ("classic lipsynch; staged, coiffed, cos-tumed") on St. Mark's Place.[15] Jackie 60 was a "laboratory," Valenti says, a combustible admixture of the explosive outrageousness of the Pyramid and the artful glamor queens of the Boy Bar, where Dynell DJ'd. In this heady atmosphere, the older idea of drag as 'impersonation' commingled with the more experimental approach to drag as 'performance.' So when one of Jackie 60's cofounders, a dancer named Richard Move, was assigned one of "these theme nights [we did] every fucking Tuesday," as he remem-bers, he decided to organize a "Dance Legends" show, which would benefit the HIV Action Network (Landini 2007). In an appropriately legendary cross between impersonation, performance, activism, historiography, and the queer claiming of kinship, there would be "someone doing Nijinsky's faun, someone else as Ruth St Denis," and a raucous auction of dance-belts (Gilbert 2001).[16] The theme of the evening would be "Acrobats of God," which was both the title of a Graham piece—"one of the last ballets she performed in," Move noted (Bell and Move 2017)—and a fair description of Jackie 60's aesthetic of divine pandemonium.

That night, Richard Move got up on the tiny proscenium stage in a vintage dress and a wig of such ambitious proportions that his bun nearly swept the ceiling and, for the first time, 'channeled' Martha Graham. The Jackie 60 crowd loved this strange new Martha; even the "people [who] had only a vague idea who Graham was . . . immediately got that she was a diva" like "Maria Callas or Bette Davis" and worshipped her appropriately,

Move noted with satisfaction (Landini 2007). And this was, as Move said later, the night that launched "my odyssey with Martha"; almost immediately, *Martha @ Mother* began to take on a life of its own (Levine 2014). After the second show, Bertram Ross—one of the Graham company's stars, and a longtime confidante of Martha Graham's—came up to Richard Move to give him costume advice (Lepecki 2010, 43). Soon, "old videotapes in the ever more decaying and neglected archives of the company would be secretly smuggled out by company members and lent to Move so he could continue his research and compose his short re-enactments," Lepecki reports (43). By the end of 1996, Joan Acocella was commemorating dance-themed nights at Jackie 60 as historic events (1996, 79), and *Martha @* had officially became a show all its own. How was it that Richard Move's reincarnation of Martha Graham, five years after her second death, had enthralled both the Jackie 60 crew—for whom diva drag was like catnip—and the dance people who took Martha Graham most seriously?

## Second Bodies

In an evening that is part séance and part showcase, Richard Move begins by showing a short video by Charles Atlas: an assemblage of dance footage, excerpts from television, and film clips in which someone—anyone—says the name "Martha."[17] In a sly and humorous way, Atlas's video establishes the visual sense that there is something spooky about Martha Graham: that she flickers in and out of montages, that characters in other films suddenly call out her name, that this is an uncanny homage to someone who is still haunting the theater. When the video ends, Richard Move appears onstage, standing very still for a moment in a dramatically pooled spotlight that glitters off his spangled Halston gown. Long, spiky shadows fall from his modestly lowered false lashes as he says in a weary, regal voice, "Yes, I *am* the mother of contemporary dance." There are scattered, knowing laughs in the audience. The image of Martha Graham is instantly recognizable: the high dark bun piled up on her head, the severity with which she holds her shoulders, the way she intones her grand truths in that studied, deliberate alto voice, so slowly that she almost drawls. The spotlight intensifies. You can see her teeth shining, the hollows of her collarbones. "Movement never lies," Martha declares imperiously, and sweeps offstage.

Holding court at Mother, Move sought to convey Graham's dramatic and self-willed fatefulness, her flair for taking center stage with an iron grip, and, most especially, the terrible and worn grandeur she brought to aging. He also danced abridged and cramped excerpts of her pieces, but mostly he performed her as a character—*la Graham*, the grande dame of contemporary dance. Not only did Move ventriloquize Graham's "sentimental" dance philosophies, as David Román put it, but he also seemed to share "Graham's romantic sense that art and religion are linked" (2005, 168). It was a mystical, melodramatic summoning, edged with the kind of camp Susan Sontag would recognize: Move described his Martha as poised on the cusp of self-performance, a 1950s Martha who "'was already a living legend'" and "'would still out-dance the girls who were 19 in the company'" with the dregs of a wild joy that was beginning to turn to grim ferocity (Carman 2000). But Move was especially interested in what happened when Martha tilted over the edge of her first life, when she was losing dance and super-adding character, so he decided to perform her just as the "decline was starting . . . maybe even rumors that she was drinking a little."[18] This was a Martha who was beginning to look backward as she slid forward, scrabbling at the past, riven by her forebodings about the future—a Martha who could see the onset of her own second body.

Richard Move is at least six foot four, which is generally the first thing mentioned in any article about the *Martha @* show. This statement is most often followed up by the observation that he is a good sixteen inches taller than Martha Graham ever was.[19] In one way the rhetorical gambit of these articles echoes Graham's idea of the two bodies, emphasizing how the death of the first gives rise to the appearance of the self-consciously performative, pointedly unnatural second body. As Charles Atlas's video flits through its clips, we see a multiplication of Marthas, and then the images resolve into a second body, that of the male dancer Richard Move, which is remarkably tall and resoundingly solid. His body projects, above all, the same quality that Martha Graham hated about her own second body when she watched her dancers from the audience: it is *there*.

Writers choose this opening hook because their readers will be interested in the disjunction between these two bodies, and because the difference in height is a sign that Richard Move has the 'wrong' body to perform Martha Graham. It also mimics a trick that is the hallmark of stereotypical drag performance, which is that after the breathless and magical illusion of the drag show, the performer takes off his wig, or, more daringly, flips up his skirt, and the audience is reassured that, underneath it all, the man is still a man.[20] These writers are not reflecting the structure of Move's show itself—Martha would never flip up her skirt—but instead responding to a certain cultural narrative about drag performance: first, evidence is summoned of its freakishness, then its playful naughtiness is brandished, and finally, its threat of transgression is neutralized through revelation. In reviews of Les Ballets Trockadero de Monte Carlo, the signs of masculinity are often trumpeted in the same way—it is rare not to read of the dancers' "chest hair," "linebacker" builds, and "size 12 toe shoes"—just before the drag ballerinas' technique, precision, and grace is praised effusively. As Victoria Thoms writes, this rhetorical similarity might be attributed to the fact that "both Move, with his statuesque difference from the diminutive Graham, and the Trocks, with their hairy armpits and chest hair, present themselves so that certain things about their performance restrict the potential for them to be understood as 'real'" (2013, 138). But it is not Richard Move's fault that he is extremely tall, just as it is not a Trockadero dancer's decision to have large feet or a broad chest.[21]

In fact, the "real" that Move and the Trockadero are primarily presenting is not gender revelation but rather the queer potential of reembodying dance that includes difference within itself. By conducting dance across the presumed boundaries of gender, time, and bodily difference, these dancers point out that these are not borders that ought to demand of you a passport or a proper reason for entry. Martha Graham can be channeled by Richard Move not *in spite of* the fact that he is a very tall man, but rather because, as a drag performer, he already knows that resemblance and representation are a terrible basis for judging what is "real" about the body. In drag dance there is no repetition of what Deleuze calls "the Same": to host other bodies and dances within your own is to incorporate their difference so that it animates your dancing. Recently, when Move reflected on the trajectory of his career as Martha, he told performance scholar Abigail Levine, "'Right now I am saying that we perform together. I choreograph, perform, appear with her. I used to say 'as' her, and now I'm saying 'with' her" (Levine 2014). Instead of producing a representation of Martha, in other words, Move has come to see himself as coexisting with her, open to her presence and mystically attuned to her spirit.[22]

Drag has enabled Move to bring Martha back into the heart of the New York dance world: to bring tremulous breath and that droll, dry, almost invincible tone of pronouncement back into the proud old stories from *Blood Memory*; to restage her explicit portrayals of feminine sexuality in the new wave of sex-positive feminism; and to make her seem, once again, a woman ahead of her time. If Martha Graham, grimly aging, had felt time passing with the keenness of a blade on her skin, Richard Move's drag

Figure 7. Richard Move as Martha. Photo by Josef Astor, courtesy of Richard Move.

Martha summoned the capacity to temporarily arrest time and to suspend its ravages. In "coming back around," as Lepecki put it, Martha embodied a presentness and a centrality that suited Graham's self-conception; she saw herself as an artist whose time was more continuous and expansive than that of ordinary mortals. But as Martha, her longevity was at the expense of singularity: she could stop time, but she had to share a body and a stage.

The generosity, tenderness, and ethereal attachment that Move feels for Martha are, as Thoms concludes perceptively, "not based on the manifestation of a shared material resemblance but on shared and simultaneously queer forms of kinship and belonging" (2013, 139). In fact, when Deleuze writes about a "bare" repetition of "the Same" that is based in

representation and concept, he opposes it to a repetition "of the Other":
the first is "material," while "the other [is] spiritual . . . [and] carries the
secret of our deaths and our lives"; whereas bare repetition "concerns accuracy, the other has authenticity as its criterion" (1994, 24). If someone
wanted to represent Martha Graham, the "accurate material" would be
a body that resembled hers. But what would it mean to go beyond bare
accuracy, beyond the proper borders of bodies, beyond what binds life to
live bodies alone, beyond the concept of dance? It would mean, as Move-
with-Martha intuits, acknowledging that we do not know where our own
bodies end and where other bodies begin again. It might even mean we
do not know the edges of dance (22).[23] If what moves dancers is, in fact, a
kind of repetition that embeds difference within itself, then Richard Move
has exactly the right body in which to carry the secret of the deaths and
lives of Martha.[24]

　　After all, what is more generous than giving your body over to an artist
who is watching her own body fail her, who knows that there is no blood
in the memory she will leave behind? What is more an act of love than
this very queer kinship—this feeling that is neither exactly choosing an
intimacy nor being delivered abruptly into it, but rather an acceptance of
the ways in which bodies connect with and depend on each other? In this
space of permeability, bodies are not called out for their perceived imperfections of morphology or technique. They are recognized, instead, for
their potential to open their borders, to care for foreign bodies, to harbor
memories that are not their own, and to be willing to be together with the
lost and the dead.[25]

## Hosting

Mary Hinkson, who began dancing with the company in 1951, said that
Graham's way of performing was "to almost empty the body, so that it was
possible to pull somebody in with you" (2001). Even in Martha Graham's
dancing, Hinkson implies, there was a dynamic that foreshadowed the
second body—and its potential to be inhabited by somebody else. When
Richard Move chose to perform a drag version of Graham, he seemed to
see his body in the same terms of generous emptiness that Graham had
imparted to Hinkson: he could make space in himself. He had the capacity to give himself over to something else, to hollow out a part of himself
at the center, almost the way that one of Graham's signature contractions

would—not to self-abnegate, but to invite someone else in. By teaching himself to replicate Graham's act of 'emptying' the body for performance, he created a physical space in himself for her traits and voice. Working with Janet Stapleton of Dance Theater Workshop, who coproduced the early *Martha @ Mother* shows, Move learned to collect the lingering, often outsize impressions of her character and embed them in his own body. In this way, he came to be inhabited by visual, kinesthetic, and aural echoes of Martha in her later years: he employed her low, semi-divine voice, the proud set of her small shoulders, the way she slathered her mouth in lipstick, the fact that she didn't like the words 'modern dance.'

"The show's structure is essentially Martha hosting, in monologue, and then I create synoptic deconstructed versions of her epic ballets," Richard Move explains (2003). It is striking that Move has chosen to give his show (which is always called *Martha @,* followed by the name of the theater in which he is performing) this cabaret or vaudeville format, which mixes spoken routines with dance pieces. In part, the show derives its pace from its Jackie 60 days, when the rule was that every piece had to be less than ten minutes long. In another way, as Move notes, it is also an ironic "nod to Graham's days in vaudeville," a period Graham disdained later in her life as vulgar (Landini 2007). However, above all, it echoes that structure of leaving the center empty, in order, as Mary Hinkson said, "to pull somebody in with you."

Richard Move's explication makes the show sound like Martha has graciously granted the stage to Move while he dances abbreviated versions of her pieces. In a 1998 version of *Martha @ Mother,* for example, Move stars as Phaedra in *Phaedra,* thrusting an agonized leg out as she tosses around on her troubled bed, clawing her way up the chest of a stern Hippolytus (played with blond and chiseled resolve by Reid Hutchins, who also graced a *Playgirl* centerfold that year). But even when Move danced two acts of *Phaedra*—from the first fateful vision of Hutchins clad in gold lamé briefs with a scimitar stuck down the back of them, all the way through to Phaedra's dramatic decision to stab herself in the crotch—he made space for other artists. In the parts where Martha isn't performing, Move fills up the cabaret structure by inviting local choreographers and dancers to show their own work while he reigns over the proceedings as hostess.[26] "My whole premise is that Martha never died," he says. "It's just that now she's hosting a dance series in which she performs and introduces other people's work" (Fisher 1999). In hosting Martha in his body as she hosts other artists onstage, Richard Move has opened up the heart of the *Martha*

@ show in a way that Graham, who arrogated center stage to herself as an inalienable right, would never have done.

Over the years, Richard Move's Martha has been seen onstage with many of the stars of the dance scene, from Mikhail Baryshnikov and Matthew Bourne to Yvonne Rainer, Merce Cunningham, and Mark Morris. The people were real—Chi Chi Valenti remembers lifting Judith Malina, founder of the Living Theater, over the bar so that she could get to the stage—but Martha also got them to perform themselves as characters (Valenti 2016). Furthermore, Martha determined the chronology, genealogy, and hierarchies of dance history, warping time around herself; she introduced Merce Cunningham by saying, with a resigned sigh, "He was always a very good student." In this context, Martha's domain was not dance but speech, not the power of movement but the sheer force of personality; she faded away to the wings as soon as other dancers begin to perform the work of other choreographers. It is in this role that Martha is most purely a voice; she prefaces the pieces, fawns over her favorites, and limits her movements to the occasional sweeping arm gesture or heavy batting of eyelashes.

In fact, the rights to Martha's voice and the authority to represent her character had become the focus of intense litigation that lasted for a decade. When Martha Graham had passed away in 1991, having created 181 ballets, an ominous legal battle for the rights to her dances began at the headquarters of the Martha Graham Dance Company. While Move was culling phrases from *Blood Memory* and hunting up vintage dresses in the East Village, the company's dancers and board were entangled in an increasingly vicious fight with Ron Protas, Graham's legal heir and companion of some years, who claimed ownership of her choreography and technique.[27] For a few years, the dancers in the Graham company were legally prohibited from performing the pieces in repertoire. In August 1996, three months before *Martha @ Mother* debuted, the *Daily Telegraph* ran Ismene Brown's skeptical write-up of an interview she had done with Ron Protas, noting that he "backs up everything he claims with those two words, 'Martha says . . .'" (1996). Linda Hodes, who danced with the company for many years before serving as associate artistic director from 1977 until 1991, reported, "When I told Ron I was leaving he said, 'You can't do this to Martha'—and this was after she was dead" (Tracy 1996, 184). In this case, it was not only drag artists who were invested in the ghostly presentness of Martha and the persistence of her voice.

In Move's original vision of the Martha character at Mother, Martha was the voice—the spirit—and Richard Move was the body.[28] "There are moments onstage in the Martha show where I am definitely not myself," he told me. "I'm filled by her and by what I am doing. . . . Then I come back and I'm myself, a performer" (2007).[29] He draws upon the structure of the séance both for the sake of authenticity—essentially, it is the same tactic used by Ron Protas, with his eternal recourse to what "Martha says"—and as a metaphor for the feeling of being inhabited by her words. "She keeps calling me," Move explains; "I have to answer" (Kourlas 2011). As *Martha @* has developed over the years, Richard Move has continued to perform some of Graham's choreography himself, but is more often accompanied now by current or former company dancers like Katherine Crockett and Catherine Cabeen, who perform adapted excerpts from Graham's oeuvre.[30] In other words, he has moved away from a concept of trying to unite the first and second bodies—being inhabited by Martha's voice *and* embodying her dance—and now leaves more of this center empty as well, to be danced by other, younger, more professionally trained bodies. In undermining Graham's conviction about the singularity of the fulfilled artist, Richard Move has come to embody her more haunting intuition about dancers' bodies: once a dancer dies her first death, she sees the ghosts come dancing in to take her place.

## Being Martha

Besides the fact that Richard Move is notably taller than Martha Graham, what critics overwhelmingly write about is the spooky accuracy with which Move captures Graham's distinctive voice and intonation. "Move is a foot taller than his subject and cannot recreate the unique shock of her dramatically ravaged face," Judith Mackrell of *The Guardian* wrote in a 1999 review. "But his make-up is perfect and when he speaks he gets Graham's voice down to its deepest diva vowels and brittle girlish overtones" (1999).[31] If this were a club drag show, this focus on Move's vocal imitation would be fairly standard, and would probably be accompanied by some comment on his skills at lip-synching. But Richard Move is a dancer, performing a woman who was consummately and insistently a dancer. *Martha @* is booked by presenters into dance theaters, as part of subscription dance series, marketed to dance audiences, and reviewed in the "Dance" sections of newspapers. Why don't critics emphasize his dancing as the essential aspect of the performance? Marcia B. Siegel

(2003), a respected dance critic who clearly loved the show she found "ever-more-exquisite," had to admit, "Move's dance impressions . . . don't really translate into Graham's choreography." Wendy Perron (2000), the editor in chief of *Dance Magazine*, couldn't help but note the quality of his technique: "an experienced dancer, tall and statuesque, he captures her glamorous despair, but lacks the fierce torque in the center of the body that Graham flaunted." From these reluctant but unmistakable critiques, it's clear that Richard Move's technical ability to dance Martha Graham's choreography with exemplary virtuosity is the least compelling part of the *Martha @* show.

Richard Move's career began with a dance class in high school from former Graham company dancer Helen McGehee and continued with a degree in dance from Virginia Commonwealth University. This led to stints with New York choreographers such as Karole Armitage, Mark Dendy,[32] and Pooh Kaye, and ultimately to several memorable years as a go-go dancer at clubs like the Roxy and Limelight (Reardon 2001). "I can remember one night coming offstage at the Joyce, and then putting on a much more fabulous outfit and getting into a go-go cage and being lifted three floors above a crowd of 3,000 people at the Palladium," he reminisces fondly (Goodwin 2006). However, he insists that he has "equal respect for the work that can be done at 1 A.M. in a nightclub and something performed at the Joyce Theater, and I don't see one as superior esthetically or more important than the other" (Harris 1998). As a dancer, he was never fully immersed in the preciousness of the concert dance world, which also meant he wasn't dedicated to its rigorous professionalism. His idea of the dancer's body was not about burnishing your technique in the searing fires of intensive dance training—Martha Graham said it took at least ten years of this to make a dancer (1991, 4)—but about bridging different dance spheres, bringing downtown performance elements into dance theaters, and making sure you still had the energy to go out clubbing at night. "I was working with these great companies on one hand and then seeing this kind of underworld," Richard Move told Jennifer Fisher of the *LA Times* (1999). "It really opened my eyes to what [concert] dance was missing—it has to be a necessity and a real communication." The idea of "communication" from an "underworld" of dance gave Move the impetus to bring concert and club dance closer together—and the phrasing does imply a sense of ghostliness—by shaping his idea that dance was not about immaculate technique, but about using your body as an instrument.

This openness to the afterlives (and nightlives) of dance was not always well received by critics. The venerable Anna Kisselgoff, who spent decades as a dance critic for the *New York Times*, hated everything about Richard Move's *Martha @ Town Hall*. She dismissed it as "a drag-queen act," and then, in her review, she reenacted the revelatory moment of drag with venomous intensity, ripping away every illusion she could get her hands on: "As Richard Winberg, Mr. Move studied dance in college and was a go-go dancer. Graham technique is not his strong suit." Kisselgoff (2001) concluded archly, "His big moment as Phaedra came when he staggered around after stabbing himself in the crotch." Here is the usual drag revelation of masculinity (his crotch), but in addition, the reader is being shown that "Richard Move" himself is a fiction, with a real name underneath his adopted identity. Moreover, when Kisselgoff decries him first as an amateur and then as a frivolous denizen of the demimonde, she attacks his very claim to the identity of a dancer. She is so intent on unveiling Richard Move as a drag act inside a drag act—all the way down to his right to say, as Martha Graham famously did in *Blood Memory*, "I am a dancer"—that she ignores the fact that he is performing Graham's actual choreography for Phaedra, in all of its intended violence.

"Drag-queen act" was Anna Kisselgoff's way of saying to greater New York City that Richard Move was nothing but a wig and some lipstick: there was no real dance to see here. Dance critic Toba Singer, who sat a few rows away from me the night that Richard Move performed *Martha @* in San Francisco in 2007, shared Kisselgoff's outrage but explained it more thoroughly. Singer was especially affronted by the sight of Graham dancer Katherine Crockett "suffering through the humiliation of having to take a back seat to Move's incompetent mimicry of Graham" as she performed the choreography while Move was "making a mockery of a figure the entire dance world revered" (2007). Singer ended her review by metaphorically throwing Move off the stage: "it is conceivable that this event could have been credibly staged at Josie's Juice Joint—a former Castro District drag artist night spot." In order to preserve virtuosity and singularity from the perceived threats of dilution and multiplication, Kisselgoff and Singer would like to close the archive. At the level of choreography, only Graham's proper disciples would be admitted to the temple of virtuosic technique; at the level of bodies, Move seems to imperil a cisgender claim to be the only 'real' thing.

By dismissing Move as a "drag queen" whose work is "mimicry" or "mockery," these accusations also invoke the queer, lingering touch of camp. "Camp is art that proposes itself seriously, but cannot be taken altogether seriously because it is 'too much,'" Susan Sontag wrote in "Notes on 'Camp'" in 1964 (1999, 59). When dance is based primarily on the expressive movement of bodies—the muscular, solid, virtuosically physical first bodies of dancers—it is, like Martha Graham at the height of her performing career, ostensibly fulfilling itself entirely through this instrument. There is no emptiness, no sense of lost time, and no space for camp's wry, haunting pathos. In this ideal of the body that fully expresses itself, without supplement and without nostalgia, both the tenderness and the irony that Sontag saw in camp are precluded.

But famously, exploring the modes through which a camp aesthetic elevates "character," Sontag gives this example: "in every move the aging Martha Graham makes she's being Martha Graham etc etc" (1999, 61). What is the substance of this "etc etc" that Sontag identifies as "camp" in Martha Graham as she so unwillingly grows old? Graham took aging to be the acrid intensification of the second body, a brittle and bitter ossification, a loss of the dancing that was her essence. Sontag seemed to think that this was not a loss at all but rather a surfeit: that Graham's character was "too much" for her body as she aged—that it overspilled her physical form, creating an excess, and that excess was "camp." When the aging Martha Graham moves, Sontag claims, you don't see the movement: you see the Martha-Grahamness. This is a logic of overabundance and afterlife. If the Grahamness of Martha Graham stays in her body long after the dancing is gone, and maybe even after the body itself is gone, where then does the Grahamness go? Perhaps this is the role of the "etc etc": to point onward to the others, to the open-ended *et cetera* who follow, to those who may find themselves "being Martha Graham."

When the critics agree that Richard Move gets Martha Graham's voice and character but not the dramatic power and fierce expressiveness of her first body, they see this as a flaw in his performance. Richard Move—who says that he chose not to go further than basic Graham training because he "was never really interested in that company, it didn't seem right for me"—draws his philosophy of performance precisely from the difference of his body from a virtuosic ideal, playing on its affinity with Graham's aging body (Landini 2007). He sees Graham's choreography not as itself but as infused with character, with the pathos of her later years, when she wrote bitterly, "I only wanted to dance. Without dancing, I wished to die" (1991, 238). Graham envisions a stark opposition—there is dancing, or else there is death—but in fact there are many years between, all the years of the second body, in which her character sharpened and expanded in inverse proportion to her artistic abilities as a dancer. As she ages, she becomes excessively herself: self-aware, self-dramatizing, self-staging. Mark Morris, one of Move's close friends, lovingly dubbed him "a genius," because he was "more Martha Graham than Martha Graham ever was"—but what makes Graham such an imitable figure is exactly this combination of emptiness and excess (Move It Productions). And this is what Richard Move has intuited about Martha Graham: in her second body, *she* was more Martha than Martha ever was.

## Reversals and Universals

The first time that Richard Move ever saw Martha Graham perform live, he only really remembers "Martha Graham taking a bow, held up by nearly naked beautiful men. . . . The dance was beyond my comprehension at the time, but I understood it was mythic and dramatic and so sexy and violent. Clearly it was one of her Greek pieces," he concluded (Reardon 2001). It makes sense that Move would be drawn to Martha Graham in the full glory of her character, foregrounded by a compliant entourage of male dancers. Graham's vision of her own choreography was manifestly and righteously female—the men in her company were, as Move notes wryly, "painfully gorgeous and for the most part did very little onstage and had no clothes on. They became props for these fierce women who were doing this incredible movement and were the stars of the show" (Harris 1998). This was essentially a performance of male bodies that appear—the limited, passive choreography and the skimpy draping of their costumes only made them look more like "props," drawing attention to their underutilization—with Graham at the center, infusing the heroine's role with her character.[33] But it is worth noting that Move doesn't remember Martha Graham dancing that night. As a drag artist, he remembers her flawless curtain calls, and he remembers her as part of a tradition of classical Greek theater.

In that tradition, of course, Medea and Jocasta and Phaedra were played by men (as were all roles). Women's dancing had been part of the emergence of Greek theater: the Dionysian maenads, women who had been moved by ecstasy to dance, had participated in the ritual celebrations that eventually developed into state-regulated Athenian drama. However, once Athenian theatrical practices had been codified, the all-male chorus took on the function of dancing, and women were thought unsuited to perform tragic roles like Jocasta in *Oedipus* and Clytemnestra in the *Oresteia*. Women were barred from the stage—it has been much debated whether they were even allowed in the audience[34]—and the male actor's body was understood to be 'universal,' in the sense that it could perform both male and female roles, with the aid of masks and costumes.[35] In other words, the audience would have expected Medea to be a man in drag; Martha Graham's idea of performing Medea herself would have been shocking in classical Greek theater, but Richard Move's interpretation would have been perfectly 'straight.'

Martha Graham, who famously used to tell the women in her company to dance from their vaginas, in some ways espoused a theory of female dramatic potential that was, ironically, not unlike the theories that underlay classical Greek productions (1991, 211). Both shared the sense that a female performer could reach a state of divine excess and ecstatic physicality. As god-possessed maenads, women had been permitted in the rituals that predated organized Athenian theater, but this was exactly the reason that they were not going to be seen onstage, in public, in the midst of the citizenry, acting in an important civic event. According to part 15 of Aristotle's *Poetics*, "the woman may be said to be an inferior being" even if she is good; female protagonists were shown onstage as emotionally driven, blood-bit creatures, who could be maddened to unthinkable passions (Butcher n.d.). Graham, however, used this concept to counter the argument that reasoned, temperate male bodies ought therefore to be models for universality and insisted that the charged state of the female dancer's body was the ideally expressive instrument for the roles of Greek tragic heroines. She herself choreographed with the fervid faith of an oracle, not just listening and responding to divine instructions but actually feeling "the driving force of God that plunges through me," as she put it (BBC 2001).[36] Until Erick Hawkins joined the company in 1938, the whole Graham company was female. She didn't think you could perform an authentically anguished Medea unless you could feel the maternal horror and the vengeful femininity coursing in your veins; you just didn't have the driving force of God plunging through you.

It was as Graham began to contemplate the fact that her body would age that she was increasingly drawn to the tragic heroines of classical Greek drama and myth, producing pieces like *Cave of the Heart, Errand into the Maze, Night Journey, Clytemnestra*, and *Phaedra*.[37] She created these particular ballets with dark, hollow forebodings of her second body; she made her first major Greek work, *Cave of the Heart*, in 1946, twenty years after she had made her debut as a choreographer; at that point, she was fifty-two years old. The following year brought *Errand into the Maze* and *Night Journey*; *Clytemnestra* is from 1958, and *Phaedra* premiered in 1962, when Graham was sixty-eight. It was at a screening of *Night Journey* in 1961, in fact, when a film editor "casually asked Graham what she had thought of the film" and was quite taken aback when Graham replied that seeing herself on screen was much like facing death (Thoms 2013, 114). She continued to choreograph stories about classical female characters— Circe, Andromache, Persephone, more Phaedra—until she was in her nineties. In other words, Greek heroines became Graham's preoccupation well after the zenith of her career as a dancer, and they inspired the choreography of many of her most memorable dances.

These are works, Graham said, that are essentially about "passion"— more precisely, they are dances about the rage of having lost the thing you most loved, about the jealousy of women who will take your place, and about the shame of knowing what your body is capable of doing. When she declared that dancers, more than anyone else, suffered two deaths, she gave a single example from her own life: she admitted that she "had changed steps in *Medea* and other ballets to accommodate change. But I knew. And it haunted me" (1991, 238). According to Aristotle, in Greek tragedies like Euripides's *Medea* (which was the basis for Graham's *Cave of the Heart*), the performance will cause an effect of catharsis, the "special pleasure" of tragedy—an emptying, an evacuation, a purgation (Ford 1995). "Catharsis" was a medical term before Aristotle had employed it in his *Poetics* for theatrical purposes (he himself had used it in an earlier work to refer to the removal of menstrual substances from a woman's body), and Martha Graham seemed to take it in its bloodiest and most female sense (Belfiore 1992, 300). By returning catharsis to its specific location in female experience, Graham could accomplish a double maneuver: universalizing women's bodies and transferring the "special pleasure" of tragedy to the performer.

When Richard Move first saw Martha Graham perform, perhaps he doesn't remember her dancing because she could barely dance then; there would come a time in her life when she would summon her dance therapist just before opening night so that she could appear at curtain call "with two strong male dancers at her side, who had just lifted her from her wheelchair when the curtain was down and who stood beside her as she bowed on stage" (Horosko 2002, 162). But perhaps what Move saw that night was an artist reclaiming a performance tradition from its history of gendered exclusion. In the tragedy of her own aging, Martha Graham took up Greek drama as material she could use to explore her corporeal and emotional experiences. These were stories about women that had been made by men, staged by men, and judged by men; she would make them into autobiographies, and the men would stand around onstage in decorative gold lamé briefs. Graham's reversal of these gender roles shifted the model of the 'universal' body enough for Richard Move to believe that this was an inclusive tradition—a tradition that would include bodies like his, and Graham's, and everyone else's. "Martha's universal themes are timeless, like in her Greek ballets—full of love and hate, lust and revenge," he would tell people (Fisher 1999). "It's tragedy that applies to everyone." And because Move sees the drag potential in Martha Graham, he sees his own drag performance not as a "mimicry" or subversion of dance history, but as part of the grand lineage of Western classical drama: "people have forgotten that this comes from ancient theater!" he notes (2007). In a world where misogyny, homophobia, and transphobia manifest in brutal ways, "drag can be the most welcoming kind of thing for people," as Move sees it (2007). And once Martha Graham decided that she didn't have to be a man to play Medea, Richard Move realized that he didn't have to be one of the nearly naked men who just stood next to her.

*Anthropometries*

When Graham made her Greek ballets, no dance critic villainized her performance as a "mockery" of the male Athenian actors who had played Medea and Phaedra. But it is sometimes claimed that men in drag, inhabiting masculinity as a neutral, universalized position, have the impunity to 'take up' or 'put on' femininity.[38] There is a fear that drag might be, at best, a vulgar joke that men make about women by 'dressing up'; at worst, as Toba Singer asserted, men in drag are seen as a "humiliation" of the "real" women who are present. It is virtually impossible for Richard Move to defend *Martha @* against this charge: that counterclaim would have to come from someone who could speak to the experiences of being a woman, being in drag, and being at *Martha @*. It would be even better if that woman did both male and female drag so that she could talk about her own embodied experience of moving between gender performances. And it would be best if she were a trained Graham dancer who, onstage with Move, could say firsthand whether that felt like a "humiliation" or not.

Catherine Cabeen, who has all of qualifications listed above plus a strong interest in gender theory and a choreographic practice of her own, came to New York to study Graham technique when she was still a teenager (Cabeen 2016). When she finished the Graham professional training program at nineteen, she was promptly hired by Bill T. Jones, despite the fact, as she recounts, "that everyone had always told me that I was too tall to be a dancer." At five foot eleven, strongly built, with broad shoulders and narrow hips, Cabeen felt marvelously at home in the Bill T. Jones/ Arnie Zane Company, with its "testosterone-driven" choreography and "grappling" approach to partnering. The dancers around her were a broad range of "gigantic and tiny and wide and narrow and black and white and purple Mohawks and no hair": no one told her she was too tall, and no one told her it was weird that she was "always the bottom in lifts." She stayed with the company for seven years, gradually being given more of Jones's and Zane's roles. She felt honored, and she worked hard, but she was also aware of how natural it felt to "dance strong and masculine—how *easy* it is for me to be that dancer." For one of those years, Cabeen decided to shave her head and wear only men's clothing; it was an "experimental moment offstage," she explained, when her body felt "free" in the world, unremarked and unconstrained.

Because her masculinity was so accepted in the company, Cabeen could delve into other questions about the politics of bodies in dance: What did it mean, when she was cast in Jones's iconic roles, that she was white and he was black? How did speaking onstage change the way audiences viewed a dancer's body? When she danced Arnie Zane's part in a duet, what was she channeling from this person whose name was still half the company's and whose death from AIDS had made his body so public? But when she left Bill T. Jones/Arnie Zane and took a job with the Graham company, all of those interesting questions stopped. In their place stood a gender binary: strong masculine men on this side, dramatically feminine women on that side; no crossing, no blending, no ambiguity. It was a terrible shock. "It was *wildly* uncomfortable for me all of a sudden to have to dance decidedly female roles—though those roles are very strong," Cabeen remembers (2016). It was not only the "artifice of the theater" that the Graham look required—"eyelashes out to here, and fake hair, and long dresses for all of the women"—but also the fact that "the rehearsal director would push down on my shoulders and sigh, '*You're just so tall. You just don't fit into this line.*'" Suddenly she was too tall to be a dancer again, and the lifts were all heteronormative, and the breadth of her shoulders was a problem: the general sense was that she "wasn't woman enough to do those roles, or to be in that world." She lasted just one season. Then she met Richard Move.

Catherine Cabeen describes her season with the Graham company as the time when she "had to dance small"; by contrast, she feels that Move has provided "a catalyst" for her growth as a mover and a thinker.[39] Ten years later Cabeen is still regularly performing with Move, not least because of one "beautiful moment in the dressing room," as she recalls. "We were doing a two-person show: he was putting on his drag as Martha, and I was putting on my makeup, and I suddenly realized that *I was also putting on my drag* as Martha's minion." In that moment Cabeen saw what she called "the artifice of the original": she had to do just as much work as Move did to perform femininity. This faux-queen *Gender Trouble* epiphany has been liberating, but it hasn't been only about access to femininity; Cabeen went on to choreograph a piece of her own, *Into the Void* (2011), in which she danced the lead role of Yves Klein, the postwar male artist famous for creating a darkly radiant shade of "International Klein Blue" paint, rolling the bodies of his female models around in it, and calling them "Anthropometries." As Klein, whose work she adored, Cabeen was bound and packed and wearing a short black wig with a rakish tousle of hair—very '60s, very jaunty, with a cool little rock to the hips as he strode forward, resetting the collar of his white button-down shirt under a brown vest, tie, and jacket.[40] Without hesitation, Cabeen says, "I feel honestly that I am performing more in drag when I perform with Richard Move as one of these hyper-feminine Martha creatures" than as Yves Klein. It's not that the Yves Klein costume takes less work to put on than the Martha costume (it doesn't). And it's not that femininity is an excess, a set of highly visible markers for gender, while masculinity is neutral and universal (it isn't; it's just historically been made to look that way). It's that Catherine Cabeen more or less grew up as an artist in a company where a female-bodied person who danced "strong and masculine" was unremarkable, even encouraged.[41] And from that experience, she learned that if your body is given opportunities to move in a variety of different styles, rather than being constrained by a binary that will always be too small for you, you can ask more interesting questions about embodiment.

The view from the dressing room has given also Catherine Cabeen another kind of insight: a glimpse into the drag dance as séance. Precisely "two-thirds of the way through getting his makeup on," Richard Move eerily transforms before her eyes. The lashes go on and Martha arrives in him, imperious and absolute. And then, from that moment at the mirror until fifteen minutes after the curtain goes down, backstage or onstage, Richard Move is solely the "conduit" for the "lifeblood" of Martha Graham, pouring her afterlife through his body. From Cabeen's perspective, "he's channeling Martha, and I'm doing everything I can to honor that vision." Cabeen's responsibility is to support Move as he gives himself over to this ghost, not to channel Martha herself—"I don't think she wants to come to my party!" she remarks, smiling a little—almost as if she were partnering him in the role he has taken on, offering him her shoulders to lean on, her taut muscularity, the decisiveness of her movement, all those years of Graham training. She doesn't have to "dance small" to do Graham choreography in *Martha @*, and the giant insectile eyelashes seem like part of a game she's choosing to play that evening. For both Move and Cabeen, drag does not mean that femininity is any more artificial or performative than masculinity. And if drag dance is an anthropometry, it does not measure how bodies fall short of ideals or exceed allotted spaces, but rather how open they are to otherness, and how they might dance it together.

### Stretching Inside the Skin

Perhaps the dance piece Richard Move most often performs (and is, by far, most often photographed performing) is a version of Graham's early, well-known solo work, *Lamentation* (1930).[42] Martha Graham explained that she had created the solo to portray "the tragedy that obsesses the body, and the garment that is worn is just a tube of material, but it's as though you were stretching inside your own skin" (1976).[43] She designed the costume for *Lamentation* herself, creating something that could be a sort of partner in this solo, by engaging the body agonistically. "At once both body and moving malleable mass," as Thoms writes, Graham seemed almost otherworldly, a cowled figure on a low bench (2013, 140). Because Graham often told the story of a woman who had seen her child killed in an accident, and who had come backstage after a performance to thank Graham for finally provoking her to cry, the piece became associated with a supremely feminine mourning. It was seen as a universal keening of mothers and widows, the raw grief of women. The wrenching, angled body showed its outlines clearly through the fabric, and this diminished the abstraction of the piece while heightening its association with the female body.

Figure 8. Richard Move as Martha in *Lamentation*. Photo by Josef Astor, courtesy of Richard Move.

Graham's idea of "stretching inside your own skin" is a particularly useful way to understand Move's performance of *Lamentation*. There is footage of Martha Graham performing this piece, and she is wearing a purple leotard underneath the stretch jersey costume, along with purple eye shadow and red lipstick.[44] When Graham company dancer Peggy Lyman performed the piece in 1975, she wore a dark red long-sleeve leotard underneath the costume. Richard Move doesn't wear anything underneath the costume, as far as it is possible to tell, and when he stretches the purple jersey over his body, you can see both the masculine contours of his body and the nakedness of his chest. Dance critic Deborah Jowitt grasped the essence of Move's version of *Lamentation* when she wrote, "A degree of gaucheness or of dislocation lies at the heart of parody; knowledge of the subject has to be thorough, but the rendition can't be a perfect copy of what it sends up" (2001). She sees the bare torso as Move's deliberate sign that he will always be an "imperfect" copy of Martha, a gesture he makes "as if to remind us that he is not Martha Graham, but has definitely gotten under her skin."

Richard Move's *Lamentation* strips the abstraction and the feminine melodrama from the piece at the same time, showing the body as it struggles to dance against the constraints of its costume. The "dislocation" that delineates Move's body occurs in the space between "stretching inside your own skin" and "getting under her skin," between his own body and the body he invokes. When he stands onstage in what he calls "the hair, the warpaint, and of course the gowns," and declares grandly, "I am a National Treasure," and then, rolling his eyes, dryly, "in Japan," he is playing Martha Graham as she came to play herself: excessively (Gilbert 2001). In *Lamentation* it is the costume that allows Move to give the impression that he is faithfully stretching inside his own skin—an authentic acolyte of Graham, performing her signature solo. Paradoxically, though, it is also the costume that reveals that he is naked under there, in drag.

When Richard Move performs *Lamentation*, it could be said that he bares the 'wrongness' of his body for Graham's solo role. But Move's version of *Lamentation* also demonstrates how the body can go on dancing, even when it is not the same body. By performing one of her early works, he restages the lives of her body: on one layer there is the 1930s Graham who is resolutely a dancer, stark in her conviction that the first body is a solo that will never end. But woven into that is a moment when Richard Move lets Graham's own tragedy obsess his body: here is the Martha who made herself a Delphic vessel for Greek tragedy, and later the Martha who suffered the haunting knowledge that she had altered her own choreography in order to keep dancing lead roles, the Martha who could "barely walk"—as Agnes de Mille noted (1991, 379)—during the last season of her dancing career, but whose careful, ossified gestures of grand artistry were still carried out, despite her age, arthritis, and alcoholism.

Dancer Glen Tetley recalled an illustrative period during the creation of *Clytemnestra* when Graham was struggling with possible endings for the ballet (Tracy 1996, 262). She had improvised a last scene in which she left the stage and exited into the darkness while the other dancers remained onstage, bathed in light. After the company had rehearsed the scene this way, an entirely new ending took its place—"a strong theatrical ending and very Martha," Tetley said—in which the group of dancers disappeared into the dark as a scrim lowered, while she "came running out toward the audience, to Hades, to death. But in full light." She could bear the tragedy of her role, but she would not accept that she might simply fade offstage. When Move is performing *Lamentation*, he acknowledges that the body under the costume is not Martha Graham's first body, and he stretches under its skin, moving toward the place Graham would not permit herself to go. And so, with his particular body, and with his drag dancing of her iconic solo, he grieves for Martha Graham so that she might not be so afraid of the darkness offstage.

## The End of Straight Dance History

Sometimes it seems that Move's drag version of Martha has overtaken the 'real' one and actually filled an emptiness left by her death. He describes the initial hesitation of some Graham company dancers to attend, much less to endorse, *Martha @ Mother*:

> These were people who deeply loved and respected Martha and gave their lives to her, so to find out that some 6-foot-4 drag queen is doing her regularly at a tiny night club in the meat-packing district of New York was probably a lot to handle. But when they finally came, they embraced it. Now they love to tell me stories, because they don't think anyone really cares about Martha anymore. (Fisher 1999)

Most people who come to see Richard Move on tour in the United States and Europe have never seen Martha Graham, but "of course, in New York, they come out of the woodwork to see me do Martha," he notes wryly (2007). Excerpts from Graham's choreography "span the history of the Graham oeuvre," Victoria Thoms points out, and are even overseen by "elite dancers and teachers from the Graham past like Linda Hodes and Yuriko Kikuchi" (2013, 132). The dancer who most often joins Catherine Cabeen onstage in *Martha @* is Katherine Crockett, a principal dancer in the Graham company for decades. It is also true that his shows are notably well attended by an insider dance crowd: Mikhail Baryshnikov has gone on record saying that *Martha @* is "the essence of Martha" (Move It Productions).

The most striking thing about Move's official involvement with the Graham company, however, is the way he has become a repository for an authentic history of Martha. If Graham's dancers think no one "cares about Martha" anymore, they confide their memories to Richard Move. "I'm convinced Martha would love him," said Stuart Hodes, a company dancer from 1947 to 1958. "In fact," Hodes continued, with the same sly temporality that imbues Move's show, "I'm convinced she does love him" (Fisher 1999). When Hodes was appointed director of the Graham school in 2000, not only was it illegal for Graham dancers to perform works in repertoire (Ron Protas held the rights), but the situation was so dire that the entire company had been disbanded several months earlier. The dancers were laid off, the lawyers kept fighting, and no one knew if there would be a Martha Graham Dance Company ever again. For four years, Richard Move was more or less the only person in the world publicly performing Martha Graham's choreography.

Stuart Hodes seems to see Martha's spirit hovering over Richard Move, approving and guiding his performance; he's one of the former company members who agreed to perform in *Martha @ Mother*. Bonnie Oda Homsey, another retired Graham dancer, mostly concurs with his extrapolation of Martha Graham's opinion: "On the one hand, I think she'd feel flattered, and on the other, the haughty part of her would make her say that no one could ever replicate her persona. . . . But she was the first one to say that if you're going to steal, steal from the best" (Fisher 1999). After her dancing career, Homsey became the artistic director of the American Repertory Dance Company (ARDC) and invited Move to perform in Los Angeles. The ARDC is primarily concerned with re-constructing and preserving historic dances—in an emphatically con-servative way—but Move was invited to dance one of Martha's Greek pieces, despite the fact that his understanding of these works reflects the perspective of someone whose most vivid memory of Martha is from her bows at curtain call. "The Greek stuff is total soap opera," Move says (Gilbert 2001), and describes his versions of these ballets—the longest of which, Graham's masterpiece *Clytemnestra*, is three hours—as things "I do . . . in ten minutes, you know, where I eliminate all of the minor characters and go right for the love triangles and the murders and the suicides" (Move 2003).

It might appear startling that Graham's former dancers have such sym-pathy for Richard Move's impersonation, but, then, they knew Martha in her second body, as Homsey says, when she was very much a "persona."

The company itself, which was supposed to be where passionate dancers in their first bodies kept the spirit of Martha alive, failed even to hold on to the legal rights to her choreography. The school's teachers weren't allowed to give classes in Graham technique, and the costumes and sets couldn't be seen onstage. There was a threat that just as Martha Graham the dancer had become unwillingly evanescent, perhaps her dances would also disappear—and not just her choreography but her history, her character, her voice, her stories, her whole "persona," which had seemed so admirably and terribly excessive. It is a great triumph of drag performance history that Richard Move, with his minimal Graham training and go-go career, with his six-foot-four frame and Jackie 60 tastes, who could say dismissively that Graham's Greek pieces were "total soap opera," seemed like the most reliable place to keep Martha Graham's legacy.

But as André Lepecki explains, "the affective force of the ghostly" was powerful enough that "it turned him [Move] into a corporeal archive, a system or zone where works do not rest but are formed and transformed, endlessly—like ghostly matters. Or simply, like bodies" (2010, 44). There came a point when it must have seemed to Graham's former dancers that the possibility for authentic, original, 'straight' dance history was gone. The genealogy that was supposed to protect the treasures of choreography, handing them down from the great artist to the chosen company of dancers, and then down to the junior company and the school, was wrenched out of joint. What was, so to speak, cisgender and heteronormative about the way that Graham's dances were enacted and inherited over time was turning out to be a spectacular failure. In place of these structures, Richard Move offered his body—his second body, a drag body—to the ghost of Martha Graham, who was growing a little more faint with every court injunction and disenchanted company dancer.[45]

One of the fascinating things about drag dancers' bodies is that they are built up in permeable layers: they are intercalated, like the feathers of a bird, or striated, like muscle tissue. When Richard Move took his first class in Graham technique, he was sixteen years old, and "It wasn't like I just said right there and then, 'I want to be her,' or anything," he recalled. "That would be a little too weird, even for me" (Ickes 1998). Gradually, though, he acquired the synthesis of drag techniques and dance experiences that led him to the idea of channeling Martha, and he "began to feel more and more possessed by her brilliance and vision and oracular qualities" (Ickes 1998). Four years after the official rebirth of Martha, Richard Move could no longer tell himself apart from the body that coexisted "with" his:

Figure 9. Richard Move as Martha in *Lamentation*. Photo by Josef Astor, courtesy of Richard Move.

"Martha has renewed my faith that art is communicative and transformative," Richard Move declared. Then, hearing his own voice, he exclaimed, "That sounds like a Martha quote! I can't separate us, I guess" (*Time Out New York* 2000, 24). Martha conceived of herself as driven by divine inspiration; Move seems to see himself as a cross between an oracle-once-removed, a medium in a séance, and a hostess of lost histories. He was willing to empty a part of himself so that her ghost could have a body again, and he was only slightly unnerved when she sometimes took over. And he is giving something back to Martha Graham that she would never have given herself: tenderness for the second body.

In a way, when Move is onstage "with" Martha, he is speaking to her as much as he is speaking to the audience; he is telling her that to let your body be governed by a concept of dance that precludes your particular body is to make yourself miserable. By recuperating the second life of the body for Graham in particular, and for dancers more generally, Move shows that dance can still be done, but with a difference, as the body differs within itself over time and as it differs from other bodies. Lepecki calls this kind of dance "an intimacy to whatever insists to keep happening," and he identifies it as a strategy that keeps dance from obsessing about its "vanishing point" (2006, 130). From the insight that Richard Move offers to Martha Graham—and from the layered and transformative perspective of drag dance more generally—what makes something a dance is generosity and discipline, not virtuosic mobility. These are not easy things to give, and they require an attentive practice of embodiment, but they are not cruel in the way that Martha Graham was cruel to her second body.[46]

In 2003 Richard Move made a film in which he played Martha; he called it *Ghostlight*, which is the term for the light that is left on all night, always, in a dark theater.

## CHAPTER THREE

# Admiring

## *The Returns of* La Argentina

Too little importance has been attached to the use of this word "multiplicity."
—Gilles Deleuze, *Bergsonism*

I think that if we take voguing as a theoretical concept, I would say we are always all voguing. It's like what RuPaul said: "Who isn't in drag?"
—Trajal Harrell to Ariel Osterweis, in *Twenty Looks or Paris Is Burning at the Judson Church (XL) Finale*

### *Beginnings after Endings*

One evening in November 1977, the butoh dancer Kazuo Ohno applied a thick layer of white face paint; coated his mouth in bright red lipstick; penciled in the dramatic arches of eyebrows; put on a stiffly old-fashioned black dress with an extravagant flounce of white lace at the throat; fastened over it a floor-length, silky, pale dressing gown that he wore as a cape; topped the ensemble off with a large and precariously flower-laden hat; stepped onto the stage of Tokyo's Dai-ichi Seimei Hall; and began to perform a new dance called *La Argentina Sho* (Admiring La Argentina). He was seventy-one years old. He had declared his retirement from the theater a decade ago. It was the eve of All Souls Day—a Day of the Dead—in the Christian calendar.

La Argentina, the object of 'admiration' in Ohno's dance, was born Antonia Rosa Mercé y Luque (1888–1936) in Buenos Aires to Spanish parents who danced at the Teatro Réal in Madrid. She studied ballet from a very young age before turning to flamenco, the traditional dances of Spain, and

'Gypsy' dances (Bennahum 2000). Captivating early twentieth-century audiences on her international tours, La Argentina was a whirlwind of castanets and driving, ornate footwork. Ohno had seen La Argentina perform only once, from the rear of the third floor of the Imperial Theatre in Tokyo, in January 1929 (Ohno and Maehata 1986, 159). He was merely a gymnastics student then, but La Argentina was at the height of her career: her publicity photo shows off her dark, glimmering eyes under arched brows, the quick flourish of a smile, her hands clasped alluringly to frame her face, a fringed shawl draped around her shoulders. The poet Paul Valèry proclaimed that she danced to music "of the inner self," and the critic André Levinson fell in love with her (Bennahum 2000, 112, 181).

There is no physical sense in which Kazuo Ohno resembles La Argentina. A Japanese man with large, expressive hands and a body carved to such taut thinness that his limbs seem to hang off his joints, Ohno (1906–2010) was trained in Ausdruckstanz by the Japanese followers of German modern dance choreographer Mary Wigman, steeped in the postwar atmosphere of trauma and experimentalism from which butoh emerged, and employed for many years as a physical education teacher and janitor in a girls' school (Klein 1988, 6–7; Ohno and Ohno 2004, 158).[1] Ohno began dancing in the 1930s and had participated in the first recognized public butoh performance in 1959, in a controversial piece called *Kinjiki* (Forbidden Colors) choreographed by Tatsumi Hijikata, which also featured Kazuo Ohno's young son Yoshito. In the years following this infamous first performance, Ohno and Hijikata collaborated prolifically, creating dances that drew on utter darkness and numinous light, on the scandalous books of Jean Genet and Yukio Mishima, on the slow gliding ghostliness of Noh theater and the dramatic contortions of Ausdruckstanz, and on a corporeal "praxis that aimed to shatter language and thought itself," as Miryam Sas described their practice in *Experimental Arts in Postwar Japan* (2011, 135). By the mid-1960s, Ohno had already assured himself a respected place in the annals of twentieth-century dance history as a cofounder of butoh.[2]

In 1967 Kazuo Ohno finished a few cameo appearances in Tokyo theaters and then bid farewell to live performance. Nearly ten years passed, and it seemed as though his stage career had come to its natural end. In 1976, a year before the premiere of *Admiring La Argentina*, Kazuo Ohno's son Yoshito, his closest collaborator, had never heard his father mention La Argentina. It had been forty-one years since Antonia Mercé's death; she was buried in Neuilly, a quiet suburb on the outskirts of Paris, with a modest gravestone that read "*Elle vecut pour son art et mourut pour lui.*" ("She lived for her art and died for it.") It took a sequence of extraordinary events—a catalytic series of images—to reanimate Kazuo Ohno as a dancer and to spark the creation of *Admiring La Argentina*, which came to be known as his masterpiece.

*Admiring La Argentina*, Yoshito Ohno declared, was not only the consummate dance of Kazuo Ohno's career; it was also his "first ever butoh performance" (Ohno and Ohno 2004, 150).[3] Hijikata, who directed the premiere, agreed with Yoshito (150): *Admiring La Argentina* somehow marked the moment of Kazuo Ohno's true birth on the butoh stage. But it is exceedingly strange to suppose that Kazuo Ohno had somehow been absent during the first twenty years of a dance form he had cocreated; that only now, a septuagenarian neophyte, was he beginning to dance. What qualities did the ghost of Antonia Mercé possess, to bring out the will to dance when it had lain dormant in Ohno's body for ten years? If La Argentina had been such a cherished source of inspiration for Ohno since 1929, why had he never mentioned her until 1976? As both Yoshito Ohno and Hijikata recognized, an ineffable force had animated this dance, as if an eggshell had cracked open and revealed Kazuo Ohno dancing for the first time. The drag practice of "admiring" was not only a form of dance for Kazuo Ohno; dancing in a dress became a dissolution of the boundaries of his body, a porousness of identity, a way of hosting other histories. Ultimately, this practice of "admiring" would transmit itself beyond Kazuo Ohno and beyond butoh, moving artists at a mystical distance. By the time Trajal Harrell's *The Return of La Argentina* came into being in 2015, a dress pressed to the body had become a mode of speculative historiography.

## Admiring

One of the most striking things about *Admiring La Argentina* is its almost bewildering profusion of costumes. In footage from a 1994 performance, Kazuo Ohno dances in a multitiered dress of purple and red flounces, a black velvet jacket with starched transparent sleeves, a silky white fringed scarf, and a red paper flower to pin in his hair.[4] Live tango music accompanies Ohno as he darts and stamps, giving coy little hops and trilling runs that rustle under his skirts, while twisting his wrists in graceful, twining circles. In a film of her dance "El Embrujo," La Argentina appears joyously flirtatious, accenting a series of sideways slides of her hips with a quick,

Figure 10. Kazuo Ohno in *Admiring La Argentina* in 1977. Photo by Hiroaki Tsukamoto, courtesy of Kazuo Ohno Dance Studio/ Canta Co. Ltd/ Kazuo Ohno Archive.

knowing look from under her long eyelashes. Her eyebrows go up merrily as she traces tiny circles with her foot on the floor, and her mouth makes a suggestive moue of mock surprise as she does a side kick that throws the flounce of her skirt up to her knee (NHK 2001). Ohno's fluidly winding arms, sinuous turns, and full kicks to the side and back are full of faded grace and a theatrically feminine coyness that recall La Argentina's stage presence. However, Ohno's affect of delicate femininity is punctuated by ragged falls to the floor and a way of shrinking inward that hunches the shoulders. He may be "admiring" her, but he is not imitating her.

Yet Yoshito Ohno declared without hesitation that "one can clearly see La Argentina taking bodily form in his dance. . . . As they begin to merge and become as one, a metamorphosis takes place. Kazuo becomes La Argentina" (Ohno and Ohno 2004, 166). Ohno's manager, Toshio Mizohata, also voiced the conviction that something impossibly corporeal was happening in *Admiring La Argentina*—that Kazuo Ohno could, as Mizohata says, "reincarnate the presence of La Argentina onstage" (Ohno and Ohno 2004, 6). It is these beginnings after endings, mystical hauntings, and uncanny resonances that ask us to think more closely about Ohno's own understanding of "admiring": what animates this practice, how it operates, and how it evolves as it is inherited by others. It might seem at first that *Admiring La Argentina* intends to re-perform or reconstruct lost dances, replicating specific qualities of La Argentina's style. In this piece, it is true, Kazuo Ohno dances to tango music while wearing vintage dresses and loosely echoing gestures that La Argentina might have made with her castanets. But his dance is inherently and irreconcilably *not* like her dances. The piece includes sections such as "The Death of Divine," restaged from a dance called *Divinariane* (originally choreographed by Hijikata in 1959 and inspired by Genet's novel *Our Lady of the Flowers*), which has no relation to La Argentina. More strikingly, this dance foregrounds poignant and deliberate differences between two bodies in terms of gender, age, ethnicity, cultural history, movement training, era, morphology, nationality, ability, dance form, and physical affect, while proposing that they "become as one."

"We produce something new only on condition that we repeat," Deleuze writes in *Difference and Repetition*, "once in the mode which constitutes the past, and once more in the present of metamorphosis" (1994, 90). The metamorphosis in which Kazuo Ohno somehow takes the "bodily form" of La Argentina into his own involves both a repetition that proposes to constitute a past performance and a repetition that can only produce something new. It is this avowal of repetition, in fact, that necessarily causes something new to be created, because both resemblance and imitation are impossible. Kazuo Ohno's body cannot physically align with Antonia Mercé's in any way that would make them alike, nor can he represent her movement as someone with similar technical training might.[5] 'Admiring' is a term of implacable difference even while it is a proclamation of becoming.

Almost disdainfully, Kazuo Ohno rejects the idea that he would "mimic any person, or spirit, as they were when alive," concluding, "We've got to go beyond mere resemblance so as to create something more substantial" (Ohno and Ohno 2004, 218). Ohno 'admires' La Argentina by incorporating the traces of her dance into his body, but this mode of memory avoids the directness of body-to-body transmission, the presence or physical proximity of its object, and the attempt at imitation. Instead, Ohno's admiring embraces what has long been buried or what has drifted into a spectral distance. With the spark of an evocative image, the process of reanimating a body begins;[6] when the costume touches the body, it opens up an interior space that can be inhabited by multiple others. As Ohno explains, because "the spirits of the dead are alive and breathing inside of us," it is "those manifold spirits living in me" that are his primary motive force (255, 267). In the same vein, when Deleuze writes that "representation fails to capture the affirmed world of difference," he explains that the basic problem with representation is that it does not help anything to move: "it mediates everything, but mobilises and moves nothing" (1994, 55–56). Both Ohno and Deleuze are theorizing an opposition between resemblance or representation, with its emphasis on likeness, and an intensified connection based in difference, which Deleuze calls "repetition" and Ohno calls "substantial" dance: in each case, it is *difference* that enables movement.[7] The effort of surfacing a memory that is already as flat and fragile and faded as a photograph from decades ago is justified, for Ohno, by the potential of "becoming"—becoming other, becoming another, "becoming as one" with many others—and by the dancing that makes it manifest.

"Admiring," then, is Ohno's mode of going beyond mimicry, resemblance, impersonation, representation, re-performance, reconstruction, or linear transmission. Rather than 'transcending' or obscuring the disparity between his body and La Argentina's, he heightens it with flamboyant gowns draped by eyelet-lace capes, shaky coats of black eyeliner that run into the deep wrinkles around his eyes, and a "crumpled pink hat and high-heeled shoes" (Stein 1986, 107). This is the context in which we can understand Ohno's statement that "my intention in dressing as a woman onstage has never been to become a female impersonator, or to transform myself into a woman. Rather, I want to trace my life back to its most distant origins" (Ohno and Ohno 2004, 76). For both Deleuze and Ohno, the elements of the strata of past time are prickling, live, larval. In each present body, Ohno proposes, there are teeming, animate multitudes underneath the skin; these are the manifold spirits of the dead who inhabit "distant origins" before birth and after life.[8] Ohno seeks a dimensionality in drag that rejects both resemblance and impersonation, instead seeking a volatile, haunting connection to other histories, other dancers, other ways of being moved.

## Moving Under the Surface

In the year before Kazuo Ohno premiered *Admiring La Argentina*, he "couldn't face standing in front of an audience," Yoshito Ohno attests (Ohno and Ohno 2004, 143). Wandering around the countryside with filmmaker Chiaki Nagano—who captured him consorting with turnips and pigs for his film *Trilogy of Mr O* (*Portrait of Mr O*, 1970; *Mandala of Mr O*, 1971; *Mr O's Book of the Dead*, 1973)—Kazuo Ohno did not seem like someone eternally enthralled by the memory of La Argentina or destined to reanimate her spirit. If anything, in *Portrait of Mr O* he appears to be traumatized by his own embodiment, alienated from human community, harrowed by mortality. In one scene his face is so grotesquely encrusted with mud that it resembles the scars of a burn victim; in another scene, in the forest, his body is rent by forceful, uncomprehending twitches. Smearing blood from a fish on a white cloth, crouching fearfully in an overgrown graveyard, feeling his way forward from behind a long wooden mask topped by a thorny wreath of twigs: Mr. O looks like a man who has suffered through years at war.

Kazuo Ohno was, in fact, conscripted as a soldier beginning the month after Yoshito was born in 1938; he returned nine years later, following a year of captivity in New Guinea (Ohno and Ohno 2004, 310). He rarely spoke of what had happened in those years, but Yoshito, explaining the "ghost dances" that his father created, traced them back to his "battlefront experiences in World War II," suggesting that "when Kazuo dances as a man," the "shadow of death" surrounds him (37, 104, 83). Trailing the body after the event, the echoes of mass violence can continue to move the body in ghostly ways; the soldier is disarmed, but the body of the dancer still holds its memories of weapons and wounds. In *Ghostly Matters* (1997) Avery Gordon investigates how traumatic histories—racialized oppression and state-organized terror, in particular—manifest in haunting. She is clear that haunting is "not the same as being exploited, traumatized, or oppressed," but happens when "a repressed or unresolved social violence is making itself known," especially when the violence has been "denied" (2008, xvi). She distinguishes haunting as a phenomenon that is "producing something-to-be-done": it is a *moving* thing, an impetus, an animating and disruptive force that rattles the way things have settled and reminds us that those things are not over, just overlaid.

The conditions of haunting, for Gordon, begin with an enforced silence, clamping the trauma down into an unspeakable pastness. But it also creates the potential of "knowing ghosts," which means becoming "the slightly mad one who kept saying, 'There's something in the room with us'" (22). Like anthropologist Michael Taussig's idea of "sympathetic magic," Gordon writes, this kind of knowing is a willingness to be affected by what is felt, even if it cannot be analytically, objectively known—an experience that "draws us affectively" into "a transformative recognition" of spectral life (8). It is in this sense that a soldier might 'know' that the pale clouds of jellyfish in the water are the floating souls of dead companions, left on other shores—or that a dancer might sense that memories are ebbing in and out of bodies in a room, looking for movements that will materialize them. For Kazuo Ohno, the unspeakable war years created the conditions for a haunting that made it impossible to dance as a man. If what the bodies of men did, over and over, was to fight and die, and to kill and bury the corpses and crouch in their holes, then those bodies were all the same, and there were no dances in them. It was the bodies of women that were not only full of life but full of *lives of their own*, lives of strong character and memorable stories—like the story of La Argentina borrowing Bronislava Nijinska's corps de ballet for her show in Buenos Aires in 1933, shortly after receiving the Order of Icham Iftikar from the king of Tunisia (Bennahum 2000, 193). If the shadow of death lingered around men's bodies, in their identical uniforms and drab suits, what could be lived in the dresses of women was the possibility of a different relation to the past.

In 1976, while leaving an art gallery in Tokyo, Ohno was suddenly drawn to an abstract painting—white swirls on a zinc background—by Natsuyuki Nakanishi. "La Argentina, it's you!" he exclaimed (Ohno and Ohno 2004, 145). "Nailed" in front of the painting, transfixed by visual recognition, Ohno "felt her come to life again" (Ohno and Maehata 1986, 159; Ohno and Ohno 2004, 184). When Kazuo Ohno came home from the gallery, he revealed his experience to his son Yoshito, who was understandably quite surprised to learn that an Argentinian dancer he had never heard of "had cast such [a] spell" on his father "that the emotions he felt at that time had lain dormant in him throughout the intervening forty-seven years" (Ohno and Ohno 2004, 145). In Kazuo Ohno's conception, the initial encounter with Antonia Mercé's dance in 1929 had been only the formation of a seed, and the seed lay "dormant" in his body, preserved by a sort of "spell" that kept it immobile but alive, and—underneath the decades of artistry and trauma that Ohno's body acquired—the seed very slowly gestated. The war came and went, leaving its dead strewn over sea and land, and shadowing its survivors with nightmares. Then, in 1976, the flash of an abstract image ignited the potential of that seed: the vision of La Argentina moving in the still, flat, painted surface struck a resonance with the buried image preserved in Ohno's body, and that shock echoed through him. This "transformative recognition" sounded the reawakening of the dancer's body after nearly ten years away from the stage, and Ohno was caught between the urgings of these two resonant images—one floating on canvas, one sunken in the depths of his body.[9]

In Ohno's practice of admiring, the task of the body is to give memories a place to materialize; in turn, the body is moved by the rushing in and out of these memories, the eddies and currents of their passage. In the year of preparation between the painting and the premiere, Ohno undertook a set of practices to open his body to the movements of La Argentina's image, now active inside him. Like Hijikata, he was seeking a way of inhabiting "a liminal place between interior and exterior, between internalization of something from the outside and externalization/exteriorization of something from within" (Sas 2011, 162–63).[10] Although butoh often asks the dancer to actively make room in the body for other presences and forms, including the ghostly,[11] Ohno's process of creation in *Admiring La Argentina* was highly specific: becoming as one with La Argentina was not like becoming a flower or a jellyfish or a fetus. In particular, Ohno generated movement by using costumes: dresses, shawls, hats, and high heels were like paintings placed on the skin instead of before the eyes. The flat image of Nakanishi's painting produced an unforeseen depth; the tautness of fabric across skin produced movement deep in the body. Touching his body with some material strange to it, apparently, could create not only a connection with other bodies but also the impetus to dance.

When Kazuo Ohno puts on a dress, he gives his body over to a world of "spirits alive inside of him" that he "can't encounter" merely "by dressing as a man," in Yoshito Ohno's words (Ohno and Ohno 2004, 81).[12] For Kazuo Ohno, dance occurs when a series of differences are touched off: when the community of ghosts moves inside the living body, when the dancer returns to the womb while giving birth to the dance, and when the dancer becomes as one with someone else. Yoshito Ohno describes the essence of Kazuo Ohno's performance as "an occasion on which those ghosts dormant in him come to life" (33). Taking the residue of the past into his own body, he allows the embryonic movement of memories to guide him: "I try to carry in my body all the weight and mystery of life, to follow my memories until I reach my mother's womb," he says (Velez and Velez 1990). For this reason, *Admiring La Argentina* is not only a work of repetition and difference, but also of gestation and rebirth, of mortality and gravidity, of embryonic movements deep under the surface of an image or memory—and of drag.[13]

### Dresses

Partly because Japanese theater traditionally casts men in female roles,[14] and partly because butoh embraces all kinds of provocative possibilities for the body—full nudity, tattered rags or strange sculptural garments, white-powdered skin, grotesque contortions, explicit sexuality, exaggerated expressions, denaturalized gender—Kazuo Ohno's dances are not often analyzed as 'drag' in the Western theatrical sense. Mark Franko, who calls *Admiring La Argentina* "Ohno's cross-dressed performance," is a notable exception (2011, 109), as is performance theorist Richard Schechner, who wrote, "Ohno concentrated on being an old man in a kind of drag that referred to but did not attempt to imitate a woman" (1989, 8).[15] Although butoh scholars such as Susan Blakely Klein and Sondra Fraleigh do refer to Ohno as having "broadened Japan's gender-bending dance techniques" (Fraleigh 2010, 98) and as sharing "Buto's interest in the marginal characters of the Kabuki stage" (Klein 1988, 37), they avoid terms like 'cross-dressing' or 'drag.' Fraleigh and Tamah Nakamura emphasize, for example, that although Hijikata and Ohno may be wearing "white Western style gowns" in the duet *Rose Colored Dances* (1965), they "dance unassumingly in the dresses, not to parody women, but simply to be themselves"

(2006, 83). Butoh scholar and choreographer Norbert Mauk declares, "this doesn't have anything to do with transvestism" (1994, 59).[16]

Yet it must be said that Kazuo Ohno is particularly attached to dresses, especially démodé ones—floor-length, fin-de-siècle dresses in dark velvet with lace ruching, or pale chiffon dresses with pearl buttons at the wrists, which cry out to be worn with outsize silk flowers pinned in one's hair and elbow-length gloves. "Ohno has an immense wardrobe boasting an array of gowns for all occasions," dance critic Bonnie Sue Stein records. "During a recent trip to New York, he purchased an exquisite off-white satin beauty, circa 1890, with puffed sleeves, a high collar, and a four-foot train. At home, he tried on the dress and immediately began to dance" (1986, 117). The strong causal connection between putting on the right dress and the impulse to dance turns out to be central to Kazuo Ohno's creative process. "Kazuo's dance doesn't come to life unless he's deeply charmed by what he wears," Yoshito Ohno asserts. "A gown, let's say, that doesn't become a second skin, won't do anything for him" (Ohno and Ohno 2004, 76). Western dresses act as catalytic images for Ohno: they activate the movements that become dances. In this sense, drag is fundamental to the creation of *Admiring La Argentina* as a strategy for conceiving the body as a place that can be inhabited by others.

A continuum of dresses spans Ohno's entire career as a dancer, beginning with his first performance and continuing well into his old age. The origins of Ohno's dance career are linked to dresses: he says he first began to wear them at his debut, in 1948 (Schechner 1986, 164). This was also the first time Hijikata had ever seen Ohno dance—"a man wearing a chemise," he said, whose movement was so powerfully intoxicating that it felt like poison was seeping into his veins (Hijikata 2000, 36, 42).[17] A biographical documentary made (in collaboration with the Ohno studio) by NHK, a Japanese television station, relates that "when the Ohnos perform abroad they often search for and buy costumes in second-hand clothing stores." If rummaging through frilly vintage gowns in foreign cities seems frivolous, it is worth considering that, for Kazuo Ohno, the costume can determine the nature, duration, and essence of the dance: "In rehearsals, costumes are chosen and when the costume is done, the dance piece is completed. It often happens that the costumes make the dance piece" (NHK 2001). For Kazuo Ohno, the dress is an invitation to the body to dance. The interaction between costume and body is full of generosity, permitting the entrance of the unknowable and the forgotten.

Sometimes, as dance critic Nario Gōda told butoh scholar Maria Pia D'Orazi in an interview in 1996, Ohno's attachment to dresses even overwhelmed the fixity of a piece that had already premiered: he would rework earlier dances in order to incorporate more lavish gowns. After Hijikata's death in 1986, Gōda noted with some disapproval, Ohno decided to change the costumes for his role as Divine (both in Hijikata's *Divinariane* [1960] and in the related "Death of Divine" section of *Admiring La Argentina*). Instead of the dirty smock and simple straw hat Hijikata had envisioned, Ohno "put on a very beautiful black gown decorated with silver and gold, and a hat full of flowers" (D'Orazi 2001, 65). The aesthetic of ever more elaborate dresses governs *Admiring La Argentina* as a whole; the majority of the evening-length solo is performed in opulently feminine gowns. In footage from a 1994 performance, for example, Ohno can be seen dancing vivaciously in a floor-length dress of tiered red and purple flounces, paired with a black velvet frock coat whose outlandishly puffed shoulders threaten to dislodge the giant red paper flower in his hair; around his neck he wears a black velvet choker and a white fringed scarf, which is not only embroidered with flowers but also embellished by an explosion of cream-colored feathers on one side. When he is dancing in a costume this ornately overwrought, it looks rather like the dress is dancing him.

It makes sense, then, to avoid a reductive definition of drag as a 'parody of women' and instead to grant it the place it deserves as a creative practice: as central to Ohno's work as music, Hijikata's influence, or his long collaboration with his son Yoshito.[18] Why would we see Ohno's dances, as Catherine Curtin does, "as a 'camp' satire of femininity, played out within a variety of intensities that range from the theatrical to self-parody" (2011, 481), when Ohno himself remarks, "We're not alone; we share our bodies with many, many others" (Ohno and Ohno 2004, 255)? The unwillingness of some butoh scholars to associate Ohno's work with drag may well be due to a misperception of drag as something that takes place on the surface of the body, as a parody or facile simulacrum of gender. But as Deleuze notes, "By simulacrum we should not understand a simple imitation but rather the act by which the very idea of a model or privileged position is challenged and overturned. The simulacrum is the instance which involves a difference within itself" (1994, 69). Ohno's use of drag counters a prevailing model of binary, fixed gender with the concept of a body populated by "difference within itself." It is the dress that opens the body to this play of difference, making a place for the coexistence of corporeal histories. This is the potential that drag invokes—a body not simply divided into "self" and "someone else" but rather simultaneously co-inhabited by the "many, many others" to whom Kazuo Ohno often alludes.

## Births after Deaths

*Admiring La Argentina* does not begin with La Argentina. In fact, it begins with one of the queerest characters in the Western artistic canon: Genet's Divine, who was translated into butoh through Hijikata's fascination with bodily decay and the limits of depravity. Ohno opens his performance with this tribute to Hijikata, incorporating in his solo masterpiece a version of their collaboration—but having added vastly more elaborate costumes, and within a structure that affirms the animate simultaneity of bodies. As *New York Times* dance critic Jennifer Dunning wrote of the US premiere at La MaMa in 1981, Ohno rises from a seat in the front row of the audience, "dressed in a lavender gown with amazing furbelows and a frumpy bonnet . . . like a glittering old hag" to make his way with "totters" and "flounces" to the stage, accompanied by Bach's *Toccata* (1981). At the end of this section, with a weary and faltering grace, Ohno takes the white eyelet-lace cape from his shoulders and carefully lays it down in the pooled spotlight. He picks up the hems of his dress daintily in order to step onto the pale fabric, showing his silver high-heeled shoes and bony ankles, and then, bending at the knees, one hand pathetically outstretched, appears to melt down into the fabric of his own cape, his body sinking into the costume as the lights fade out.

When the lights come up again, the voice of Maria Callas singing Puccini's "Senza Mamma" introduces the reincarnation of the aging male prostitute as a young girl who arises, a large bow pinned lopsidedly in her hair, from the pile of Divine's clothes. Childishly clutching the edges of her white dress, the girl finds Divine's garishly flowered hat and tries it on, taking little spinning steps across the stage. She wraps Divine's discarded cape around her shoulders, lurching forward in her high heels, as if overcome by the clothes she has inherited. "Birth of a life is attained through a death of another life," Kazuo Ohno said as an introduction to this piece in 1994. The dance of the living emerges not only from the place of the dead, but directly from the overlapping layers of their costumes: as a man in drag (Kazuo Ohno) dances the role of a man in drag (Divine), he gives birth to a man in drag who is a young girl, and whose dance seems inspired by a gradual accumulation of the clothes worn by Divine as she was dying.

Figure 11. Kazuo Ohno in *Admiring La Argentina* in 1977. Photo by
Hiroaki Tsukamoto, courtesy of Kazuo Ohno Dance Studio/ Canta Co.
Ltd/ Kazuo Ohno Archive.

Although, as Yoshito Ohno says, "Kazuo identifies himself totally with" La Argentina in this dance, there is still room for other ghosts (Ohno and Ohno 2004, 166). "Admiring" does not mean the straightforward translation of one identity into another; it is a continual movement through the interwoven strata of bodies that inhabit each other, emerge from each other's deaths, sink back into each other's clothes, and draw each other into movement. An audience is brought into the world of *Admiring La Argentina* not by witnessing Ohno re-performing La Argentina in any direct or mimetic way, but by seeing Ohno in drag, rising from the amorphous darkness of the house to take the stage. Then the "admiring" of La Argentina is initiated by characters who are pointedly not like her and who bear no historical relation to her. That these characters share clothing—that "admiring" is framed through costumes that prompt impossible transmutations and reincarnations—means that dresses, not likeness, are the common ground for Hijikata's Divine, the young girl, and Kazuo Ohno himself.

In this sense, butoh and drag share a feminine metaphor of bodies developing inside bodies: intimately connected and yet constantly engaged in nurturing and growing their state of difference.[19] Ohno's capacity for somatic metamorphosis—much praised by Miyabi Ichikawa in "A Preface to Buto" (1983)—is closely related to a butoh practice that Sondra Fraleigh describes as developing a "relational body" that can expand "the self to include others" (2010, 48–49). In butoh, the preparatory state of the body is to make an interior space available; it does not steadfastly proclaim its own plenary identity. In other words, the self does not fill up the body with itself. Instead the body lies open to other forms: flowers, ash, eggs, stars, mothers; the dead, the invertebrate, the eyeless.[20] "Acts come upon us and become the act-ors," Sas writes of Hijikata's vision of the artist overcome by the 'object' of artistic expression (2011, 163–64). Like butoh, drag can catalyze the body to transform itself into a densely populated cohabitation of selves: to become many things at once, to be both what it is 'outside' and what it is 'inside,' because those things are no longer separate—rather, they are soldered together in a kind of creative difference that impels the body to move. "The costume the soul has on / Is flesh," Ohno wrote in his poetic notes for the choreography of *Ishikari no hanamagari* (The Ishikari River's Hooked-Nose Salmon), a dance from 1991 that restages a section from *Admiring La Argentina* (Fraleigh and Nakamura 2006, 63–64). This disjunction—that wearing the flesh of your own body is, essentially, the experience of being in drag—is crucial to *Admiring La Argentina*.

Figure 12. Kazuo Ohno in *Admiring La Argentina* in 1977. Photo by
Hiroaki Tsukamoto, courtesy of Kazuo Ohno Dance Studio/ Canta Co.
Ltd/ Kazuo Ohno Archive.

## Copying the Diva

For a downtown dance and theater audience at La MaMa in the 1980s, it would have been difficult to hear any Maria Callas soundtrack 'straight,' even if the diva's voice *weren't* being used by a man in a dress channeling Divine in the first act.[21] The drag opera star Dagmar Onassis, for example, was born late one night when John Kelly taught himself to sing like Maria Callas, somewhat accidentally, by lip-synching in front of a mirror while tripping on acid in his East Village apartment (Kelly 2001, 41). As David Román made clear in an early article, tellingly titled "'It's My Party and I'll Die if I Want To!': Gay Men, AIDS, and the Circulation of Camp in U.S. Theatre" (1992), Callas was perceived as a gay icon in the pantheon of indisputable divas. "Callas was a refuge," Wayne Koestenbaum declared, a site where "a forbidden sexuality . . . could spread its wings" (1993, 153). Between Divine, Maria Callas, Ohno's sumptuous drag, and the idea that *Admiring La Argentina* was channeling a beautiful, passionate dancer from long ago—a woman who "lived for her art and died for it," as her gravestone proclaimed dramatically, an icon of her time, a star known only by her single stage name—it made sense that certain audiences would sense a queer strain in Ohno's work.

Perhaps it is not surprising, then, that one particular aspect of *Admiring La Argentina* has continued queerly into the present: the Japanese dancer and performer Takao Kawaguchi, who has neither studied butoh nor ever seen Kazuo Ohno perform live, has taken up a project to "embrace the abject copy," as his artist statement says, in *About Kazuo Ohno— Reliving the Butoh Diva's Masterpieces* (2013). Using archival materials from the Kazuo Ohno Dance Studio, Kawaguchi has studied a number of Ohno's pieces, laboriously transposing each step and gesture onto his body as precisely as he can, despite the fact that Ohno often improvised ecstatically onstage rather than adhering to a strict choreography. Notably, Kawaguchi has learned to perform *Admiring La Argentina* from the grainy 1977 premiere video alone, imitating Ohno's movements as exactly as possible while noting in his artist statement that, paradoxically, "The closer it gets, however, the clearer the gap becomes," to the extent that "copy is original." For Kawaguchi, the video representation of Ohno performing has become an original that he copies back into performance, but imperfectly: it is an artistic experiment in eternally approaching a model, an asymptotic performance.

Onstage, Takao Kawaguchi is painstakingly attentive to detail. He fixes the middle finger of his right hand in a dramatically crooked bend, where it stays for the length of the performance; he attunes his wrist to the flowing figure-eight movement that Ohno made when he loved the music he was dancing to, and his mouth is held open in Ohno's transported expression. In the "Tango" section of *Admiring La Argentina*, Kawaguchi picks up his skirt, in all its layers of pale ruffled tulle, to show his feet in their simpering steps. After a lively pivot on the ball of one foot, he stamps. Half a second later, the echo of Ohno's stamp is heard in the theater, a soundtrack projected in ghostly resonance from 1977. There is a little catch in the temporality of Kawaguchi's performance, a slip out of simultaneity. In the willingness to do everything possible to imitate the details of another body—to study a dance down to the angle of a finger in the air—there must also be some willingness to show the disjunction between these two bodies. In this light *About Kazuo Ohno* could be seen as a failure: it is a copy that comes so close that an audience can *hear* its gaps. But it does convince those who see it—not least, Toshio Mizohata, who was Ohno's production manager and is now Kawaguchi's, as well as the Japan Society in New York, which presented Ohno in 1993, 1996, and 1999, and then hosted Kawaguchi in September 2016—that Kawaguchi has done meticulous work in order to re-perform the 1977 video. Even the showing of tiny slips and errors attests to the singularity, authenticity, and historical significance of the 'original' to which he devotes his efforts.

If Ohno understands his dancing as 'with' La Argentina and the other ghosts 'within' his body, Kawaguchi is very much making a piece 'about.' As Jaime Shearn Coan observes in his insightful review of Kawaguchi's show, "Perhaps we could consider the 'about' in *About Kazuo Ohno* in a spatial sense—as an ambulatory, circuitous cruise, over and around and through the revered performer's work" (2016). The 'aboutness' of Kawaguchi's dancing is the topical, indexical, documentary aboutness of the archive, not the channeling of spectral others.[22] After the show in New York, I asked Kawaguchi if he ever felt haunted by Ohno. "That's the last thing I feel," he replied, somewhat ruefully. "I *wish* he would possess me. [But] this is copying." In taking the video as the origin of his dance—in the sense of a 'master copy'—Kawaguchi engages in a practice of surfaces and costumes, but in the opposite direction from Ohno: "I focus instead on the very tangible forms on the video screen, and wear them as if putting an armor or a costume on my body," he explains in his artist statement (2013). The outer layer of images still galvanizes the body to move, but without any interior transformation or resonance.

In fact, what Kawaguchi is doing with his body is not catalytically re-animating a dance inside himself, but rather re-performing the *"diva."* As Coan points out, putting "diva" in the title automatically "engages a campy aesthetic that also asks us to consider Ohno's work anew in light of its transgression of gender norms" (2016).[23] Takao Kawaguchi, who ran the Tokyo International Lesbian and Gay Film Festival for two years, is presumably clear on the rhetoric of the diva. So when he mused aloud during a 2016 workshop at the Japan Society in New York, "Why, to learn about Kazuo Ohno, why not learn his *dance?*" instead of memorizing and re-performing one single recording, he answered himself: "Copying is an interesting thing: not parody, not caricature. How much can you do [with] different bodies?" As it happens, there *is* something you can do in queer culture that involves different bodies, reliving divas, meticulous copying from recordings, live performance, and campy transgressions of gender norms, and that thing is lip sync. *About Kazuo Ohno* is a work of keeping the surface on the surface: the dresses never get under the skin of the dancer, and the history stays flat, like a video screen. The impressive labor Kawaguchi dedicates to his project is pinned to one piece of videotape—infinitely repeatable, always the same—that fixes *Admiring La Argentina* to one November evening in 1977. The differences between "copying" and "admiring" are differences of depth, temporality, and, ultimately, of openness to multiplicity and transformation. To lip-synch, you learn to mouth the words exactly: you match yourself to the recording, and the recording never changes. To admire, you dance without knowing what will happen in this present past, in this ghostly communion, in this dress.

## *The Return of La Argentina*

Through a doorway, in an adjacent room, a figure is distantly dancing. He holds a dress pressed against his body, tenderly, like a fragile partner. The dress falls full-length to the floor with frilled hems: it is pink, as pink as lip gloss and candy hearts, patterned with flowers. He dances in swooping little waltz steps, through the doorway and along the back of the room, holding the dress under its sleeves so that his hands press its neckline to his chest. In the turns, his elbows and hips jut out, and the dress swirls away from his body. He looks impassioned, riveted, intense; his hips and shoulders are mobile and slinky as he leads the dress up the aisle toward the stage space at the front of the room. Extending one proud bare foot forward, he tucks the full skirt to his other hip and presents himself in counterposed profile, like a flamenco dancer.

The dance quiets. He carefully folds the dress against his body until it is a ragged bundle of pink fabric, and then lays it to rest gently on a low chair. There is something funereal and touching about the way he lays the dress down—once a partner in the dance, the dress has become nothing more than a thing on a chair. But it is also an opening invocation of a larger ritual: "a very special ritual," the program notes from ImPulsTanz 2016 say, "of artistic reanimation" through an "intimate, queer aesthetics." Trajal Harrell, the choreographer and performer of this piece, describes it on his website as "fictional archiving," which is the work a dance does when it "fictitiously remembers, stores, accounts for, forgets, registers, memorializes, ritualizes, and gives home to" earlier dances and the bodies that have animated them.[24] Under the title *The Return of La Argentina*, this piece alludes to a ghostly lineage of Kazuo Ohno's *Admiring La Argentina*—which in turn owes its ethereal inspiration to La Argentina, its earthly form to Tatsumi Hijikata, and its multiplicity to the endless returning of spectral others. Harrell, whose work tends to burrow back into specific dance histories, reinhabit them, and mix them into new hybrid forms, does not claim to be a flamenco dancer or a butoh dancer, just as in his long-running *Twenty Looks or Paris Is Burning at the Judson Church* series (2009–2013), he did not claim to be a voguer. ("The world doesn't need me to be a Butoh dancer," he told Gia Kourlas wryly in 2013, after spending time in Hijikata's archives and in the butoh community in Japan.) Instead, with a markedly queer reverence, he claims, "Harrell is voguing Ohno voguing La Argentina and/or Harrell is voguing Hijikata voguing Antonia Mercé." In other words, he is being moved by forms that are themselves being moved by the bodies they channel.

Trajal Harrell approaches voguing as both a theory of historiography and a practice of dancing that values performative experiments in 'realness' over all other claims to authenticity or truth. Voguing can be used to fabricate a lineage—even simultaneous and seemingly contradictory lineages, these "and/or" forms of inheritance—and to break through the orderly lines of normative transmission (Harrell never saw Hijikata dance live, voguing didn't exist in Japan in 1977, etc.). This is "dancing in the subjunctive," as performance theorist Tavia Nyong'o calls Harrell's approach (2017, 257): what would have happened, what might have been, what could still be called into being after it has long been gone? Harrell explains that *Return to La Argentina* was formed partly in recognition of the multiple drag channelings already embedded in *Admiring La Argentina*, "because of course there was this element in *La Argentina* which could be compared to voguing, because Ohno dresses as this character Divine," he told me the week before the piece premiered in Paris, "and also I could project or hypothesize that he is voguing Antonia Mercé, La Argentina" (2015). The queer potential of Divine in drag opens out onto other possibilities of embodying dancers—dancers who are as different from each other as they are from Trajal Harrell. In this multilayered drag practice of haunting, dresses, and "the performative effect of turning to history in a propositional or speculative mode," as Nyong'o puts it, there must also be an element of incorporation (2017, 254). Therefore, the second phase of this ritual involves food—a careful ingestion of a precise series of ingredients that has been designed, Harrell says to the audience, to make "the dance go better," and the resonant scrape of a metal spoon against the inside of a ceramic bowl that gradually becomes more and more like the tolling of a bell. But before he finishes eating, he stops to reclothe himself, draping each of his four limbs in its own elaborately filmy or ruffled garment. As he rises and begins to move, striking the bowl and extending it like an offering, the garments follow him loosely, trailing off his arms and puddling around his feet.

A red dress and a black dress float like ghostly streamers from his shoulders as he dances; when he is still, they divide his body at the midline, splitting him in half. Like the dresses, multiple histories wrap and fragment Harrell's body: he grew up in a small town in southeastern Georgia, and "I really fought," he remembers, "even to cross my legs, to be who I really was—my sensibility and the way my sensibility got expressed in me physically" (Osterweis and Harrell 2017, 114). He began dancing at twenty-two, after getting a degree in American Studies from Yale and doing theater. But he confided to art scholar Claire Bishop that he never would have started dancing at all, were it not for the "democratic principles and inclusiveness" of the postmodern Judson Church artists, who "gave me the courage to believe I too could be a dancer and choreographer" (Harrell et al. 2017, 301). In 1999, during a residency at Movement Research in New York, he went uptown to his first vogue ball (Moore 2014, 7). Although Harrell always emphasizes "that I am not a voguer. I don't make voguing. I make contemporary dance," ball culture gave him a new way to think about redefining realness, a place where dressing and moving had a status of their own (Osterweis and Harrell 2017, 110).[25] He went on to make a whole series of works called *Twenty Looks or Paris Is Burning at*

Figure 13. Trajal Harrell in *Trajal Harrell: Hoochie Koochie, a performance exhibition* at Barbican London, 2017. Photo by Orpheas Emirzas, courtesy of Trajal Harrell.

*the Judson Church*—historiographical voguings of what might have been if the Harlem ball scene had dropped in on the postmodern Judson dancers in 1963—and he did them with a costume wardrobe that had its own legendary proportions.

When the red and black dresses have been folded away, a new ensemble takes their place: a black long-sleeved collared jacket and a long black skirt, frilled sumptuously along the lower hem, which Harrell begins to shake up and down with an air of defiance, glaring at the audience as he pumps his arms. In this new skirt, Harrell's gestures become lighter as they take on a kind of frippery of their own: a wobbling head, a graceful trailing of the wrist through the air, a touch of the ball of the foot to the floor. There is a trace of the elderly Ohno in that elegant wrist, that perched foot, that wavering head—but only for a moment, and only as a resonance that passes through Harrell's body. It is not like watching someone imitate Ohno, or even like watching someone do a loose impression of Ohno: it is like watching someone try Ohno on for a minute, as if he were a strange dress temporarily pressed to Harrell's skin. Dance scholar Sara

Figure 14. Trajal Harrell in *The Return of La Argentina* at MoMA: The Museum of Modern Art, New York, 2015. Photo by Orpheas Emirzas, courtesy of Trajal Harrell.

Jansen (who is also the dramaturg for Harrell's 2016 *Caen Amour*), notes that while Ohno would wear dresses that he imagined La Argentina might have worn, Trajal Harrell tends to hold dresses and skirts at a slight distance from his body.[26] This "provocative gesture of spacing evokes Ohno's uncanny ghostly presence," she writes, but also "makes concrete the space Harrell opens up for himself to re-imagine the work in the present" (n.d. 3). Intensifying, these movements start to shake Harrell's body and then to produce other, more vigorous sequences of stamping, grunting, hopping, labored breathing, and raising a fist in the air like a matador.

To end *The Return of La Argentina*, Trajal Harrell spends a long time waving good-bye. First he puts small, bright pink bags on his hands. Then he begins to twirl the bags around his hands, like flashing semaphores. And then, swaying from foot to foot, he starts to wave good-bye to the audience, looking at each of them, waving individual and collective farewells, smiling magnanimously as he catches the eyes of spectators. Graciously, earnestly, he makes his way slowly down the aisle, toward the doorway, looking for all the world like a departing queen. He looks benevolent, enamored, so glad just to be dancing in a hallway of a museum. He looks fabulous. Or as Tavia Nyong'o would say, he looks "afrofabulist"—like someone who has imagined "an alternative tradition within which to position his own dancing body and, in and through the same gesture, to mark out a space for blackness and queerness" (2017, 257). He looks like someone who is no longer fighting for the right to cross his legs in public in his hometown, or someone who doesn't need the Judson Church to anoint him as a legitimate dancer, even if he isn't, as he remarked to Claire Bishop, some "ideal human specimen who can stand on one leg and lift the other up past their ears" (Harrell et al. 2017, 301). He looks like he is enjoying this interlude of not having to explain, for the umpteenth time, that this piece is not a reconstruction or a re-performance of Kazuo Ohno's *Admiring La Argentina*.

He also looks like he has something to give the audience as he goes—as if those little pink bags on his hands *were* semaphores, and they were flashing out their final message, a gift in parting. But what would Trajal Harrell want to communicate to each unknowable person in a room? Maybe he would try to transmit to them something that he said repeatedly to me: that above all he was struck by Ohno's "freedom," by "his ability to dance from a place that was really unknown and unprecedented" (2015). "He was such a wonderful amazing dancer, with so much *freedom*," Harrell said again, wistfully. Dancing out of the open doorway and into the distance, Harrell doesn't look like he is voguing or doing butoh or flamenco, and he doesn't look like Kazuo Ohno or Tatsumi Hijikata or Antonia Mercé. But he does look like a dancer who sees a way to be free.

*Ongoing*

"dear trajal," André Lepecki begins in a dream letter, and goes on to explain, in a rush of febrile gratitude, how it feels "to learn, thanks to your work, what it is *to redirect history*, and to redirect it corporeally, collectively, just as you do" (2017, 96). It feels liberating, apparently, but also dizzying, agitated, bereft of the regularity of punctuation in the same way that "ongoing going," as Lepecki calls it, has lost its usual temporal markers of periodicity and directionality (97). The whole letter feels coursed through by hot, tender spirits of radical historiography—difference and repetition, if they stayed up all night together. This might be because the process of "speculating corpo-affective-historically" immerses a body in the middle of swirling currents of events, encounters, and inheritances—but also in counter-streams of lost stories, lack of permission, nights that never happened, and barely conjectural connections. This seems true to the ethics of pieces like *Twenty Looks*, with its 'what-would-have-happened-if' premise, and to *The Ghost of Montpellier Meets the Samurai*; the *nouvelle danse* choreographer Dominique Bagouet and Hijikata never met, and even if they had, it's doubtful that they would have crossed paths in a gay bar in the West Village, and it's even more unlikely that the jukebox would have inspired them to spend the evening making dances in each other's styles, on the theme of love.[27] But this "redirecting" might also explain why, when Trajal Harrell performed the final butoh-related piece of his Museum of Modern Art (MoMA) residency, *In The Mood for Frankie* (2016), he chose as his stage an awkward hallway flanked by an escalator and asked that the dance not be videotaped.

The hallway, MoMA curator Ana Janevski pointed out, had very limited seating for spectators, and the performances were held late at night; it was a kind of "non-space in the Museum" (Janevski and Harrell n.d., 1). Moreover, in the planning stages, Harrell had voiced his desire to dedicate this final piece to "voguing Yoko Ashikawa," a butoh dancer who had inspired Hijikata and then vanished enigmatically. It would make a nice trilogy: *Used, Abused, and Hung Out to Dry* (2013) had channeled Hijikata, *The Return of La Argentina* was fictionally archiving Kazuo Ohno's masterpiece, and then the third piece in the series would explore, "corpo-affective-historically," Hijikata's mysterious muse. But it didn't exactly happen that way. And Trajal Harrell didn't want the actual, unplanned dance that had emerged to be recorded for posterity, even though MoMA was understandably eager to archive the products of his residency. It would be too dark to see, he demurred, and it would feel more precious, anyway, if you just had to be there for the show. But perhaps Harrell's overarching reason was to transmit to the audience his own practice of "historical imagination"—to ask this small collective of spectators, clumped in the transitional space of a hallway, to fictionally archive his dance. "In the performance," Harrell explained to Janevski, "I am working strongly on togetherness and how we imagine things together as a performative belief system" (2); if someone later wanted a record, he would connect them to a member of the audience, whose responsibility it would be to conjure *Frankie* in their own way. Speculative historiography was not only a practice for the choreographer; it could also be given to an audience.[28]

What happened to the nice, logical plans for a piece dedicated to

Yoko Ashikawa is what unexpectedly happened to Trajal Harrell when he began admiring Kazuo Ohno—"particularly the Ohno of *Admiring La Argentina*," he specified (3). Having seen Ohno perform live when he was still "too young to appreciate" it fully, Harrell reencountered *Admiring La Argentina* on video in the Hijikata archives in Japan, and it was as fatally, wondrously fateful as Hijikata's first sight of Ohno dancing in a dress: quite simply, Harrell says, "I fell in love with the way Ohno danced" (2015). Catalyzed by these moving images, drawing on years of practicing "how to be open to that openness, to that ethics you choreograph so well," as Lepecki put it in his letter, Harrell was drawn to Ohno, transfixed by his movement, and changed by the resonance that this dance produced deep within him (2017, 97). Admiring, in all of its differences and repetitions, had returned, and with it came not only *The Return of La Argentina* but also *In the Mood for Frankie*. And so, in the middle of making a piece that he hadn't intended to make, channeling a dancer he thought he had got over, Trajal Harrell took this unsought love, along with an armful of dresses and a little food, into the studio, and found a freedom that he hadn't been looking for:

> For sure, my work on Ohno was the pivot. I couldn't believe the way he was dancing. I saw him dance when he was alive; and I certainly didn't get it. And now I watch the videos; he leaves me speechless. I can say, "He was the best dancer in the world." But the minute I say that, I know Ohno didn't care to be the best dancer in the world. He just immensely loved dancing and couldn't stop dancing. Seeing him freed me in a way. (Janevski and Harrell n.d., 3)

The "freedom" of being compelled to keep dancing sounds a little perverse, perhaps in the way that the temporality of Harrell's falling in love with Ohno's *Admiring La Argentina* on video, after his death, years after seeing the live performance, is a beginning after an ending. However, Kazuo Ohno believed that "the future lies in the past, and the past lies in the future," with "some perpendicular matter which penetrates both the past and the future" (NHK 2001). Like Bergson's model of temporality—which Deleuze glosses as "defined less by succession than by coexistence" (1991, 60)—Kazuo Ohno envisioned a bodily simultaneity that persists through planes of time and across corporeal differences. It is for this reason that Ohno's insistence that "La Argentina and I are *together*, at all times" is a statement of both co-embodiment and co-temporality. "I don't care if my flesh is cremated and reduced to ashes, for my ashes will continue to walk at her side," he declared, emphasizing that this capacity for movement does not come from physical ability or a stable materiality, but rather from a definition of corporeality itself as a layering of bodies within and beside other bodies (Ohno and Ohno 2004, 265). Admiring, for Ohno, unbinds the dancer from the constraints of one temporal plane, allowing him to wrap death around rebirth, or to slip out of his own body and into an afterlife of ashen duets.

In the last section of *Admiring La Argentina*, Ohno presses his hands repeatedly over his heart, clasping them to his cream-colored beaded bodice with an expression of ecstatic gratitude. He was certain in his conviction that the dead dwelled within him and that La Argentina was alive and dancing in his dance. He thought deeply about the past, the lost, the ghosts: they were the movers under his skin. In this framework, drag is essential, as the body simultaneously wears its existence and is worn lightly, theatrically, without recourse to the singularity of fixity of a bodily identity. "The body wears the universe, and at the same time the body—the dress of the soul—is also a costume," Ohno said (D'Orazi 2001, 148).[29] It is through drag that the body is moved to dance, animated by the dead spirits who treat the dancer's body as their womb, confounding the assumed constraints on gendered bodies. André Lepecki calls this mode of dance "embodying otherwise," explaining that "a dancer's labour is nothing else than to embody, disembody, and re-embody, thus refiguring corporeality and proposing improbable subjectivities" (2012, 15). When Ohno "admires" La Argentina through drag, he dances the potential to be populated, the willingness to know ghosts, and the shiver that memory gives before borrowing the warmth that will bring it life.[30]

In Ohno's openness to the spectral past, he created potential queer futures for his own body and dance that he could not have conceived. That Takeo Kawaguchi would refigure him as a "diva" to be copied, or that so many proliferations of La Argentina would emerge after his death, or that the dancers who would be most drawn to *Admiring La Argentina* would be outsiders to butoh: these were unforeseeable permutations of the "perpendicular matter" conjoining past and future. Who would have guessed, moreover, that Trajal Harrell, so many years later, would take Ohno's practice of admiring as the mode of "discovering how I want to dance and practice dancing, perhaps for a long time to come" (Janevski and Harrell n.d., 2)? And that, as Harrell insisted, the process of "trying desperately to accept myself in all my strengths and weaknesses"—that freedom he had sought for his body in dancing—had finally been catalyzed by "Ohno as muse"? This was an almost dangerously utopian queer future, in which difference was a crucial condition of repetitions that produce something new, something mobilized, something that finally got past resemblance and representation.[31] This was dancing beyond the subjunctive and right up to the borders of the contrafactual, commingling bodies in impossible duets. It was claiming for the dancer a right to cross over into other bodies and histories, but that right was also a compulsion to be haunted—to recognize that bodies were not proper unto themselves but animated by other bodies. Anywhere that dances happened—in cramped hallways, on old videos, in abstract paintings, in collective imaginings and fictional archives, in the folds of dresses—they might be transmitting something to us. Dances could secretly be full of admirings and returns, and we would never know until years later; we were more open than we had thought. Maybe, when we thought we were only watching a dance, we were being given something to hold.

## CHAPTER FOUR

## Genealogies for Ballet

*Les Ballets Trockadero de Monte Carlo*

It's all very real to me.
> —Antony Bassae, the self-proclaimed "Black Rhinestone of Russian Ballet," to journalist Henry Post, "Prima Donalds," 1975

and we do need queer ontologies within dance, because so often we are told to not *do* queer in dance . . . and yes, we still need the doing to confirm the being.
> —thomas f. defrantz, "Queer Dance in Three Acts," 2017

*Origin Stories*

Once upon a time, on the eleventh story of the edifice of ballet history, there was a biography of a ballerina named Nadia Doumiafeyva:

> Banished from Russia, she made her way arduously to New York, where she founded, and still directs, the Ecole de Ballet de Hard-Nox. Her most famous exercise is the warm-up consisting of a martini and an elevator.

Before Nadia, this bio had belonged to Vera Namethatunenova, and before her, to Irina Kolesterolikova, and, somewhere along the way, to a whole perverse lineage of ballerinas who take the idea of 'bio' not only with a grain of salt but with three olives and a slosh of vermouth. The genealogy of these ballerinas, all of whom have danced with the drag ballet company Les Ballets Trockadero de Monte Carlo, is one of the most storied counter-stories in dance.[1] Nadia's bio is, in itself, a perfect little mock history of the beginnings of American ballet—a Russian émigré with a French pedigree, hard up in New York, swilling the glory of the new world and pushing all of the buttons at once, recalling the legends while becoming rapidly legendary herself. But this is historiography at the hands of someone whom Foucault, in "Nietzsche, Genealogy, History," would call a "genealogist"—someone who sees "history in the form of a concerted carnival," and who would not only "know what to make of this masquerade" but would also be "not too serious to enjoy it" (1984, 93–94). In this carnivalesque practice, the history of ballet is best done by people with cod-Russian names who think 'getting your leg up' should mean a pint of vodka by the twelfth floor.

Traditionally, ballet has been a kinesthetic discipline that has gradually ritualized 'ideal' forms for bodies; every time dancers take class, their bodies are reinscribed with its aesthetic values (e.g., perfect turnout, 'beautiful' feet, virtuosic extension). Western classical concert dance is, in fact, one of the most visible examples of Foucault's idea that history, through its parade of dominant ideals, "establishes marks of power and engraves memories on things and even within bodies" (1984, 85).[2] Historically, ballet has subscribed to certain codified forms of the body: the courtly body; the royal body; the Romantic, ethereal, disembodied feminine, among others.[3] An embodied genealogical practice, then, would interrogate the terms that ballet has gathered around itself since the Renaissance: whiteness, lightness, femininity, ethereality, desirability, perfection, nobility, grace, geometry, effortlessness, pageantry, virtuosity, youth, 'pure line.' In this airy assemblage of ideal qualities, an inquiring genealogist would identify what has been suppressed by the impetus to achieve and perpetuate the semblance of perfect form. What is underneath lightness, for example? Who is kept out by the collocation of whiteness and femininity? In order for 'pure line' to maintain its 'purity,' what lineages must bodies disavow? In investigating these questions *by dancing them*, the Trockadero undertake historiography not only as an embodied practice but also as a potentially political act.[4]

When a monolithic history of ballet is cracked open, a querulous multiplicity of other origin stories spills out, each with its own queer cast of characters and its own crooked timeline. The dancers of Les Ballets Trockadero de Monte Carlo are genealogists of this order: they inhabit the eddies and accidents of ballet, embodying what it used to be, what it might have been—and perhaps even what it might still become. The Trockadero company itself has at least four origin stories, which range across centuries, rife with ghosts. In one version the Trockadero were called into being by a theater trick that happened to become the hallmark of Western classical ballet: the rigging up of certain eighteenth-century ballerinas so that they could dance on their toes. Before ballet treated pointe work as if it were a *function* of gender—as if women were naturally built to rise to their toes and dance—it was clearly a technology, a prosthetic, a *figment* of gender. The Trockadero belong to that misty past, in which getting up on toe was an act of artificiality and visible labor for dancers of any gender, not some ethereal result of God-given ballerina ankles. In a different origin story, the Trockadero passionately animate the afterlife of an "old, broken-down Russian touring company" that no longer exists, as Peter Anastos, one of the company's founders, explained (Shulgold 2008). In a third version, the Trockadero were born one night in 1974, sui generis, in a rattly firetrap loft in the West Village, where they first performed under the auspices of what used to be called a "homophile" association, on a twelve-by-twelve-foot plywood stage (Acocella 2005). And the Trockadero are also the direct descendants of their drag mother, Charles Ludlam of the Ridiculous Theatrical Company, whose chaotic camp theatricality they cherish as if it were, in fact, the family jewels.

Like the haunted bio of Nadia and her comrades, the history of the company is a labyrinthine interweaving of multiple births, lost twins, accidental deaths, and queer inheritances. The "intersections between genealogical inquiry and practical research can be used," dance scholar Kate Elswit proposes, "to facilitate the mapping of present understandings of choreography as process onto the past," producing a "heterogeneous" form of historiography (2008, 65, 64). The Trockadero dancers bear in their bodies a tangle of bloodlines, some invented and some abandoned, that traverse a chronological history of ballet like rhizomes. They ask us to laugh at some of the most sacred narratives in ballet: Anna Pavlova lying pale upon her deathbed, Queen Victoria left speechless by Jules Perrot's *Pas de Quatre* (1845), Pierina Legnani whirling through her famous thirty-two fouettés, Maya Plisetskaya so bewitched by the music of *Coppélia* as a child that she wandered into the middle of the street to dance to it. They tell these histories not as triumphs or tragedies, but rather as agglomerations of jokes, longings, lost dances, backstage secrets, and the jostlings of bodies subject to failure.[5] Genealogy, in Foucault's terms, is an "analysis of descent," a move from the lofty heights of abstraction toward the materiality and contingency of bodies (1984, 83). In dance, a virtuosic leap into the blazing halo of the spotlight succumbs, at its zenith, to a downward pull: that is the teleology of the grand jeté, the descent from an illusion of lightness into weight and mass. For classical ballet, by extension, descent would mean coming down out of the abstract Platonic ideals of the body—particularly of the ballerina—and into lived corporeal realities. As Jennifer Fisher writes, this ethnographic work is still necessary: the figure of the ballerina has not yet "been woven into the kind of complex, contextualized analysis that includes practitioners who embody the form" (2007, 3). An analysis of descent, then, would show us the disciplines that have molded balletic bodies and the discontinuities that still fissure the concept of the ballerina.

Regardless of what the body under the tutu looks like, the Trockadero insist, the body in the tutu can do the steps. In fact, the tutu and the pointe shoes may well be what *enable* the body to do the steps—it is disciplined devotion to the costume that makes a drag ballet dancer. And it is a devotion to the company as a collective—not just showing up for rehearsal, but being kind to others, learning extra roles, believing wholeheartedly in the company's queer balletomania, helping out, accepting failure as part of the practice of ballet itself—that makes a Trockadero dancer. In the proliferation of their drag personae and their variant genealogies for ballet, the Trockadero envision how ballet might enact Deleuze's insight that "the internal genetic elements of repetition itself" are inherently theatrical, like false eyelashes and pancake makeup (1994, 17). "The disguises and the variations, the masks or costumes, do not come 'over and above,'" Deleuze writes; "they are, on the contrary . . . its integral and constituent parts" (16–17). Nadia Doumiafeyva, in other words, with her cod-Brooklyn airs and her vodka *tendus*, has as much claim to the history of ballet as Catherine de Medici or Maya Plisetskaya. Not only are the "genetic elements" of the Trockadero repetition of ballet opposed to everything that is heteronormative about traditional genealogy; they also take "repetition" in a queer way, insisting that those who have the right to repeat ballet are those who show up for *répétition*—the French word for 'rehearsal.'

### Norma, Madame, and Marguerite

Before there was Nadia Doumiafeyva, there was a proto-Trockadero ballerina who wasn't a man and didn't dance. She was the creation of Charles Ludlam, an actor who believed that "drag embodies the paradox of acting," and whose Ridiculous Theatrical Company was part of the madcap ferment of nearly feral creativity and newly liberated gay identities of late 1960s and early 1970s Manhattan (Kaufman 2002b, 104).[6] These were the years when publicly performed gay and lesbian identities were both political and highly theatrical; the Stonewall riots had kick lines of drag queens, singing. On the one hand, sexual preferences were becoming a form of politics—gay liberation—that seemed to imply an ontology for queer identity. On the other hand, queer theater was about a proliferation of roles, a provocative and vitally askew perspective on fixed, normative identity. Sara Warner chronicles, for example, how closely the "zap actions" of the lesbian activist group Lavender Menace were related to the lesbian feminist theatrical performances held at WOW Café. Both "were dramatizing the performative dimensions of theater and sexuality through their recognition that identities are transformed in real time by actors and spectators, in electrifyingly close proximity, who produce alternative, subversive interpretations of bodies and how they matter onstage and off" (2012, xix). This kind of theater was unnervingly live and interactive; there were no 'bystanders,' no safety behind the fourth wall.[7] Sometimes this was quite literal: one evening Charles Ludlam pelted the audience with vegetables and then threw his ventriloquist's dummy—whose name was Walter Ego—at them (Isaac et al. 1968, 116). They threw it back.

In 1967 Charles Ludlam staged his first play for the Ridiculous Theatrical Company, a chaotic caravanserai of a piece called *Big Hotel*. Its premise was that anything that could be imagined to go on under one hotel roof would happen onstage, "with lots of room for improvisation," as journalist Calvin Tomkins put it (1976, 72). Ludlam featured himself prominently, and he also created a role for Susan Carlson, whom he had christened "Black-Eyed Susan." As Tomkins relates, Black-Eyed Susan played "Birdshitskaya, an unhappy Russian ballerina who periodically flings herself (in effigy) from the roof. (Desk clerk: 'Is she hurt?' Bellhop: 'No, but she will never dance again.')" (72). A camp scrambling of other plots, *Big Hotel* ransacked the 1933 film *International House*, with its vaudeville assortment of characters, and romped through another 1930s film, *Grand Hotel*, which included Ludlam's idol Greta Garbo playing the worn-out ballerina Grusinskaya (Kaufman 2002b, 61–62). It seems likely that this multiplicity of deathless divas was the prototype of the Trockadero's ballerina personae. It would be fitting that, in at least one origin story, the Trockadero arose from histrionic fictions of a Russian ballerina who had never been Russian—and who was both indestructible and unfit for the stage.

Like Ludlam's dummy, Walter Ego, Birdshitskaya was hurling her persona at the audience; that she would "never dance again" was exactly the reason she was melodramatically encamped at center stage, again.

In 1969, when Ludlam was trying to distinguish his Ridiculous Theatrical Company from its forebearer, John Vaccaro's Play-House of the Ridiculous, he took to calling it "the Trockadero-Gloxinia Magic Midnight Mind Theater of Thrills and Spills" (Kaufman 2002b, 94).[8] Ludlam loved the Ridiculous too much to give up the name, but when a few dancers who often performed with the company started a drag ballet project in 1972, they called it the Trockadero Gloxinia Ballet Company, and Ludlam approved (94). One of these dancers, Larry Ree, whose stage name was Ekaterina Sobechanskaya, took up the artistic direction of the company and began to arrange performances at La MaMa and other small venues in downtown Manhattan. Ree had been a spectacular presence in several Ridiculous performances: in *Turds in Hell* (1969) he led an armada of ballerinas across a stage sluiced with soapy water, and reportedly sometimes halted the whole show so that he could descend into the audience, "caressing various men" (Kaufman 2002b, 102–103). One evening during the run of Ludlam's *The Grand Tarot* (1969), Ree usurped the intermission with a cassette tape of "Rite of Spring" and a white tutu in an improvised homage to Stravinsky (139).

Moreover, Ree—whose *Dying Swan* solo was highlighted by the *New York Times* as "the only bright spot in the Cockettes' disastrous season" in New York (McDonagh 1972, 28)—had enough charisma and ambition to gather four other male dancers and garner a six-show run at the Jean Cocteau Theatre in August 1972 (Coleman 1993, 31). The Gloxinia, following Ree's vision, were the conquering camp heroines of center stage. They were enamored of white tulle and bejeweled bodices and sweeping, gauzy gestures: "basically," the *Times* review of the Gloxinia debut concluded, "a cameo art form" (McDonagh 1972). Madame—as Ekaterina Sobechanskaya liked to be called—fully embraced the cult of the ballerina; she "styles herself after pictures of Anna Pavlova," Arlene Croce observed in a *New Yorker* review (1974, 187). The Gloxinia dancers "seized on the look of ballet, wafting and wilting," Jennifer Dunning concurred in the *New York Times* (1990). If, as art critic John Berger proposed, "*men act* and *women appear*," then the Gloxinia wanted to be the women appearing (1972, 47). Creating a cartoon of mincing, beribboned femininity, the Gloxinia's camp drag stayed safely on the surface of gender roles in ballet.[9]

But for Charles Ludlam, performing was a practice of becoming animated by someone else, of turning your body over to the dictates of a costume, of being deeply moved by a character who appeared, over time, to inhabit you. His theory of theater was stridently anti–Method acting; he found Konstantin Stanislavski's emphasis on the actor's own feelings to be "deadening" (Shewey 1987). Instead, Ludlam explained his theatrical practice in terms of

> the craft of role creation . . . before he learned one line, he went to the costume room, stood in front of the mirror, found the costume, did the makeup, and, when the character was staring back at him out of the mirror, then he could begin to work on the role (Argelander 1974, 86).[10]

The kernel of the role, in other words, came from the costume and the makeup, not from the actor's personal experience or understanding: it wasn't about *you*. Ludlam spoke of actors "possessed by their roles," whose melodramatic performances were attempts to fill the space of costume and character (Ludlam and Dasgupta 1978, 73–74). Channeling a character who appeared to you—as you—through a reflection in the mirror was not "a cameo art form," in which you styled yourself after a picture and waited for the applause, but rather a durational drag practice of making space inside your own body so that it could be possessed by someone else.

In an interview in 1968, Ludlam described an experience that "changed my life" (Isaac et al. 1968, 116): the first time he performed in drag, as Norma Desmond from the noir film *Sunset Boulevard*, in Ronald Tavel's *Screen Test* (1966)—a piece that was supposed to star Tavel and the Warholian drag icon Mario Montez, not Ludlam improvising for hours as Norma. Until that night, Ludlam had "needed weeks of rehearsal for any part," but then, just before he went onstage, he said, Henry Geldzahler gave him a wig (which he claimed to have gotten from Salvador Dalí); "I put on the wig and POW! there was Norma" (116). The costume had produced what Susan Sontag called "instant character" (1999, 61). Moreover, Ludlam insisted, two contradictory things were happening simultaneously: he was "teetering on the edge of being a man and a woman," and he utterly believed that he was Norma, ready at last for her close-up (Isaac et al. 1968, 116). This fervent, mystical, incorporative, layered drag identity championed by Ludlam would become fundamental to Les Ballets Trockadero de Monte Carlo.

Casting against type, Ludlam asked everyone in his company to play drag roles at one time or another. "It's evoking reality by showing us what isn't real," he explained. "If a man can put on makeup, false eyelashes and mascara, all the artifices of being woman, then obviously all those things are not part of being a woman" (Ludlam and Dasgupta 1978, 79). It seems noteworthy that twelve years before the publication of Judith Butler's *Gender Trouble* (1990), Ludlam was offering a quite lucid theory of drag as a tactic for denaturalizing gender. But what is even more striking is Ludlam's insight into drag's potential for animating bodies, for *moving* them in both physical and psychic senses. When Ludlam put on a wig and a "brown silk beaded dress," he felt impelled to get up onstage and improvise his lines (Tomkins 1976, 68). Many years later, when Ludlam wrote "a quasi-autobiographical play" called *Galas* (1983), he attributed his inspiration to an "amazing gown" that his boyfriend Everett Quinton had bought in a thrift shop (Kaufman 2002b, 372–73). Drag was not a superficial form of dress-up, but rather a vector of startling emotional intensity, an excessive sentimentality, an open channel for overwhelming affects—the power of the costume to move the body to tears.

Ludlam's most famous creation was a pastiche production of *Camille* (1973), in which he played the heroine Marguerite Gautier, in drag, but in a low-cut gown that showed off his chest hair. That excess of the body relative to costume—the deliberate sign of a body "set against itself," in Foucault's terms (1984, 88)—would come to be a hallmark of Les Ballets Trockadero de Monte Carlo dancers. "'I didn't want to engage in the kind of trickery that would make people think I was a real woman, and then suddenly unmask at the end,'" Ludlam said (Tomkins 1976, 86). "Wanting to look like a woman was not the point" (Samuels 1992, 41). In his long black wig, décolletage, and "personal anguish," Ludlam was working against one traditional telos of drag performance, in which the performer's 'real' gender is reassuringly revealed at the end of the show (Ludlam and Dasgupta 1978, 71).[11] Even "his voice would also descend occasionally into a more masculine register during the performance," playing against the delicacy of the "oyster-colored silk nightgown" he wore in the third act (Kaufman 2002b, 186, 192). By foregrounding the signs of his male body in Marguerite's costume all throughout the performance, Ludlam created a layered drag transformation. Clive Barnes of the *New York Times* called Ludlam's portrayal "completely convincing" (1974, 31), and Calvin Tomkins of the *New Yorker* praised Ludlam's "virtuoso performance in an almost forgotten style—the style of Bernhardt or Duse" (1976, 87).[12] This critical acclaim was an unexpected triumph, given that this was a play in which when the suffering, penniless heroine asks for another log to be thrown onto the fire of her bedchamber, her maid responds dolefully that there is no more wood; "What," cries Marguerite/Ludlam, peering into the audience with a moue of mock astonishment, "no *faggots* in the house?" (Shewey 1978; emphasis mine).

But people in the audience actually wept when, in the third act, Ludlam's Marguerite died of tuberculosis. And Ludlam, overcome by his own role, wept with them: "Sometimes, at the farewell scene with Armand at the end of the play, just before I died in his arms, I became so totally wrapped up in Marguerite that my mascara ran down my cheeks in my own tears," he recalled (Samuels 1992, 42). The surface of the drag costume—which did nothing to disguise Ludlam's body—had collapsed into the depth of Ludlum's "whole soul and being," as he put it, and brought him to tears (Ludlam and Dasgupta 1978, 78–79). At the end of the evening, the tears were part of his makeup.

## *Believing*

Ludlam believed in his costume; Madame Ekaterina Sobechanskaya believed in her cameo. But some of the newer Gloxinia dancers were less thrilled by the wafting and the appearing—and especially with having to appear under the billing "Ekaterina Sobechanskaya dances with the Trockadero Gloxinia Company" (Coleman 1993, 46). Instead, these newer dancers were ready to believe in the dancing. One of them, Antony (Tony) Bassae, born in London in 1943 to British and Caribbean parents and raised in Cleveland, had started his own ballet company in New York in 1961 (38). By all accounts, Bassae was an extraordinarily talented dancer; moreover, his Ballet Players of WPA was one of the very few racially integrated classical dance companies in the United States. (Dance Theatre of Harlem was not founded until 1969.) Ballet Players ran valiantly on and off into the 1970s, held together by a shoestring budget, Bassae's dedication, and the goodwill of Trutti Gasparinetti, who acted as ballet mistress and sewed costumes (41). Gasparinetti also recruited new dancers from her classes at Alvin Ailey, including an extremely tall, red-headed, wealthy twenty-four-year-old from New Mexico named Natch Taylor (41–42). In 1972 Natch Taylor was not only dancing with the Ballet Players; he was also financially supporting the company, and Antony Bassae moved in with him (43). It was Bassae who took Taylor to see the Gloxinia's debut at the Cocteau theater over Labor Day weekend in 1972; by the end of December, both of them were performing with Madame (44). Tamara Karpova (Bassae) and Suzina LaFuzziovitch (Taylor) were born, and they were joined by Olga Tchikaboumskaya (Peter Anastos), another new Gloxinianette who happened to have prodigious amounts of body hair and a gift for choreography.

Throughout 1973 and into the spring of 1974, rebellious ballerinas murmured against the autocracy of Madame. Natch Taylor felt that Larry Ree "had a great idea but that it had to be worked on," and told him so (Christon 1989). Taylor meant "worked on" in a literal sense; he wanted the bodily discipline of ballet at the center of the aesthetic so that the humor would emerge from the choreography, technique, and historical styles of ballet. Bassae's zeal for ballet was matched by his omnivalent talent: he could dance, he could choreograph, he could stage ballets, he could manage a herd of dancers, he could design and sew costumes, and he could paint and build sets (Coleman 1993, 38). He had a college degree, and he had danced with professional companies both in the United States and in Europe, including the New York Negro Ballet, Laguna Beach Civic Ballet, and the Munich Opera ballet (Coleman 1993, 41; Dunning 1976). Peter Anastos was the kind of balletomane who could tell the gay magazine *Christopher Street* what drag ballet had been like in St. Petersburg "just before the end of the Romanovs": "there was a lot of travesty" then, he explained to journalist Sharon DeLano, "when the nobility were so decadent—Youssoupoff and his crowd. You know, the guy who bumped off Rasputin" (DeLano 1976). As a triumvirate, they had a lot of knowledge, a little money, and an almost fanatical love of ballet. And they were dancers who wanted, impatiently, to dance.

One night at La MaMa, in March 1974, the great schism that was to rend the Gloxinia from the Trockadero made itself manifest (Coleman 1993, 46). It happened when Natch Taylor decided on the spur of the moment that he would go onstage and partner Antony Bassae—that Taylor would appear as a danseur, a male dancer, rather than as a ballerina. "That was the first time there was a boy" in the Gloxinia, Taylor said, and "Larry hit the fan" (46). In a loud flurry of backstage profanities, Taylor was excommunicated from the Gloxinia. He had done two things wrong at once: he had presumed that drag ballet was more than just men dressing up as ballerinas, and he had taken the stage to be a place where he could dance—or, more precisely, where he and Antony Bassae, and people like them, could dance together. In the Gloxinia these were crimes against the company.

So, from midnight on September 6, 1974, until 3 A.M. on September 7, Les Ballets Trockadero de Monte Carlo gave their *"première saison russe,"* starring Tamara Karpova. There were eight men and one woman in that first performance, and the program listed ten ballerinas and two danseurs: this was Trockadero arithmetic, where dancers could multiply themselves across gender binaries in order to do the ballets (Greskovic 1974, 17). From the very beginning, the Trockadero had an expansive view of drag: there was a broad range of masculinities and femininities onstage, and dancers could perform both male and female roles in the same evening. Pretty much anyone could be a Russian. There was partnering, which meant that bodies relied on each other, lifted each other, balanced and steadied each other. In particular, a number of gay men got to perform romantic duets together that had always otherwise been done heterosexually. Carrying on the Ballet Players' commitment to antiracist ballet, the Trockadero crowned Antony Bassae, listed in the program as "the black rhinestone of Russian ballet," as their *prima ballerina assoluta*, the highest rank a ballerina can achieve.

Drag, for the Trockadero, was as much a strategy of historiography as it was a politics of gender, sexuality, and race. In a move that queer theorist Elizabeth Freeman calls "temporal drag" (2010), the Trockadero were undertaking a queer practice of genealogy, traveling back into outmoded histories in order to claim inheritances that had long been dismissed.[13] For one thing, Les Ballets Trockadero de Monte Carlo had been named for one of the most melodramatic moments of twentieth-century ballet history—when Diaghilev's Les Ballets Russes de Monte Carlo fell apart and splintered into quarrelsome bits (including René Blum's Ballets Russes de Monte-Carlo, Colonel Wassily de Basil's Original Ballet Russe, and eventually Sergei Denham's Ballet Russe de Monte Carlo). Even when the Trockadero were newborn, they were already of an old world, dusty and slightly delusional. Dance critic Robert Greskovic wrote of Bassae's Tamara Karpova, who danced Odette in *Swan Lake* and Kitri in the *Don Quixote* pas de deux that night, that she was not only a "brilliant interpreter" of these roles, but that she danced them as "a personal loving comment on 19th-century ballet" (1974, 17). Peter Anastos recalled how he "went to the ballet every night" in order to see "all the aging dancers." He explained, furthermore, that "Natch and I joined a drag company [the Gloxinia], but we quickly got fired because we actually wanted to dance" (Shulgold 2008). This conjunction of experiences—admiring the *aging* dancers, *actually* wanting to dance—was formative for the Trockadero.

Figure 15. Tamara Boumdiyeva as Odette with her swans, from a 1970s *Swan Lake*. Photo by John L. Murphy, courtesy of Les Ballets Trockadero de Monte Carlo. © Estate of John L. Murphy.

Les Ballets Trockadero de Monte Carlo emerged from the division between two polarities: drag that was drag for the sake of light camp, and drag that was *dance*. Arlene Croce championed the Trockadero on this basis, cuttingly, in a well-known 1974 review of the two companies: "The Gloxinia is so good at being girls that, for me, it's boring theatre," she wrote (185). For Croce, the Gloxinia had succeeded in terms of gender impersonation and were failing to do any ballet. She found Les Ballets Trock-adero, on the other hand, so "dead on target and hilarious" (182) that she concluded, "I don't think anything in ballet can be safe from it for long" (186). However, she noted, the Trockadero were not simply triumphing through their mastery of technique; on the contrary, they "totter, gallop, or bourée in a flatfooted scuffle through the scene, or else lumpily deco-rate it in poses" (185). But if, as Croce said, the Trockadero were gracelessly galumphing their way through the repertoire of swans and sylphs, how could they possibly embody something wickedly true about ballet?

Larry Ree's "Sobechanskaya believes in herself," Croce proposed; "Bas-sae's Karpova believes in her role" (187).[14] This crucial distinction between self and role echoed Ludlam's conviction that costume could produce character: it was the job of the self not to get in the way of the character. The self was supposed to commit itself thoroughly to the bodily practice, and then, when the role took over, believe in it utterly. Antony Bassae might have been, as Croce put it unkindly, "built like a pug version of Lou Costello, and on point looks a little like a bulldog standing on its hind legs," but, like Ludlam in *Camille*, he threw his whole body, *as it was*, into Tamara Karpova's dancing (187). The Gloxinia, by contrast, stopped short of exposing their bodies working at the discipline of ballet, because to fail in this regard would have ruined the picture of a ballerina they were projecting. The origins of the Trockadero were a heterogeneous admixture of bodies: some were men, some were women, some didn't dance, some were fictions, some had been dead for a century, some weren't real Rus-sians, one was Greta Garbo, and almost all of them were queer. But, as the Trockadero biography of the three Legupski Brothers explains,

> Ivan, Vladirmir and Vyacheslav are not really brothers, nor are their names really Ivan, Vladirmir, or Vyacheslav, nor are they real Russians, nor can they tell the difference between a pirouette and a jeté ... but ... well ... they do move about rather nicely ... and ... they fit into the costumes.

## Bending the Daisies

Meditating on Mallarmé's assertion that "a ballerina is not a woman danc-ing, because she isn't a woman and she doesn't dance," Arlene Croce had conferred a new legitimacy on the Trockadero ballerinas: they, too, were poetic vessels conveying the essence of ballet to a discerning audience (1974, 182). Mallarmé saw the dancer's body as a "metaphor": "her poem is written without the writer's tools," he proclaimed ecstatically (1983, 112). In Mallarmé's pale and feathery metaphysics of ballet, the ideal ballerina was a weightless form "summoned into the air," in the phrase he used to describe the dancer Elena Cornalba (111).[15] "She might pirouette on a daisy and it would not bend," as one London critic wrote admiringly of the ballerina Adeline Genée in 1911 (Sayers 1993, 180). Mallarmé's Symbolist interpretation of ballet was useful for Croce because it allowed her to make the point that ballerinas need not be women and to imply that drag ballet had a poetry all its own. However, it also led Croce to conclude that in ballet "the arabesque is real, the leg is not" (1974, 188). This is a problem; whether the leg belongs to Elena Cornalba or Antony Bassae, it is a real leg, especially from the dancer's point of view. Croce wanted to say that the Trockadero had transcended camp drag to pierce the pale-pink heart of ballet, and she saw that Tamara Karpova was a ballerina who deserved the same kind of recognition as Nina Sorokina of the Bolshoi. But to deny the corporeality that was behind the whole edifice of classical ballet, holding it all up, linked Croce's analysis to a pervasive and problematic view of gender in ballet.[16]

"'The principle of classical ballet is woman,'" Balanchine declared imperiously to a journalist from the New York Times one evening in 1976 while his dancers were busy performing the second act of Jewels (Daly 1987, 17). "The woman's function is to fascinate men." This kind of comment infuriated even people who thought Balanchine was a brilliant choreographer, and it spurred dance scholar Ann Daly to undertake a sharply feminist analysis of the third theme of Balanchine's The Four Temperaments. "As long as classical ballet prescribes Woman as a lightweight creature on pointe and men as her supporters/lifters, women will never represent themselves on the ballet stage," Daly concluded vehemently (17). More broadly, she stated, it was necessary "to recognize ballet as a cultural institution that represents and thus inscribes gender behavior in everyday life" (19). For a nascent company of drag ballerinas like the Trockadero, this capital-W abstraction of women dancing presented both an obstacle and an opportunity. On the one hand, if ballet was exclusively about women appearing as fascinating images for men, there was no place for men who actually danced as ballerinas—the only possible parody would have been the stylized Gloxinia version. On the other hand, if Daly was right, and one of the problems of classical ballet was the categorical narrowness of

"Woman as lightweight creature," perhaps what the art form needed was to be grounded again by some anti-normative bodies—bodies from which the daisies would never recover.

Whether or not *The Four Temperaments* is misogynist—and Daly later shifted to a more nuanced reading of gendered movement in an essay titled "Feminist Theory across the Millennial Divide" (2000)—it is clear that Balanchine's "ballet-is-woman rhetoric" was part of a widespread understanding of ballet in the 1970s and '80s (Daly 1987, 17). In those years Balanchine was a towering figure—the genius who had brought ballet to America and then made it superbly *American*—and his aesthetic for ballerinas irrevocably redefined the bodily ideal.[17] If the choreography was not pernicious in itself, and even if, as dance critic Marcia Siegel generously supposes, Balanchine made these statements because he just "liked to be enigmatic" or didn't quite "know how to make contact" with his female dancers, the rhetoric still had real effects on individual ballerinas and on the context in which ballet was created and received (1987, 133).[18] Gelsey Kirkland, for example, bitterly recalls the day when Balanchine "halted class and approached me for a kind of physical inspection. With his knuckles, he thumped me on my sternum and down my rib cage clucking his tongue and remarking 'Must see the bones'" (1998, 56). Kirkland became anorexic; this is one possible result of idealizing the effacement of the fleshly body. For Kirkland, the simultaneous injunction to embody ballet ("ballet is woman") and to shed the characteristics of having a body ("Must see the bones") produced an impossible double bind.[19] This is why Mallarmé's proclamation that a ballerina is "a poem free of all writing apparatus" (Shaw 1993, 3), while very pretty, is also a potentially dangerous idea of a dancer's body. Acknowledging that an abstract idea of feminine lightness can harm the bodies of real dancers is crucial to understanding how the Trockadero intervene in the ballet tradition.

Unlike New York City Ballet—past or present—Les Ballets Trockadero de Monte Carlo employ dancers whose bodies are remarkably diverse from each other and from the bodies idealized by classical ballet. As the aging *étoile* Ida Nevasayneva, Paul Ghiselin continued dancing into his fifties. Joseph Jeffries, described as a "linebacker" by Gia Kourlas (2008), appeared in ballerina roles as Minnie Van Driver, while the elfin, agile, Cuban-trained dancer Carlos Hopuy, who is five foot five, is regularly cast in major male roles. Christopher Lam recalls that when he auditioned, he was "kind of overweight"; Joshua Grant is six foot four even before he puts on his 17W Sansha 202 toe shoes; Long Zhou (who wears a 7.5W in Gaynor

Minden and grew up in a town in Hunan Province) could more or less pass under Grant's leg in arabesque without ducking (David 2009, 20). Philip Martin-Nielson, who was severely autistic as a child, discovered the Trockadero when he was twelve and joined the company at eighteen; now dancing full time as Nadia Doumiafeyva, he describes himself as "very sociable" (Mackrell 2015). At least one former Trockadero dancer, Julia Horvath, is trans. In the tradition of Tamara Karpova, the company's leading ballerina for many years has been the talented black dancer Robert Carter, who appears *en pointe* as Olga Supphozova. In terms of age, height, weight, race, nationality, morphology, gender expression, ability, training, and myriad other ways in which bodies are read and categorized, the Trockadero dancers are strikingly diverse. Their common ground is that they take class and rehearse together, again and again, and the belief that, as Christopher Lam puts it, "To anyone who says a man can't be a ballerina, I say, 'I put on those shoes and get up there, and it hurts, so I'm a ballerina'" (David 2009, 20). This is a literal expression of the idea that ballerinas are actually made of toe shoes and pointe classes—as Ludlam's Norma was made of a wig and fanatical devotion to experimental theater—and not of bone structure or a particular ratio of muscle to body fat.

In the Trockadero's drag genealogy for ballet, the costume is essential and 'ballerina' is a bodily discipline, not an inherent identity. From Antony Bassae onward, Trockadero dancers have devoted themselves to the physical and durational work of ballet, absorbing its technique into their bodies over the course of many years of class, rehearsal, and performance, often touring forty weeks a year. What they have *not* done is hide the bodies they have. One of the results of this open, visible working of moving bodies has been to show up the performance of airtight, 'natural' femininity as an illusion—to the same effect as Ludlam's chest hair. Another consequence is that Trockadero dancers can often be seen trying, sweating, falling, struggling, and failing to maintain the perfect semblance of their roles onstage. To fail to get a leg up, to fail to lift a ballerina, to fail to enter on cue, to fail to maintain the unity of the corps de ballet because you got bored and decided to eat a banana, to fail to notice that you have accidentally kicked another ballerina in the head: these are highly particular forms of failure, because they brazenly detach the shame from the failing. Ballet nightmares are such a staple of the Trockadero repertoire that they have been drained of their psychic force.

Often, when a Trockadero ballerina fails to get a leg up or a danseur can't lift a sylph by himself, other Trockadero dancers will gather around and pitch in. Failure is not isolating; it does not foreclose the possibility of that person doing that role; it might simply mean that a three-person lift is in order, or that a leg needs to be propped on a shoulder. Conversely, when a Trockadero dancer is succeeding at something difficult—especially at a round of fouettés, which are a long-standing indication of a ballerina's technical virtuosity—the other dancers will stop pretending to be swans or Spanish village girls for a minute in order to give a heartfelt round of applause. At first it might seem that visible public failure isn't a catastrophe for a Trockadero dancer only because drag operates as a kind of comic insulation: they're men, so it's funny, so it's OK. But this is the same dismissive bloke-in-a-frock view of drag that drove Antony Bassae, Natch Taylor, and Peter Anastos out of the Gloxinia.

The real reason that the Trockadero embrace 'failures' onstage is because the company has an ethos of collective corporeality akin to the value that disability studies places on interdependence, or to the perspective Jack Halberstam describes in *The Queer Art of Failure* (2011): "under certain circumstances failing . . . may in fact offer more creative, more cooperative, more surprising ways of being in the world" (2). "Targeted" queer failure in particular, Thomas F. DeFrantz elaborates, "provides an important space for humor and irony."[20] Failure, in this framework, is not a sign of a personal failing; it is an occasion for support. It is a call to work out queer configurations of affirmation and vulnerability so that there can be laughter—even ridiculous theater—without exclusion and alienation. As Tory Dobrin, the Trockadero's artistic director, told dance critic Ismene Brown, "You have to have the harmonious teamwork, and you have to have the possibility of doing the role, so that you know you will be supported and cheered on" (Brown 2013). In fact, when a dancer auditions for the Trockadero, "'we look for a person who is first of all eager, somebody who's nice to be around," ballet master Paul Ghiselin said in an interview in 2011 (Parry). "So we may choose a dancer who perhaps isn't that great but who is friendly to be around, polite with the others, and who learns quickly. A team player."[21] If the idea of a company as a "team" in which everyone is playing ballet together sounds bizarre, it is because mainstream ballet has traditionally been such a vicious hierarchy that we cannot really imagine a world in which dancers would be evaluated on how kind they were to others. The Trockadero, graciously, do not chide us for our failure; they simply imagine it for us.

*Leaving the Earth*

In the field of ballet, men traditionally have not trained on pointe, except in very limited cases (such as minor comic travesty roles).[22] When Tory Dobrin first began dancing with the Trockadero in 1980, "there were only two teachers in New York who would let me take class on pointe," he recalls vividly. "The others all turned me down" (2012). Finis Jhung, one of the teachers who accepted him into a pointe class, remembers that Dobrin was extremely discreet, even wearing black socks over his toe shoes (Jhung n.d.). In 1995, when Paul Ghiselin joined the Trockadero, he says, "Thank goodness we had a ballet mistress who was training us like little girls—she was giving us those little-girl classes, where you do those horrible exercises, day after day," because less than half of the dancers were prepared to do classical pointe work (Ghiselin 2012). "For years, it was frowned upon when a male dancer wanted to put on toe shoes," Ghiselin reflected. "But that's all changed now. Guys show up to audition well trained in pointe work, and some even know our repertory, thanks to YouTube" (S. Smith 2012). "In my generation joining the Trocks was a career wrecker; now we are getting dancers out of the academies," Dobrin remarked, explaining that this dramatic shift is due to an increased cultural acceptance of homosexuality (Sulcas 2010). "It's part of a trend in society that makes young gay guys feel really comfortable expressing who they are" (Dobrin 2012). In a larger struggle against homophobia and transphobia, it is a tiny victory that pointe shoes might be understood as a prosthetic that someone could choose to put on rather than as the natural extension of a gender. But if you believe you are a ballerina, despite all of the tropes of the 'wrong body' being deployed against you, it matters. And if you are a dancer who wants to be both a ballerina and a danseur, like Natch Taylor partnering Antony Bassae, it matters.

Tory Dobrin modestly downplays the Trockadero's role in this cultural shift: "It's not really that important," he says; "a cure for AIDS would be important" (Wolf 2000). But Paul Ghiselin emphasizes that "because Trockadero has been around for so long, it definitely has" had an effect on the way male pointe work is viewed (Ghiselin 2012), and Robert Carter agrees with him (R. Carter 2012). Since 1974 the Trockadero dancers have stubbornly and publicly believed that their bodies could do pointe work, and instilled that belief in their metatarsals and pulled-up core muscles. After all, "God gave everyone the feet they need to support their own weight," as Dobrin says, slyly appropriating the rhetoric—so common in homophobic discourse—of 'unnatural' acts and divinely sanctioned bodily configurations (Wolf 2000). The example of pointe training for men shows that no matter how rigid and self-evident the prescriptions of ballet might appear, it is possible for dancers—especially when they act collectively as companies—to slowly loosen the constraints of normativity.

Of course, the Trockadero can't eradicate homophobia, body shaming, and racism in the field of ballet. As Sara Ahmed points out in "Queer Feelings," "Bodies take the shape of norms that are repeated over time and with force," meaning that "norms surface *as* the surfaces of bodies" (2012, 423). And ballet has made its racialized, gendered, and morphological norms appear on the surface of dancers' bodies with a particularly daunting efficacy. Virginia Johnson, a renowned former dancer with Dance Theatre of Harlem who became the company's artistic director, clearly states, "We as a field have become obsessed with a single body-type that is presumed to be predicated by race" (2014). It is black ballerinas, unsurprisingly, who have borne the brunt of this racialized misogyny. Raven Wilkinson, the first African American dancer to be accepted into a major ballet company (she joined the Ballet Russe de Monte Carlo in 1955), mused that one reason why black female ballerinas

> have a harder time [than black male ballet dancers is] because ballet, as Balanchine said, is woman. . . . That purity, that sense of leaving the earth and the romantic sense of being on pointe is the idea of the woman on the pedestal. Whereas the black woman is seen as more earthy and as dancing solidly. (Kourlas 2007)

In recognizing the extent to which Balanchine's ethos still holds sway in mainstream Western classical dance companies, Wilkinson called out a history of conjoining whiteness and femininity that continues to strangle ballet. Wilkinson herself left American ballet in 1961 under the strain of persistent racism: since she had light skin, the company could keep her race a secret on tours in the South, but when a hotel owner in Atlanta asked her directly if she was black, she simply answered, "'Yes, I am'" (Langlois 2007, 25). Wilkinson was thrown out of the hotel, and the Ku Klux Klan showed up to menace the company in Alabama. That was 1957; fifty years had passed, and the *New York Times* could still fill a page with all of the ways that black ballerinas were still struggling with pervasive racism (Kourlas 2007). In 2007 a writer for *Ballet Review* asked Wilkinson, "When you look at the City Ballet today or ABT, would you say we've come very far from 1955 in terms of racial integration in the ballet world?" (Langlois 2007, 24). Wilkinson replied, bluntly, "No."

In order to bring diversity to ballet, as Virginia Johnson sees it, "we will need to banish some preconceptions about what ballet is"—including stereotypes about "the wrong bodies"—and to encourage young dancers of color to continue training past the age of twelve (2014). Robert Carter, who dances female roles as the Trockadero's unofficial *prima ballerina assoluta* Olga Supphozova, is in some ways the kind of dancer Johnson envisions. At age ten he saw the Trockadero perform in Greenville, South Carolina, and told his mother, "*that's* what I want to do" (R. Carter 2012). He is muscular and elegant and dedicated, and because of the Trockadero ethos, he is not only a successful black ballerina but also a gracious one: "I have the gift and the talent on loan," he says, "and it's not for me to squander it. It's to share." Perceiving a future in which he *could* be a ballerina, Robert Carter became a ballerina—and is now a model and a mentor to others.[23] As he said in 2010, "I've been dancing 40-week years for 16 years and never had to worry about the next paycheck. And how many people in this business can say that?" (Trebay 2010). This question—how many people like Robert Carter can say they have fair opportunities and successful careers?—brings up another, more pointed question, as Ahmed observes: "How does defining a queer ideal rely on the existence of others who fail the ideal? Who can and cannot embody the queer ideal?" (2012, 427). Robert Carter can embody the queer ideal of a black ballerina—and Olga embodies it beautifully[24]—because the Trockadero are, and have always been, antiracist as well as anti-heteronormative.[25] As Raven Wilkinson and Virginia Johnson (as well as younger black ballerinas like Aesha Ash and Misty Copeland) have made clear, black women who want to be ballerinas don't yet have a Trockadero.

The dearth of "black swans" in ballet, as Gia Kourlas put it (2007), has been obvious, but there was someone else who tragically turned out not to have a Trockadero, either. It was Antony Bassae. By the time of the Trockadero's first international show in January 1976—at the Minkier Auditorium of Seneca College in Toronto—it seemed that Bassae was struggling (Coleman 1993, 89, 92).[26] Natch Taylor threw him out of the apartment they had been sharing on W. Twenty-Fourth Street, and Trutti Gasparinetti would find him holed up in bars, weeping (92–93). "Maybe," Bassae himself wondered aloud to Jennifer Dunning, "it all happened too fast" (Dunning 1976, 17). Unexpectedly, right before a big show at the Brooklyn Academy of Music (BAM), Bassae left the Trockadero. He announced that

Figure 16. Olga Supphozova (Robert Carter) as the Black Swan (Odile) in *Swan Lake*. Photo by Sascha Vaughan, courtesy of Les Ballets Trockadero de Monte Carlo.

he would start his own company—Les Ballets Trockadero de la Karpova—with just nine dancers and his own charisma. It was bold to presume that New York City could support three drag ballet companies at the same time, but Bassae was committed, as he said in a press release, "to exploring all facets of the art of travesty as it pertains to dance drama"—and, "unlike other travesty companies," the Karpova would focus on "serious dance material."

Trutti Gasparinetti remembers that Antony Bassae would say strange things on those nights when he took refuge in bars and wept (Coleman 1993, 93). He would say, "I can't dance anymore," and she would try to cheer him up, reminding him that he loved to dance, that it didn't have to be perfect; and then he would say:

> I am not a person,
> I am a thing.
> I am a dancer,
> I am a costumer,
> but I am not a person.

Maybe Antony Bassae gave everything he had to Les Ballets Trockadero de Monte Carlo so that, in future generations of queer dancers and dancers of color and dancers who would be described by critics as having the bodies of dogs, maybe, in the genealogy of ballet, there would be a place for dancers like him, a haven, a history, a form of ballet that wouldn't destroy them, a *drag* understanding of embodied potential, a way of knowing that you are a person.

## Drag and Mourning

Antony Bassae died of AIDS-related causes in 1985. Sanson Candelaria, a wonderfully comic dancer who kept the Trockadero running after Bassae and Anastos left, died of AIDS-related causes in 1986 (Brown 2013). Charles Ludlam died of AIDS-related causes in 1987. The legendary Jack Smith, whom Ludlam described as "the daddy of us all," and who used to make costumes for the Play-House of the Ridiculous when he wasn't consumed by his own spectacularly chaotic creations, died of AIDS-related causes in 1989 (Brecht 1978, 28). The actor John D. Brockmeyer, a mainstay of the Ridiculous Theatrical Company, died of AIDS-related causes in 1990. Mike Gonzales, a beloved Trockadero costume designer and dancer—and Tory Dobrin's partner—died of AIDS-related causes in 1996. In the 1980s and '90s, AIDS decimated the world of queer theater and dance.

In 1974, when a band of nouveau Trocks were showing up to dance on W. Fourteenth Street at Ninth Avenue, where the curtain went up at midnight, it was part of an exuberant unleashing of a community that was beginning to claim a place for itself. No Trockadero dancer worked full time for the company; only two of them could actually dance on pointe, but they all got up onstage in a collective insomniac balletomane fervor and poured their hearts into it. By 1982 there were fourteen company dancers in Les Ballets Trockadero, and all of them could do pointe work; ten of those dancers would die from AIDS-related causes in the next few years (Dobrin 2012). Hauntingly, Tory Dobrin alludes to a photograph from

1983, taken during one of the company's annual tours to Japan, "in which three [Trockadero dancers] are on one side of a Japanese ballerina and eight on the other side, and all those eight people are lost. There's only three of us in that photo who are still alive today" (Brown 2013). It felt as though every week brought the funeral of some other beloved, young, witty, creative, queer luminary of theater or dance. "The challenge is realizing the meaning behind the fact that they are gone," ACT UP activist and writer Sarah Shulman reflects, "and how difficult it is to individuate in the AIDS era, when the losses are so numerous and cumulative" (2012, 54). There was a terrible precariousness of bodies and a grim communal responsibility of witnessing and marking so many abrupt, unjust deaths. And "performance," David Román points out in *Acts of Intervention: Performance, Gay Culture, and AIDS*, "was part of the more encompassing ritual that helped organize peoples' response to AIDS both in space and time," when the concept of "lifetime" had lost its reality (1998, 8). But could drag performance, which had been such a glittery exploration of camp and the outer limits of theatricality, find a way to express mourning?

Diane Torr, a modern dancer based in New York City at that time, describes her seminal experience with drag in the context of this "tragic time blighted by the untimely deaths of bold personalities like Charles Ludlam. . . . I attended so many, too many, funerals," including that of her brother Donald, who died of AIDS-related causes in 1992 (2010):

> I clearly couldn't keep them alive, so I did the next best thing—I decided to keep their spirit alive by filling the vacuum that was created by their loss. I was compelled to do this when a wonderful friend, writer and columnist, Charles Barber, unexpectedly died. . . . I decided to become him for a day—to become a living requiem to him—to go to "his" café on Christopher Street, and take "his" morning espresso and croissant.

This is drag impersonation as a form of mourning—mourning the body you have lost with the body you have, whether or not your body 'is right' or 'has the right' to undertake this act. For Torr—and for similar artists like Jeff Friedman, who created a solo dance called *Muscle Memory* (1994) that used the oral histories of the friends and colleagues he was losing to AIDS—funerals were not enough (Friedman 2006).[27] There needed to be repositories in the body itself, radical ways of remembering that showed what the loss really felt like, "affective historiographies" that acknowledged how the dead remain present for those still living (Lepecki

2010, 43). Because queer theater had explored the intermediate space between 'being' and 'playing a role,' certain theatrical techniques that might have been deemed too camp or superficial to count as 'real' grief were taken up as viable modes of expressing tragic loss.

Drag allowed the border between distinct bodily identities to be crossed, and therefore enabled artists to enact a corporeal inheritance from someone who had died. In a time when, as Diane Torr remembers, the biological families of the dead often tightly controlled the funeral, refusing to mention AIDS or homosexuality or a bereaved partner but heaping anodyne hymns and platitudes upon the coffin, "the question of how best to *remember* those who had died became pressing for all of us" in the queer performance community (Torr and Bottoms 2010, 179–80). Bringing the raw emotion of grief into the theatrical-political sphere of queer public life, drag traced lines that would otherwise have remained unseen and called them bodily kinships; it became a vocabulary of mourning and a queer form of family-making. The Trockadero continue this tradition: they are genealogists, reclaiming a queer history that ballet would like to disavow by dancing it in their own ways.[28] For example, the costumes for their Balanchine leotard-ballet parody piece, *Go for Barocco* (1974), are white tights, black leotards, and red AIDS ribbons pinned prominently at the strap. This is a specifically drag answer to heteronormative pronouncements like Balanchine's about ballet; more broadly, it is a reminder that 'abstract' ballet cannot ever really efface the politics of embodiment.

When Les Ballets Trockadero inherited their drag aesthetic from Charles Ludlam, they got the wigs, the false eyelashes, and the signature chest hair. They came into being with the idea that bodies do not deny their corporeality in order to take on roles; rather, the Trockadero throw themselves lovingly into the process that Foucault called "the systematic dissociation of identity," in which identity "is plural; countless spirits dispute its possession" (1984, 94). But they also inherited from Ludlam and his cohort the knowledge that drag could be an act of mourning—that in the face of tragedy, you could offer your body to the costume.

## The Don Q Effect

When Arlene Croce penned her first review of Les Ballets Trockadero, she ended with a bittersweet note about Maya Plisetskaya, an *étoile* of the

Bolshoi. "Her glamour seems to have taken on a tinge of heaviness and sadness," Croce wrote, nostalgic for a vibrant era of Russian ballet that had already begun to fade (1974, 188). Many years later, Robert Carter was asked by an interviewer to describe his fondest memory as a dancer. He replied by telling the story of one performance, "in a Dance Festival in Sicily," when Olga Supphozova encountered

> Maya Plisetskaya, the legendary Russian ballerina, [who] was the guest of honor, and danced, but we were the main focus. We opened with the beginning of *Paquita*, and then others danced, and then we finished with the Coda. Maya was in the wings, cheering me on as I did the *fouettés*. She said she loved our *Paquita* (Jhung n.d.).

Maya Plisetskaya was the kind of Bolshoi ballerina who was so ardently, so excessively, so melodramatically a ballerina that even other Bolshoi dancers told her she looked like "a circus performer" (Riding 1996). She had a pliable, sweeping port de bras, a flair for jumps, and a feverish intensity of feeling. She would dive into her roles, immersing her whole body, sinking into each character as if willing the waters of tragic fate to close over her head while she danced fearlessly into the depths, trailing her beautiful red hair. Her memoir recounted stories of executions, exile, intrigue, near-starvation, passion; she would eat dog food on tour if she had to, as long as she could keep dancing. She danced at her own seventy-fifth birthday party.

In his decades with the Trockadero, Robert Carter has accumulated an abundance of successes and memorable occasions. The company has appeared at the Bolshoi Theatre in Moscow and performed for the British royal family in London; they have received the UK Critics' Circle Company Prize for Outstanding Repertoire (Classical) and the Positano Award for excellence in dance. A typical review of Carter's dancing is full of superlatives—and often comparatives, as critics find Olga's technique superior to that of many female ballerinas. As critic Robert Gottlieb writes, "not many of A.B.T.'s ballerinas can match" Olga's fouettés (2007). He "has greater mastery of the female technique than most females I've seen," Joan Acocella declared unequivocally (2005, 84). Moreover, Maya Plisetskaya is not even the only grande dame of dance to have honored Robert Carter as a worthy inheritor of the tradition; "when Martha Graham premiered the *Maple Leaf Rag* at the Spoleto Festival two weeks before she died," he remembers, "that night her assistant took me back to see her, and she said, 'You *look* like a little dancer, so keep dancing.' And she stuck out her gnarled little hand in her glove, and she shook my hand" (R. Carter 2012). Why, then, does this one moment with Maya Plisetskaya—a fading *étoile*, an epitome of a century of ballet that was already coming to a close, a ballerina whose decline Arlene Croce had begun to pity before Robert Carter was even born—matter so much to him?

In a queer framework, Elizabeth Freeman explains, "temporal drag" can have both historiographical and gendered dimensions: "drag can be seen as the act of plastering the body with outdated rather than just cross-gendered accessories, whose resurrection seems to exceed the axis of gender and begins to talk about, indeed to talk back to, history" (2010, xxi). Robert Carter prizes that moment when Maya Plisetskaya applauded Olga's fouettés because, in part, that is what Trockadero ballerinas do for each other: she showed that she was part of the team. She wasn't going to make catty remarks about how Robert Carter couldn't be a 'real' ballerina, or didn't have the 'right' body to do *Paquita*, or belonged in a local gay bar instead of an international dance festival. Together, Maya Plisetskaya and Robert Carter were going to have a moment of queer kinship, when what mattered was the transmission of a way of doing ballet that was so full of love and character that it overspilled both of their bodies. Olga Supphozova knows what it is like to drown yourself in ballet; she has her own fiercely effusive port de bras and exultant jumps. So Robert Carter doesn't *look* like Maya Plisetskaya. But he *dances* like her.

By cherishing what would have been lost when Maya Plisetskaya left the stage—by carrying her history in their own bodies—the Trockadero also alter the future of ballet. The Trockadero genealogy, as a practice of "temporal drag" *ballet*, is akin to a phenomenon that sociologist Pierre Bourdieu called the "Don Quixote effect" (1984).[29] Like Don Quixote, the Trockadero demonstrate their fidelity to a past now shrouded in fiction, a set of values and codes that everyone else has abandoned for more modern narratives.[30] The company roots itself in the history of lost dances—performing, for example, a version of the nonextant divertissement from Alexander Gorsky and Marius Petipa's *The Humpbacked Horse*—and lost dancers, whose names echo through the camp Trockadero biographies. "We're kind of selling ourselves as an old, dusty touring Russian ballet company that the modern age doesn't have anymore," Tory Dobrin explains, and Joan Acocella elaborates: "The smell of the greasepaint, the ballerina *in excelsis*, the demented fans: for the most part, that kind of company is now an honored ghost" (Acocella 2005, 84). The Trockadero have performed at the Théâtre de Châtelet in Paris, where Diaghilev's Ballets Russes made their sensational debut in 1909. But the "honored ghosts" might have been most satisfied when Les Ballets Trockadero de Monte Carlo were invited to Monte Carlo itself to give a performance in honor of the official centennial of the Ballets Russes. They graciously accepted, and in December 2009 the Trockadero dancers could be found in their dressing rooms at the red-velvet-lined Salle Garnier of the Opéra de Monte Carlo, gluing on their double sets of false eyelashes and looking out at the harbor of super-yachts, in preparation for the "Programme Ballets Russes" they would dance that evening. Afterward, in a haze of champagne, the princess would clasp their hands and tell them all how lovely they had been, how delightful, what an honor.

It is fitting, then, that the Trockadero actually have *Don Quixote* in their repertoire, both as a full ballet and as an excerpt. In the Trockadero version of the full ballet, which has been a staple of the Bolshoi repertoire since 1869, twinkly blue ballerinas with magic silver-star wands help Amour to untangle several twisted couples. The notoriously difficult *Don Quixote* pas de deux, which has been in the Trockadero repertoire since 1974, is described by the Trockadero website as a lineage: "first danced by the famed Sobeshanskaya . . . all the great ballerinas including Pavlova, Karsavina, Plisetskaya, Maximova, Kolpakova, and Gregory have performed this most famous of *pas de deux*." The clear implication is that the Trockadero are inheriting—and, through drag, fulfilling—this bloodline of ballerinas. Larry Ree's stage name was Madame Sobechanskaya, after all; subsequent Trockadero ballerinas have been named Fifi Barkova, Maya Thickenthighya, Ludmila Beulemova, and Irina Bakpakova, among others. Croce's review—which began the journalistic tradition of hailing the Trockadero as both utterly 'wrong' as ballerinas and also mystically 'better' than most female dancers—praised Antony Bassae as a dramatic improvement over the Bolshoi ballerina performing this pas de deux contemporaneously at the Metropolitan Opera. "There was more wit, more plasticity, more elegance, and even more femininity in Karpova's balances and kneeling backbends than in all of Sorokina's tricks," Croce wrote (1974, 187). For Croce, it was a good thing that the Trockadero were there to faithfully carry on ballet history, because 'straight' ballet was not rising to the occasion. Maya Plisetskaya was growing older, the Bolshoi ballerinas looked complacent and stiff, and the last of the splintered-off Ballets Russes companies had tottered to its end in 1968.

But the Trockadero are committed to inheriting exactly this moment, in their own queer way—not restoring Russian ballet to its glorious heights, but paying tribute to Russian ballet in its decline; not replicating Maya Plisetskaya, but embodying the way she believed in dancing. Paul Ghiselin remembers that "when I started dancing in the late 1970s, there were still many teachers from the Ballets Russes around in America, and I was able to study with them" (Parry 2011). And, like Robert Carter, Ghiselin recalls the "treasured moment" when Maya Plisetskaya watched him from the wings. After his performance of *The Dying Swan* as Ida Nevasayneva, Plisetskaya "came up to me, she grabbed my face, and she says, 'I love what you do! Nobody dances like this anymore!'" (Ghiselin 2012). Ghiselin understands that what the Trockadero have inherited from Plisetskaya is a haunting and corporeal "responsibility," as he says, to restore the missing body—corpuscles and viscera, not merely bone and line—to classical ballet. "You watch the performances of major ballet companies, and there's no *blood*, there's no *guts*. It's all about legs up in the air and how many turns you're going to do. But where's the spirit?" he asks searchingly (2012).

The *Don Q* pas, as dancers call it, is still in the Trockadero repertoire, being performed in a gold-edged red tutu by a diverse set of ballerinas (the bodices of Trockadero costumes have several sets of hooks so that many different sizes of dancers can fit into them). The fading flame of Maya Plisetskaya, the vanished legends of the Ballets Russes: the Trockadero are, like Don Quixote, both mourning a history and carrying it on. Because of their own drag inheritance from Charles Ludlam and the understanding of drag channeling as a celebratory form of mourning, the Trockadero undertake their performances in the spirit of showing the fragility and singularity of the body, its imperfections and efforts. They give their bodies onstage as they are—working at the discipline of ballet, but touchingly, sometimes laughably, collectively undermining the limitations of its ideals. The Trockadero have inherited a lost world, and they are determined to honor its ghosts; even if their attachment seems a bit delusional, Maya Plisetskaya has given them her blessing from the wings.

## The Dying Swan

Mortality is a constant specter of ballet; for dancers in general, the body is both the center of their artistry and the means by which they make a living, and its fragility is terrifying.[31] As Ida Nevasayneva, Paul Ghiselin was for a long time the oldest Trockadero ballerina, and his signature piece is *The Dying Swan*, originally choreographed by Michel Fokine for Anna Pavlova in 1905. Pavlova performed this solo thousands of times; she kept a favorite swan in her garden in London, named Jack, with whom she had herself photographed; when she was on her deathbed, the legend goes, she demanded her swan costume. Maya Plisetskaya insisted on dancing *The Dying Swan* on her seventieth birthday. *The Dying Swan* is perhaps as storied and freighted with iconicity as a three-minute dance piece can be. When Ghiselin dances this solo, it is a moving picture of the descent of the body: genealogically, corporeally, and aesthetically.

Becoming Ida Nevasayneva was Ghiselin's second life, after he retired from the Ohio Ballet; from a Trockadero perspective, it makes sense that the afterlife of the dancer is to embody the ghost life of bygone ballerinas.[32] Ghiselin already had a keen sense of "aging, injury, and retirement," those shadows that trail ballet dancers' careers, when Tory Dobrin called him to say, presciently, that his name would be Ida Nevasayneva and that he would "be a great Dying Swan" (Ghiselin 2012). Ida is very much a living persona, in terms that Charles Ludlam would recognize: "Thirteen years since he first looked into a dressing-room mirror and saw Ida Nevasayneva staring back in that Swan costume," Ghiselin describes "Ida as someone who eats, sleeps and breathes DANCE. . . . She can't do what the younger girls do. Actually, she doesn't care. She's an artiste. She believes in herself. So she's going to give it everything she's got" (Brennan n.d.). In this fond and determined embodiment of an aging ballerina, Ghiselin is committed to Ludlam's belief in the costume and to the Trockadero principle of queer bodily discipline without the exclusions of normativity. And what Ida inherits from Marguerite and Maya Plisetskaya, she gives back: as the company's ballet master and *repetiteur*, Ghiselin has transmitted ballet as a collective form of immersive, inclusive, exuberant, anachronistic, and slightly delusional love.

The Trockadero *Dying Swan* begins with a spotlight shining on the wings upstage right. No one is there. The spotlight bounces to the wings upstage left, wavers, and then streaks back to the right. This is partly a joke about the perils of touring—a shaky local crew can wreak havoc if they get the spot cues wrong—and partly a tribute to Anna Pavlova, whose death was ceremonially marked by a spotlight shining on an empty stage while the Saint-Saëns score played. This means the Trockadero version of *The Dying Swan* begins with a body missing from the stage, with a gesture of mourning that is both individual (Anna Pavlova is gone) and hauntingly collective (all of the ballerinas who dance this piece will someday be gone).

But the staging of this gesture is low camp, an approach to pathos that winks at the melodrama of deathbed scenes. The roaming spotlight is both knowing and ironic, like the moment when Ludlam's Marguerite, succumbing to galloping consumption in the third act, says incredulously that she cannot really believe there are no "faggots in the house." When Ida Nevasayneva finally does appear on stage, her back is to the audience, and she begins a series of tiny bourrées that give the impression she's gliding sideways, while her arms gently rise and fall with an airy, wistful grace. Paul Ghiselin is tall, white, and remarkably bony, with taut muscles in his arms and a very long nose. Ida's port de bras, however, is delicately expressive, and her pointe work seems to epitomize an idea of feminine lightness, of elevation without bodily effort. Still, as she turns, it is impossible not to see that her tutu is shedding tufts of feathers. It seems to be disintegrating rapidly into a trail of sad white plumes. Ida turns, does an attitude, and—continuing to bourrée across the stage—begins to demolish the fourth wall with a wicked, preening smile that reaches up to her arched eyebrows. But just as she finishes the 'swan' gesture—straight arms held out and down in front of the torso, crossed lightly at the wrists—everything falls apart. Her neck pumps out like a pecking chicken, her feathery derrière gives a little shake, and then, in the next series of bourrées, her knobby knees wobble apart so that she is nearly squatting on pointe in a second position demi-plié instead of balancing lightly upright on her satin tiptoes. Ida pushes her bony knees back together with her hands and gives the audience a look that says: we all know what's it like, these aging bodies, they don't always do what they're supposed to, but you understand, we've all got them.

Waving her arms more forcefully now, she turns as a flurry of feathers rapidly pool at her feet. Something goes wrong in the next attitude; Ida clutches her ribcage, her elbows poking out, and suddenly her elbows and knees are flapping, flailing, wildly akimbo, like the wings of an alarmed chicken. In an instant she is bowled over backward as her legs fly up straight in the air: the ballerina has not only fallen off pointe but has also come down to earth entirely, her body awkwardly real and openly failing to maintain the illusion of ethereality. The descent of the body, as the costume falls apart, is a kinetic and corporeal answer to the Platonic idea of ballet. If the ideal of the ballerina is a sylph-like swan, the Trockadero will take it too literally and produce the material body of a bird.[33] If the ideal of the ballerina is the suppression of any sign of aging, struggling, falling, or

Figure 17. Ida Nevasayneva (Paul Ghiselin) as the Dying Swan. Photo
by Sascha Vaughan, courtesy of Les Ballets Trockadero de Monte Carlo.

behaving in an unladylike way, the Trockadero will give you their oldest ballerina, falling on his ass.

The Trockadero *Dying Swan* is a wry, empathetic reminder that mortality is actually painful and awkward, not lightly borne away. It involves a whole process of achingly, creakingly falling out of the disciplines that have kept the body 'up': bodies that were supposed to represent lightness and grace have back spasms and need hip replacements. For ballerinas in particular, the injunction to remain desirable, without showing the sweaty efforts required to produce the temporary illusion of gliding effervescently across the stage, is a version of the double bind entailed by Mallarmé's ballerina-as-poem. It is for this reason, perhaps, that when Ida Nevasayneva scrambles back up from the floor, she does it facing upstage, with her back to the audience. Dusting herself off, flinging stubborn bits of feathers from her fingers, she bends over: the audience is faced with her homely, bony ballerina butt.

When Ida has composed herself, she gets back up on pointe and good-naturedly goes on with the show, but we have already seen the worst. The body of the ballerina is material and subject to all kinds of embarrassing carnalities: it will bend the daisies. Ida tries to enact the theatrical illusion, but her old bones just won't comply; she falls out of the ideal and gets real bruises. From this point on, Ida's relationship to the audience is different, because she has brought us into a shared experiential reality that is the 'backstage' of performance. A conspiratorial affection connects us to her as she tries to sneak offstage early but is shooed back on by someone in the wings—she jogs back across the stage on pointe, in a subtle mockery of her earlier bourrées—and makes a futile attempt to stuff the feathers back into her depleted tutu.

Finally, she sinks to the floor, assuming Pavlova's famous swan pose, but she can't just expire gracefully. The spotlight narrows around her raised arm and bent wrist, which is supposed to be the swan's farewell to the world, and feathers are still clinging to her fingers; she shakes them off irritably, these reminders that even costumes have messy corporeal realities of their own. The stage goes dark, but it is hardly over—Maya Plisetskaya was known to do three or four encores of her *Dying Swan*, and Ida soon appears again to take her bows before the curtain, nodding with a patronizing grace at the applause she clearly expects. Her air of regal aloofness is briefly disrupted when, in a moment straight from a dancer's nightmare, she can't find the opening in the curtain again and pokes around in the red velvet folds for half a minute, frowning. Then she finds the right place, gives the audience another big fake queen-of-the-world smile, and waltzes offstage.

A brief pause and the spotlight seizes on a toe shoe that is poised to emerge from the curtain; the leg slides coyly into view and Ida bounds back onstage, delighted to have another chance to flutter her fingers and bat her oversize eyelashes. She gets back into her final swan pose to remind us how fabulous it was—and promptly, in a nightmare moment specific to ballerinas, rolls right off her tucked-under foot and lands clumsily on her side, as her tutu flies up to show her crotch. But Ida just purses her lips, gives us a little wave, and rearranges herself in the pose, where she stays, head bent over her outstretched leg and her wrists crossed at her ankle, until she determines that the applause is not as thunderous as her performance merits. Then, with her head still bowed, Ida beckons for more with her big hands, coaxing the audience to a roar. Only then does she look up, apparently satisfied by the reaction she has just theatrically produced, and, smiling broadly, gives us the A-OK sign. We're participating in the performance of illusion, and we're doing a good job.

Three rounds of air kisses later, Ida is kneeling in a deep ballerina bow when she is overcome by emotion. She fans herself with her hand; she looks at us like, really, we shouldn't have showered her with all of this adoration—she chokes back a little sob. As an audience continuing to applaud Ida's bows, we've been persuaded to give our bodies over to the staging of an illusion. Ida Nevasayneva has simultaneously brought us into an empathetic relationality with the bodily problems of producing the ballerina ideal and given us a genuinely moving performance as a ballerina. She has broken down the stage conventions of gender and ballet: we've seen her fall flat, we've seen her bend over, and we've seen her body splayed out in all of its material fallibility.[34]

Through drag, Paul Ghiselin has woven a genealogy of ballerinas from Pavlova to Plisetskaya into his own aging body.[35] Everything that is lovable about their histories is given a place in his performance, but so is everything fractured, overblown, and unspeakable. As London dance critic Clement Crisp writes, "I love Ida Nevesayneva as her swan dies of galloping moult . . . as I once loved Markova and Danilova and Riabouchinska and Schanne and Fracci and Slavenska" (2006). Because drag refuses the idea that there are 'wrong bodies' for roles, it allows Paul Ghiselin and his fellow dancers to dismantle an ideal form by inhabiting it themselves, giving it their own weight and height and race and age until its metaphysics buckle under the strain of real bodies. Drag genealogists recognize that there are no 'pure lines', either in terms of lineage or of dancers' bodies. Embodying history is a tangled and bent thing, and to pretend otherwise is to subject real bodies to untenably abstract ideals—to sublimate the leg into an arabesque, and the arabesque into a poem that is as insubstantial as a whisper of ink on a page. In drag, the distance between body and costume is a disjunction that opens a space of possibility for multiple personae, each with its own history, to settle and take root.

The Trockadero are gracious hosts for these spectral histories. They know what it is like to love lost bodies, both because of their attachment to a bygone era of ballerinas and because of their collective experience with AIDS. Drag performance is a way of mourning lost bodies *through* the body—of entwining their multiple histories together and working them into a bodily discipline, like Ida Nevasayneva, who "does *tendus* in her bed at night, so she falls asleep thinking of ballet technique," as Ghiselin says (Parry 2011). As Ghiselin grows older, he becomes an even more poignant ballerina, because he has found a rare way to express the immanent mortality that ballet excludes from its field. He gives the ghosts of ballerinas an afterlife and a freedom they never had, and he demands that we recognize their bodies working through his own—that we, in fact, *applaud* them as aging, fallible, fleshly bodies. It is perhaps for this reason that in Ida's performance of *The Dying Swan*, the bows are actually choreographed to last longer than the solo itself.

In fact, the Trockadero *Dying Swan* is a collective pretending to be a solo. This is not because ballerinas are such lightweight creatures that they have no agency or strength or right to take up space onstage; it's because the Trockadero dancers believe we are not alone in our bodies, and they perform everything that way, even solos. They audition dancers that way, and they do AIDS benefits that way, and they channel ballet history that way. They aren't even alone in their costumes: they make the bodices with many sets of hooks and eyes so that everyone's body can fit into them. On the Trockadero website, under "About Us," they list the names of people in the company whom they have loved that are no longer alive. The Trockadero idea of "about us," in other words, is that the company is a gathering place, a belonging place, a place where the dead are remembered and held. In acts like this, when we openly acknowledge that mortality makes our bodies both fragile and interdependent, a kind of relational ethics that Judith Butler calls "queer bonds" can arise. "Bodies come into being and cease to be," Butler writes, and we all have—we all *are*—these bodies (2011b, 382–83). She asks, therefore, "How do we understand this way of being bound up with one another, of being implicated in each other's lives, a mode of interdependency that is hardly chosen and never precisely easy?" (384). The Trockadero have taken up this question as genealogists, and if Butler is right that "it helps to return to a reflection on embodied life," they are extremely helpful. The whole company is a community formed around the nonbinary potential of bodies to perform multiple identities; among those identities are always the bodies that have been lost over time. And this helps us to imagine a very different paradigm for the identification and acceptance of bodies *as they are* than the one that currently governs, for example, which acts are 'natural,' which bodies are 'able,' and which gender expressions are 'real.'

As Butler says, drag becomes part of cultural politics by "not only making us question what is real, and what has to be, but by showing us how contemporary notions of reality can be questioned, and new modes of reality instituted" (2004a, 217). In Ida Nevasayneva's *The Dying Swan* we see what dance critic Deborah Jowitt called the special Trockadero technique of "layered transformations": drag intercalations that incorporate the missing bodies of past ballerinas and illuminate the bodily materiality that ballet has historically tried to abstract (2006). Touchingly, feelingly, with a heroic and perverse tenderness, Ida Nevasayneva undertakes the responsibility of carrying lost histories in her own hardworking, aging body. She uses her delusional attachment to help us imagine how ballet history might be reanimated through drag, and then brought forward, so that the future of the form is less binary, less normative, less *noxious*. And what would happen if we imagined, like Ida, that our solos were actually collective, if we believed we were responsible for the histories of the unmourned dead, if we knew we were not alone in our bodies?[36]

## The Firebird Rises

Once upon a time, there was a dancer who loved bad puns and story ballets almost as much as the Trockadero do, and one evening, after a show at DTW (Dance Theater Workshop),[37] she and her dancer friends were reflecting on what seemed "to be symptomatic of the downtown dance scene at that time, which was really beautiful slow articulations of arm-bones, laying on the ground, in semi-darkness," which meant that "half the audience was asleep" and the performers, who clearly "had the capacity to leap, turn, fly, do these bigger joyful movements," were constrained to tiny creeping unfoldings of their ulnas and glenohumeral joints, done with the utmost seriousness. That person was Katy Pyle, and that postshow lament became a company called Ballez (Pyle 2016). Ballez's first creation was an open anti-heteronormative adult ballet class at BAX (Brooklyn Arts Exchange), and its second effort was *The Firebird, a Ballez* (2013), which was based on Fokine's *The Firebird* (1910) and featured lesbian, transgender, and queer-identified performers. It starred Jules Skloot as the proud "Tranimal" Firebird and Katy Pyle herself as an exuberant Lesbian Princess who knows what she wants. It also included a group of Polyamorous Princes who, after playing catch, not very skillfully, with a bunch of oranges, stuffed the fruits down the fronts of their black ABT-standard-issue boys' dance tights. I was there on opening night, and no one in the audience fell asleep.

Katy Pyle does not categorize Ballez as drag, but she does describe her aesthetic as being "like layered Russian dolls, each layer of which is borderline garish, an identity nestled inside multiple false versions of a self," which is uncannily close to the exaggerated multiplicity of Trockadero personae like Nadia Doumiafeyva and Innokenti Smoktumuchsky, who in turn channel the spirits of past dancers in order to perform roles like Odette, irked by her dithering prince, or the disco-villain Von Rothbart (Pyle n.d.). Jules Skloot, who "love[s] dressing up in all kinds of gender-fabulous ways," cites drag as a crucial part of what "helped me grow myself up and stay alive" (Finch 2016). One of the people Katy Pyle consulted when Ballez was just starting was former Trockadero dancer Peter Richards. Pyle affirms that she does "feel a connection" to the Trockadero, especially to its early days, when the performances came more from ardor than from virtuosity (Pyle 2016). And their similarities are striking: like the Trockadero, Pyle has an anachronistic love of "ballet as theater, as danced storytelling," with "the extreme facial expressions, the makeup." She is opposed to any kind of dance that requires "rotations with a blank face," which makes dancers like her look as if they were "straight, empty, [and] depressed"; Ballez dancers grin and pout and mug for the audience, just like Trockadero dancers do. Most importantly, if Pyle doesn't have the same sense of drag *costumes* as the Trockadero, she does share their drag *ethics*.

From the very beginning of Ballez, the company was about being a big, raggedy, diverse, queer, inclusive, celebratory collective: in a downtown dance scene of quiet ulna solos and anti-theatrical partnering, Pyle says, "I miss feeling all those bodies, the feeling of dancing *with*" (Pyle 2016). In a collective interview conducted while Ballez was creating its second piece, *Sleeping Beauty and the Beast* (2016), Pyle described her choreography as being much like a "'co-op' with worker-owners" (Hafezi 2014). Similarly, Jules Skloot, reflecting on five years of working with Pyle, explained the "uniquely 'Ballez-y'" mode of partnering—how the bodies, stories, and relationships of the dancers would change the form of partnering itself. Not only would people bear and give weight based on how their bodies felt to them, Skloot was saying, but also relationally, responding to how they knew and felt other bodies. What had been kept offstage would become an integral part of the dance, and what had too often been determined about bodies by normative categories would instead be decided by the performers themselves as they were dancing together.

Ballez was also about what Katy Pyle herself wanted out of ballet and had never gotten. Trained in ballet since she was three years old, she has the technical foundation and vocabulary a ballerina would need. But she is a jumper and a lifter—two roles that traditional ballet assigns to men—and she always wanted to do the excitingly physical things they were doing in the men's classes, instead of having to lie around listlessly in a feathery swoon on the floor (Sheena 2013).[38] At some point while she was rehearsing a variation from *Giselle*, she looked at her body in the mirror and told her reflection, "I am not that. I'm not a kind of waif-woman" (Bo 2017). The lightness, the airiness, the ethereality, the terrified maidens, the wilting swans, the idiocy of trying to make her body "look weaker" and smaller than it actually was "and like I was in need of someone": ballet drove her crazy. And yet its history contained all of the theatricality, physicality, narrative, outlandish frippery, and sheer chaotic potential—"characters, stories, ridiculous costumes, sexiness, romance, drama, intrigue, big big *big* dancing, turning, leaping, flying through the air, partnering!" (Pyle 2016)—that she couldn't find in theaters like DTW.

Before Katy Pyle could make a ballet that did all the things that she loved, however, she had to undo some things about ballet itself. In Ballez classes she would often find that the "masculine-presenting female-assigned queer people" whom she most wanted to dance with had a troubling history with ballet: if they had trained when they were younger, it had gotten stuck in their bodies like a bad habit, an unconscious physical pattern that they were still repeating. Since "in ballet you really communicate your gender through the way you turn your head and tilt your hand and regard other people, and how upright you are," Pyle explains, when "more masculine-identified" people come back to ballet as a practice, they automatically "click back into the sweet little head-tilts," and then it's her job to stop everything and say gently, "Wait a minute: is that *you*?" But the people who have never taken ballet, she finds, are just learning how to turn, or jump, or lift, or feel their legs going up: she doesn't teach ballet as a form that requires head tilts, so they aren't learning it that way. Like Trockadero classes, Ballez classes are literally about rechoreographing the constraints of normative embodiment, where half of the class can be un-doing a gendered regime that has damaged them, while the other half of the class is overcoming the assumption that they don't have the right to do ballet because they're not virtuosic enough by mainstream standards. "So that's been a revelation for me," Katy Pyle concludes: "how do I also do these movements that I want to do *in my gender*?"

One answer to this question would be failure: you fail to do them. You don't do them right. You don't have the right body to do them. You didn't have the right training to do them. You had the training, you were given all the right chances, and you still failed. You used to be able to do them, and now you can't do them anymore, because you're too old. You can't, because people like you don't do that. You can't, because people like you don't do that with people like them. If you do these movements, and you fail, it will be horrible. No one will come. Or everyone will come, and ev-eryone will see you fail, and no one will help. You will wonder, like Antony Bassae, if you are even a person.

But if you remember Antony Bassae, you could say to yourself, as Katy Pyle does, that we have not *only* inherited a form of ballet that constrains and excludes bodies. Tamara Karpova believed in a ballet of queer lineages and reclaimed histories, in ballet as an occasion for 'dancing *with*' rather than 'failing at.' In the tradition of the Trockadero's drag recasting of em-bodied potential, Ballez has a radical idea of who is really failing in ballet, as Pyle explains:

> I am taking on these monolithic cultural structures and putting these really incredible, beautiful embodied humans inside of them to show how the structures fail to hold us. If you're looking at this as a ballet and judging it from a classical set of terms, assumptions and value systems, then we are failing at every single fucking thing we do. . . . But, the ways we do them wrong are actually worth look-ing at and interesting to watch, and shows how the world is actually failing us. (Perel 2013)

When you open up a fixed structure through a collective queer reworking, you do more than simply 'fail' to reenact it correctly.[39] You put the political back into the performative—or, as Judith Butler and Athena Athanasiou write, you take the body to be "a turbulent performative occasion" (2014, 178–79). This is queer dance going beyond the threshold of the theater, marching under the camp banner of a bad pun on 'ballet.' This is queer dance doing politics and, along the way, healing some of the physical damage that dance training can wreak on non-normative bodies. As one Ballez dancer says, "Regular ballet underscores how I'm failing at this thing I'm striving for, but in . . . Ballez I'm Nijinsky!" (Perel 2013).

This is why, when dance scholar Victoria Thoms cautions against seeing drag dances by the Trockadero and Richard Move "as a utopian challenge to the status quo of a clear and knowable identity," because theater is "not really 'real,'" I cannot agree (2013, 138). Drag dances like *Martha @*, anti-heteronormative dances like Katy Pyle's *Firebird*, and the drag dance companies like Les Ballets Trockadero de Monte Carlo are helping us to reenvision what dance can be, who can be a dancer, and what dance history ought to tell us. As queer theorist José Muñoz put it so eloquently, "accomplished drag" is not merely a campy thing that guys in wigs do in Castro nightclubs for fun; it is actually "some kind of sweet revenge on gender" (2009, 69).[40] When you are enacting your very right to be this kind of body, with these kinds of desires, and you are opening up categories like gender and art and the history of Western concert dance to those it has excluded and denigrated, theater *is* really real.

## The Dying Swan *at the Meow Mix*

The sweet revenge scene of Ballez's latest piece, *Sleeping Beauty and the Beast*, is the pas de deux in the first act. It starts when the Lilac Fairy (Chris DeVita), unzips the princess Aurora (Madison Krekel) right out of her ruffly pink princess dress. Relieved, Aurora casts off the dress, which looks like the collapse of a whole kingdom of frosted cupcakes, and kicks it heartily offstage left. She is about to do the same thing with her sparkly pink tulle underskirt when the Lilac Fairy picks it up. He pauses, hesitant; then he tentatively holds it up to his own waist, as if wondering whether it might ever fit on his body. Aurora nods at him; she's down to her plain white knickers and a camisole, and busy pinning her hair back. He puts it on. As he fondly smoothes out the skirt of his new tutu, the sparkles seem to grow even more sparkly. In turn, he slips off his pearl-colored satin frock coat and helps Aurora into it; she brandishes its flounces with evident satisfaction. Finally, the Lilac Fairy takes off his extravagantly plumed hat and crowns her with it, giving it a little pat as if to say, Well, here we are then, all sorted!

He gives her his hand; she leads him center stage; the familiar Tchaikovsky adagio starts; he begins in *attitude devant* while she supports him proudly, attentively, helping him through the turns, bracing her whole body on bent knees to take his weight. At one point in the partnering, Madison Krekel is so fully absorbed in holding a body much larger and taller than hers that there is a slight risk to her feathered hat, so Chris DeVita thoughtfully plucks it up and holds it through the lift. Then, when his lilac booties touch the dance floor again, he gives it back to her, and they smile at each other. "In that moment," Katy Pyle explains, "both of those characters are *themselves*; they're just arriving at a more visible version of themselves through the use of that clothing so that they can settle into something that's really natural to them—and maybe that's happening in Trockadero, too, I don't know" (Pyle 2016). What Ballez is inheriting from the Trockadero is this expansive sense of drag: drag that *uses* gendered clothing as a cue for transformation but does not stop at a definition like "x dressing up as y." If Krekel and DeVita can be more themselves in each other's clothes—so much more themselves that they can dance a romantic pas together and smile about it—then they are upholding drag ethics as the Trockadero understand them.

Act I of *Sleeping Beauty and the Beast* is all about fairy tales and nineteenth-century workers' revolutions: it's about resistance and righteousness and true love, like the Firebird rising. Act II of *Sleeping Beauty and the Beast* was supposed to be about how "hot and awesome" it was to be a lesbian in New York City in the mid-1990s, Katy Pyle tells me (2016). Remember the Clit Club? Remember the Meow Mix? But when she started asking the older dyke activists and Lesbian Avengers about how hot and awesome it had been, everyone told her instead: "*it was a battlefield. It was hell. We were care-taking, we were nursing, we were cleaning up, we were feeding.*" As soon as she undertook this historiography of a generation of lesbians in her community, she realized that "their entire identities were constructed around their friends that were dying that they were caring for." So Act II became about caring, about dying, about AIDS, about the intertwining of queer and trans lives in ways that no one had

Figure 18. Madison Krekel (Aurora) and Chris DeVita (the Lilac Fairy) in the pas de deux, act 2 of Ballez's *Sleeping Beauty and the Beast*, choreographed by Katy Pyle. Photo by Theo Coté, courtesy of Ballez.

asked for and no one had sanctioned. It's a sort of mash-up of club life and ballet: the score is half a DJ set by JD Samson of Le Tigre fame, and half the score for *The Dying Swan*, and the two are overlaid so that the thump of the Clit Club bass resonates through the harp trills of the Saint-Saëns. The dancing is intermingled, too; there are sexy, strutting, jutting, clubby, flashy sequences of scantily clad people in black leather and crushed velvet moving together on beat, and then it fades into a ballet interlude, in which eleven people in their white underwear, with Chris DeVita downstage in front, do the *Dying Swan*.

They repeat this collective solo several times over the course of act 2, taking up the center of the stage each time. Most of the swans appear to be queer cisgender men, but not all. Some appear to have traditional ballet training (Chris DeVita went through Alonzo King LINES Ballet's professional program, for example) and some do not. Their bodies look quite different from one another, and they all do the steps in their own ways. But each time they do the *Dying Swan*, someone dies. They all go down to the floor together, and then one swan doesn't rise again. Instead, someone from the club crowd—often it's Jules Skloot, the true love of the princess

Figure 19. Act 2 of Ballez's *Sleeping Beauty and the Beast*, choreographed by Katy Pyle. Photo by Elyssa Goodman, courtesy of Ballez.

Aurora, now clad in a black leather vest and cap—comes forward and tenderly takes the swan into their arms. One by one, the swans fall. And one by one, they are cradled and carried offstage by people who look like they intended to go clubbing and pick up other hot and awesome people in leather outfits while JD Samson boomed through the semidarkness of the back bar. But instead they are here, holding the dead.

Channeling histories, especially the histories of lost bodies, is unpredictable; Katy Pyle calls it a "heart-opening connecting practice" (2016). You open your heart, and then you have this open space in the center of your body, and you invite the bodies of others into it, because "in the act of performing," Pyle says, "we're literally connecting ourselves by embodying this community across time." In the dancers' bodies, the heroines of the 1893 garment workers strike are entwined with the dyke activists of 1993, and the corporeal politics of all of those bodies are overlaid, like the score, while the dance is happening. But to undertake an embodied genealogy is not only to make a fairy tale about revolution and queer resistance. It is also to be willing to be haunted, to mourn on the dance floor, to expand the "about us" to include the dead, to let the tears become part of the costume.

Chris DeVita is the last swan, and he can't even make it through the final repetition of the solo. He slumps, he stumbles, he falls; he doesn't rise again. The last time he falls, in the silence, Madison Krekel runs to him and flings her body on top of his, but nothing happens: it isn't that kind of fairy tale. Instead, all of the dancers who are left take his body up on their shoulders and bear it in a solemn, silent procession across the stage. It was not the lifting or the partnering they had wanted, but they do it, because his body is also theirs.   ·

## CHAPTER FIVE

## To Be *Faux Real*

Dancing queerly is never done alone; there's always someone else in
my solo.
  —Clare Croft, *Queer Dance*

Would it be possible to talk about a biography of gesture, of inter-
ruption, of reciprocal coexistences?
  —Lauren Berlant to Jay Prosser, "Life Writing and
    Intimate Publics"

### To Be Real

On a stage the size of a walk-in closet, already cluttered with a rolling
clothes rack and a dressing table holding one of those old-fashioned
makeup mirrors with little round bulbs, the lights begin to come up on
pair of a long, white legs, muscled like a Rockette's, striding downstage
with a twist and a flounce. Swiveling her hips as she catwalks, the dancer
pauses in the pose of a dimpled calendar girl, one knee coyly pressed into
the other, and then, opening her fists into big showy jazz hands, throws her
shoulders back sharply and starts to slide sideways into the splits. Sinking
into her scissored legs, she turns and gives the audience a look: a knowing,
slightly sassy look, jawline hard and mouth held in a lipstick pout. We're
supposed to recognize what she's doing in that hot-pink leotard with those
glammed-up shoulder rolls. She's *working.*

  *Work, girl!* someone shouts appreciatively from the second row, right
on cue.

  As David Bowie's "Speed of Life" plays on, she gives us showgirl kicks,
aerobic lunges, pliés undertaken with proper *épaulement*, and a series of
languid, artfully draped fashion poses familiar from glossy magazines. As
the dance slows, she begins to lip-synch a few words to Bowie's "What in

the World": "What are you going to say to the real me?" she asks, eyeing us coolly. But when she addresses the audience directly, a little breathless from exertion, she preempts whatever we might say in response, declaring, "I feel real. Mighty real."

The person who famously added "mighty" to real was the African American disco star and occasional Cockette named Sylvester, and the question of realness is indebted to the working-class, urban, queer-of-color realm of drag ball culture. To ask from the stage for a judgment on your realness is to invoke a mostly black and Latinx legacy of queer and trans dancing, gendering, self-styling, and belonging.[1] Realness rises up against categories that exclude bodies from an idealized 'real': in opposition to "the hegemonic order of an anti-black, anti-queer, and misogynist world," as Tavia Nyong'o writes, balls create "a space where quotidian violence, insecurity, poverty and exploitation are transformed into extravagant beauty and beloved communitas" (2017, 255). This is partly in response to enforced distance; "realness," the world-weary queen Dorian Corey says in *Paris Is Burning*, is "as close as we will ever come to the real" (Livingston 1990). And it is partly a question of judging differently—valuing queer forms of labor, a layering and collaging of identities, and a rechoreographed presentation of self over the anatomical virtuosity prized by heteronormative beauty pageants.

In one sense, what is being judged in ball culture is how someone embodies *feeling* real. When drag does something transformative, Madison Moore explains, it is affective and participatory: the audience, valuing the fierceness of the drag artist, helps to "realize" the identity being performed and to recognize the labor this requires (2013). Drawing on Geneva Smitherman's scholarship on black vocabularies, Moore defines "werk" as an energetic, persuasive, public, physical "way of reclaiming the body" (2014, 20). The body doing this kind of werk in queer performances is almost always a body that has been judged, on the street or in the home, as not real, not enough, not quite, or too much. The "ever-receding horizon of the real" can make it feel like some bodies will never be allowed to touch the identities they reach for (Halberstam 2005, 52). Realness, then, can be a strategy of movement. By repositioning some ontological categories so that they are closer to the intricate textures of feeling and crafting a body, and by shifting some naming and narrating practices back to the communities to which they belong—so that they aren't just carried off by late-capitalist reality television[2]—realness seeks to reconfigure judgments about who gets to be what in public.

Sylvester's 1978 anthem "You Make Me Feel (Mighty Real)" emphasizes that this cannot be accomplished alone: the feeling of realness is granted to "me" by "you."[3] Feeling real depends on a community, a group of people willing to acknowledge the effort someone puts into achieving degrees of realness. This is why, when the Bowie song fades out, the dancer squints into the audience and asks the crew to bring up the house lights. People in the audience are blinking, and seats creak. Holding the microphone at arm's length as the theater brightens, she exclaims, "I don't need this mediation, right? It's an intimate house," and starts to pick out faces in the audience. This is Monique Jenkinson, being real, in the tiny black-box Climate Theater in San Francisco in 2009, in the first scene of *Faux Real*, the evening-length piece she has been working on since she was approximately four months old.[4] *Faux Real* is supposed to be an autobiographical solo piece about a woman who is a drag queen; it is only autobiographical in a queer sense, and it turns out not to be a solo at all. But it is a drag dance theater piece about the asymptotic trajectory of realness that Dorian Corey describes—and about drag as a twenty-first-century practice of gender performance that goes beyond 'cross-dressing.'

Trained both as a dancer and as a drag queen, Monique Jenkinson sees drag as "a classical practice" just like ballet: a rigorous physical discipline with its own performance values and modes of virtuosity (2013). But because she performs as a woman in drag as a woman, she is what is usually called a "faux queen" (or "FTF," for female-to-female or female-to-femme, or "bio queen," or even "RG" for "real girl").[5] Monique's drag name is Fauxnique, and she has performed at the San Francisco drag club series Trannyshack (now Mother) since 1998.[6] In 2003 Fauxnique accepted her glittering tiara as the first faux queen to win the title "Miss Trannyshack," in front of a thousand shrieking fans. If some of that shrieking was actually coming from disgruntled male-bodied queens, Fauxnique's victory was defended by none other than the founder and formidable hostess Heklina. "'I never came from a *traditional* drag background," Heklina said pointedly, "where there were all these *rules* about what it means to be a drag queen'" (Nagy 2008, 64; emphasis mine). Or, as journalist Johnny Ray Huston put it when Fauxnique subsequently won a Goldie Award from the weekly *San Francisco Bay Guardian*, "She offers a unique kind of proof that drag queenery isn't about dick size" (2009).

What ought to align faux and real drag is the fact that staging gender *always* takes work. Ana Matronic, an early faux queen and longtime Trannyshack performer, points out, "'Except for having to tuck away a penis, I do everything a drag queen does: stuffing a bra, putting a wig on my head, putting tons of makeup on. Drag is drag'" (Nagy 2008, 64). Moreover, ball culture traditionally features 'realness' as a category that has at least as much to do with *same*-gender performances across class and professional status as it does with gender-crossing: if a man who is not employed as a US Marine walks in a ball dressed in the uniform of an officer in the Marines, he is understood to be in drag (Livingston 1990). When Marlon M. Bailey, who really is an associate professor of Women and Gender Studies at Arizona State University, walked in the "Executive Realness" category at a drag ball as a professor, he won a trophy—not because he was really a professor, but because he produced the effect of looking like a professor (2013, 59). Heightening, recombining, tucking away, taping on, stuffing, painting, getting in costume, summoning affect: drag demands the work of "realness" from all bodies, not only those that are presumed to be different from the identities they are performing. In *The Drag King Book* (1999), Del LaGrace Volcano defines this succinctly: "What is a Drag King? A Drag King is a performer who makes masculinity into his or her act," not necessarily a woman in drag as a man (35–36). When what is supposed to be biologically given is *performed*, gender is pried away from its own usual ontological certainty. Repeating gender as if it were not self-identical, faux drag marks itself not as a representation of gender but as a doing, an active making of differences, a deliberate proliferating of layers that give the gendered body depth and mutability.

Instead of stripping down to a body that would divulge 'the truth,' this kind of drag takes identity to be a thickly built thing, heavy with layers of what might *also* be true for that body. This collage of identities was evident when, after performing the latest version of *Faux Real* at the Oasis in May 2015, Monique Jenkinson appeared at the bar to greet a cluster of admirers, still a little breathless from the show. Late in the second act, she had added a sort of speeded-up drag striptease whose sheer aerobic virtuosity was applauded with great enthusiasm—and even some faux catcalls. The faux striptease involved removing a layer of costume and switching wigs at least every sixteen counts, while lip-synching. Over the course of the song, Jenkinson had loosened the belt of a glamorous red dressing gown, unzipped a pointy-breasted, huge-hipped dress, shimmied out of a spangled top, and tossed her patent-leather clutch offstage; she ended the act by stalking ferociously to center stage in a long, blonde rock-chick wig with blunt-cut bangs. But we never arrived at the end-endpoint, at her 'real' hair or her 'real' identity; in *Faux Real,* there are always more layers of

Figure 20. Monique Jenkinson (Fauxnique) in her opening monologue in *Faux Real*. Photo by Robert Crouch, courtesy of Monique Jenkinson and Marc Kate.

costumes. And when the show was over and Monique Jenkinson said she would just slip into something more comfortable before meeting us at the bar, there was only a brief interlude before she appeared in an elegant gray wig, streaked aristocratically with white, and an off-the-shoulder white gown with sharp triangular cutouts that would not have looked out of place at a reception for the wives of certain senators.

## Making Yourself Up

Realness in *Faux Real* is composed of effort, style, technique, Scotch tape, falls, bobby pins, pancake, Lycra, lashes, paper, sequins, and hot glue—an aesthetic of ongoing collage, not of core identity. As a result of this werk, realness is detached from its referent in gender (a 'real' man or woman) and given over instead to a quality of performance (really a drag queen) and a degree of interaction (a real connection between stage and house). In *Faux Real* Jenkinson sometimes looks like a white female-bodied dancer moving like a white female-bodied dancer is supposed to: in the ballet section, she goes on pointe in shell-pink toe shoes. In other moments she looks like a drag queen, lip-synching in welterweight false lashes just as skillfully as any of her male-bodied drag sisters. In between, she often shows the work of transitioning; instead of concealing body modifications backstage, or masking the physical labor of presenting a gendered body in public, she puts the dressing room onstage as a performance space. Just before the intermission, for example, Jenkinson is seated at her makeup table, affixing a severe black wig with a tight chignon to her scalp and hollowing the space under her cheekbones with a darker shade of blush. She has lowered her painted eyebrows from 'drag height' (arched far up on the forehead) to 'female stage height' (closer to the brow ridge). She suddenly looks taller; her face appears gaunt with the strain of age and forbiddingly regal. She sharpens the line of her upper lip, then daubs it over in a red so dark that it looks blue-black. Blackout.

When the lights come up—dimly, barely, as in a chapel with one stained-glass window set on high—there is Maria Callas, facing upstage into a diptych mirror that reflects her image to the audience while she puts on her stage makeup. Her shoulders are tightly held, and her face is narrow, haughty, distant, with high cheekbones and a sharp, queenly set to her lips. Now she makes herself look younger: she fills in her eyebrows, powders her chin, and draws 1960s cat-eye trails of black eyeliner at the corners of her eyes. When Monique Jenkinson makes herself up to look like the aging Maria Callas, who then makes herself up to look young enough to appear onstage, thereby becoming the kind of imitable icon who circulates in predominantly gay male drag culture, she is a woman performing a woman who is performing a stage role of femininity—a diva—who is often performed by men. In reclaiming the category of 'drag queen' for people with a range of genders, this scene also stages a feminist return to Maria Callas herself. By reenacting Callas's *embodiment* rather than her iconicity, Jenkinson shows the work that it takes to make the body of a diva.[7]

"When we say a particular woman is not really as well-formed as she appears to be and that the same woman is not really a physician although she appears to be," sociologist Erving Goffman observed in 1956, "we are using different conceptions of the term 'really'" (1959, 61). In that case the real woman would be the one who alters her body—cosmetically, surgically, by dressing or moving in certain ways—in order to present as a woman, while the faux woman would be the one who pursues a profession not traditionally permitted to her. Monique Jenkinson, who is really a drag queen in Goffman's second sense, complicates his first claim by performing women who *make themselves up*, both literally and figuratively. When she performs Maria Callas, Jenkinson flips the stage so that what we see is the dressing-room performance—a woman dutifully making herself appear younger and more attractive than she really is—instead of the immaculate figure of the diva who appears ready-made when the curtain opens. Watching Maria Callas construct her Callas face, layered over Jenkinson's own faux-queen makeup, historicizes the question of realness for an identity like 'woman.'

For Jenkinson, who describes *Faux Real* as "this play on this idea of being a quote unquote real woman who does drag as a faux queen," drag ethics demand that "we don't use the word 'real girl,' or we use it in scare quotes; obviously a transwoman is no less real a woman, her reality is no less" (2013). Jenkinson's queer resistance to any straightforward reading of 'real woman' may also explain why, when she first went onstage at Trannyshack, she called herself Glory Holesome—a rude pun on what it means 'to be real' as a 'real woman' in a bar like the Stud. "The question of who or what is considered real and true is apparently a question of knowledge," Judith Butler notes. "But it is also, as Foucault makes plain, a question of power" (2004a, 215). This is why when Jenkinson does encounter the rare drag queen who disapproves of faux queens, she retorts: "OK, you're not a real woman, I'm not a real drag queen: we're even" (2013). She hopes that it is clear to any good queen that this is not the way drag judges realness—that, as Gayle Salamon eloquently puts it, "assuming a body" is *always* a process of feeling, moving, posing, accumulating, appearing, and being recognized, and this is true whether you are trans or cis or agender or in drag or nonbinary (2010). In *Faux Real*, therefore, what happens at the makeup table is an essential part of the show, "since what the example of drag sought to do was to make us question the means by which reality is made" (Butler 2004a, 217). The backstage labor of gender—the work of costumes and cosmetics in making femininity appear, the effort of rendering a gender legible through gesture and posture—is not hidden from the audience.

Like Fauxnique, the Seattle-based performer Lou Henry Hoover has an expansively autobiographical sense of drag, a showy high-kick dance sensibility, and a commitment to undoing the misogyny of the 'really' that Goffman interrogates. Both artists define drag as "the use of artifice as a means to expose truth" (Hoover 2017, 37), or "to get at what is real through what is fake: using artifice to get at authenticity" (Jenkinson 2013). In 2015 Lou Henry Hoover, a self-described "showboy of a drag king" whose

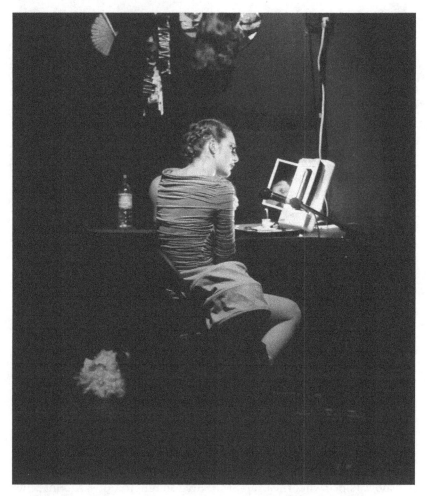

Figure 21. Monique Jenkinson (Fauxnique) at her dressing table in
*Faux Real*. Photo by Parker Tilghman, courtesy of Monique Jenkinson
and Marc Kate.

swaggering white masculinity somehow always gets bitten in the crotch
by a rattlesnake, became the first drag king to contend for the title King
of Boylesque (Pasulka 2015). Since the King of Boylesque category had
actually only been created in 2006 to make room for male performers in
a predominantly female burlesque scene, this was a twenty-first-century
gender moment that went beyond Fauxnique as Miss Trannyshack: could
Lou Henry Hoover, who was stuffing his dance belt and painting sailor

tattoos on his binder, actually be a King of Boylesque? Lou certainly didn't see why not, and neither did the organizers of the competition, who recognized this as a chance to emphasize that burlesque/boylesque should be gender-inclusive for drag kings, men, trans people, and anyone else with a feather-fan rattlesnake dance routine.

The other person who didn't see why Lou couldn't be the first *king* King of Boylesque was Ricki Mason, who had created Lou as a drag persona so that she could do what she loved about burlesque and modern dance without always having to appear as a straight woman stripping to tasseled pasties. The drag life of Lou has been so liberating for Mason that, although Lou did not conquer the King of Boylesque title, she has gained the confidence to perform as "a drag queen and burlesque artist" in addition to kinging (Hoover 2017, 39). In addition to their parallel efforts to make drag more inclusive, Lou and Fauxnique share a serious devotion to makeup, which Hoover calls a "third wave feminist approach to drag kinging, further queering the paradigm of drag" (39). By making themselves up to be drag queens and drag kings, regardless of the genders they were assigned at birth, Jenkinson and Hoover challenge Goffman's two 'reallys' at the same time. In a queer conjunction, they intersect at this historical moment, looking back at the constraints placed on a woman like Maria Callas—that in order for her voice to be heard, she had to present a certain kind of face and body—and forward, to a time when drag "artifice may look like candy coating, but it is not superficial," as Hoover writes (43). Maria Callas has long had a gay drag afterlife, but now she may also have a feminist drag future.

## Stars and Lies

To make yourself up is both self-expression and self-fabulation, a simultaneity of what is 'really' the body being presented. In the middle of the first act, Jenkinson literalizes this paradox by playing a sort of parlor game with the audience called "Two Lies and a Truth." "This is my real hair color," she says first, raising an eyebrow and pointing to her tightly braided hair, whose hue falls somewhere between 'flamingly red' and 'burnt lipstick.' "This is not my real nose," she offers as a second possibility, with a little grimace, or, thirdly, "I finally decided to inject botulism toxin into that pensive little line between my eyebrows." If this is a game about judging bodily realness, it sets up the real as a category determined by what is *made* or *done* with the body—two of the three options are plastic surgery, and the third looks a lot like a tribute to Rita Hayworth. By conjoining the categories of "lies" and "real," and by asking us to decide under that unstable rubric which parts of her body are real and which are not, Jenkinson shades autobiographical truth with self-crafting.

Before we can come to any judgment about the implication that she has cosmetically altered her body, she interrupts: "You know what I'm talking about! You've struggled with it yourself. And," she finishes knowingly, "if you haven't, you will." Reversing the dynamic between the audience that judges and the performer who submits herself for consideration, she implicates us in the process by which she has come to be "faux real."[8] By interpellating our real bodies into impossible possibilities like ageless faces, she prods us to think more about the status of 'lies' that, when told by real bodies, might assume the value of a collective or partial truth. In this way, *Faux Real* shifts the idea of what 'truth' means away from a solid first-person-singular indicative description and toward something like a murky first-person-plural subjunctive. As Eve Sedgwick writes in her critique of J. L. Austin's reliance on the utterance "I do" as defining the performative utterance, "The emergence of the first person, of the singular, of the active, and of the indicative are all questions rather than presumptions for queer performativity" (2003, 71). What would a collectively queer performative subjunctive autobiographical utterance sound like?[9] What form would it take, and what process would achieve it?

Queer autobiographical drag dances like *Faux Real* undertake the possibility of a collective, intimate presentation of a life that is not simply 'personal.'[10] In dialogue with the audience, *Faux Real* stages identities that might be derided as 'not real': self-contradictory, imitative, inverted, unmoored, transitional, excessive, altered, improper, mixed, momentary, dubious, invented, false. It proposes that these states of identity are not only experienced by Monique Jenkinson, and that they are not only about Maria Callas or being socialized as a woman or becoming a faux queen. The process of making yourself up in public is undertaken by all bodies, each with its own particular history, its own layers of risk and proposition, and its own shifting declarations of identity. In *Faux Real* Monique Jenkinson never says which are the lies and which are the truths; we don't need to know whether that is the nose she was born with to know that she is real.

The idea that the 'truth' of bodies is not a monolithic materiality to be judged from an objective distance is central to drag culture and to trans politics. But it is also a tenet of a philosophy of perception that Alva Noë calls "enactive realism" (2012). Noë, a philosopher who has collaborated with choreographers like William Forsythe, Deborah Hay, and Jess Curtis, proposes an analogy in which perceptual experience is itself "a kind of dance—a dynamic of involvement and engagement with the world around us" (2012, 130–31). Embodied movement is at the center of seeing and thinking: the whole structure of perceptual consciousness depends upon kinetic and haptic capabilities.[11] As Noë writes, the "real presence" of a perceived object seems impossible if we understand perception in a cinematic sense, as merely seeing a flat image projected in our line of vision (5). But if we take perception and cognition in a *theatrical* sense, we understand that "audience and performers are together; they share a space and they are both present to each other." For this reason, Noë thinks we ought to overturn our conception of cognition as representational, optical, and imagistic; instead, "we should think of perceiving on the model of touching" (2005, 260). To touch something, you must first believe that it is touchable at all; its "real presence" depends upon proximity and relationality.

Perhaps surprisingly, Noë also subscribes to the idea that "style" is essential to the act of perception, calling it "the repertoire . . . of available ways of achieving the world's presence" (2012, 45). Style, "the face of a practice" of connecting to the world around us, is critical to making real contact with everything in the sphere of our experience: "And what is the world but that to which the stylish being achieves access?" Noë asks provocatively (153, 45). The dangerously stylish being that is Fauxnique onstage at the Stud after midnight enacts the kind of realness that happens during live theater, through embodied movement, when audience and performer are present to each other. The world to which she achieves access has everything to do with "the face of a practice" and the interactive intimacy between stage and house. But if Noë and Jenkinson would agree about real presence, enactive realism, and even the cardinal importance of style, what would Noë say about the category of the "faux real"? What would he make of her faux queen style of accessing the world and feeling "mighty real" while she does it? Is there a place in this philosophy for the layeredness of bodies, for the faint and ghostly presence of things that hover on the edge of perception, or for the realness of falsehood in "Two Lies and a Truth"?

Alva Noë takes up the problem of "nonveridicality" in perceptual experience, as he calls it, by talking about stars. Stars are in the category of things that we fail to actually perceive: they're dead, they're too far away, we can't touch them or even conceive of a mode of touching them. We can't access them as real. "When you look up in the night sky," Noë explains, "you don't actually visually experience *the stars*; what you see, rather, are points of light in the night sky" (2005, 260). If, as Noë admits, a "direct theory of perception fails for the seeing of stars in the night sky," then we either need a new theory" of realness or a different definition of proximity. The stars are fixed in their distantly untouchable firmament, so Alva Noë solves his problem of nonveridicality in the night sky in nearly the same way that Monique Jenkinson solves the problem of not being a 'real' drag queen: by moving the category of realness. Specifically, they both move the category of the real closer to bodies, with their feelings of realness and their repertoires of gestures.

After all, Noë proposes, why do we have to take the stars as the ultimate and true referent for the lights we see in the sky at night? "Why can we not say that . . . *point-of-light-like* is just the way stars look from this distance?" (261). Why not say that a body can look like an admixture of lies and truths, of poses and faces, of constructed autobiography and collaged subjectivity, and still be real? In this "partial nonveridicality," according to Noë, we don't have to decide between an authentic and absolute kind of realness (which would mean, impossibly, touching the stars) and a disavowal of our quite real, dizzyingly *felt* experience of seeing the night sky alive with the glittering scintillations we call stars (261). Many of us, like Monique Jenkinson, can "feel mighty real" in our bodies and at the same time fail to achieve direct access to the glittering, distant, icy constellations of idealized gender normativity that seem to be set so far off in the outer universe. Any absolute veridicality of gender, as Noë says of the stars, is "just too far away!" To want to be a star is to wish to be distant, self-contained, and singular—to be an untouchable celestial body.[12] *Faux Real* is as skeptical of claims to autonomous selfhood as it is of the promise of perfectible bodies: one truth about bodies is that they touch other bodies, which are so much closer to us than stars.

*Ten Moves*

Monique Jenkinson is center stage in earnestly geeky glasses with thick black frames, crooning into the microphone. A strand of frizzed reddish hair is falling over one eye as she swings her arms to the beat. "Will Nature make a man of me yet?" she sings in a low alto voice that is both lightly ironic and heavily inflected with a melancholic English accent. "I would go out tonight," she intones mournfully, "but I haven't got a stitch to wear." Jenkinson makes a surprisingly good Morrissey in those glasses, and at first it looks like a lip-synch number: she's got the timing of the breath and facial expressions that a drag version of The Smiths's "This Charming Man" would require if performed at the Stud. But she's really singing the song, including the weird little shrieks that mark the end of the chorus, and she's still wearing spiked heels. She prefaces this song by saying it helped to get her through high school; in fact, she tells us, she's been rehearsing this "tribute" for twenty years. After twenty years of rehearsing a gestural and vocal routine gendered 'male' but explicitly wary of naturalized maleness, Jenkinson is at home with layered drag selves. Underneath Jenkinson's Morrissey drag is not a body gendered along binaries of biology, morphology, or biography, then, but a body trained for dancing. Her theory of drag is based on a dancer's understanding of the distance between performer and choreography and, more specifically, on the two kinds of potential it implies. First of all, there is space in that distance— room to move, so to speak—and, secondly, an individual repertoire can include a variety of choreographies.

A dancer's distinction between body and choreography, Susan Foster proposes, is a useful analogy for gendered bodies and the normative codes that govern them: there are "choreographies of gender" that get set on bodies, but there are also possibilities of performing these movement phrases and gestures with the particularity of your own body (1998). The question Monique Jenkinson posed for herself in conceiving *Faux Real*— "What makes me a drag queen or not?"—"create[s] that distance" that distinguishes a performer from the choreography she has culturally been given (2013). In doing faux drag, she deviates from the normative choreography for femininity —but also from the choreographies for masculinity, queeniness, effeminacy, and butchness, refusing to simply exchange one gender choreography for another. By crafting a kinetic style that is some parts queeny (with the queer masculinity that implies), some parts femme (but with a knowing wink of the oversize lashes), some parts Martha Graham, and some parts disco, Jenkinson layers gender styles one on top of the other, a collage of surfaces that have their own depth. This is why "What makes me a drag queen or not?" is not a question that can be answered by traditional ontologies of gender that separate men from women, masculinity from femininity, and realness from fakeness.

If you're trained as a dancer, and you have a lifetime of kinesthetic experience performing movement phrases that have been set on you, you understand that choreography is not just absorbed into the body but actually alters it. The layers of choreographic residue that stick to some of your bones, thickening them, and smooth down some of your muscles, toning them, make your body into something other than what it has been. If these choreographed gestures are deeply marked by gender codes, and you do nothing but learn and perform this limited set of gestures, the distance between your body and the choreography diminishes: it seems natural to do them. But as Carrie Noland notes, "If moving bodies perform in innovative ways, it is not because they manage to move without acquired gestural routines but because they gain knowledge *as a result of performing them*" (2009, 7). Performing gendered movement routines, then, can also give you the subversive awareness that gender is less like the way your body naturally 'is' and more like a choreographic phrase you've learned for one specific kind of dance. And then, especially if you've made dances for yourself, you can get the idea that your body could do other kinds of choreography. It could do gender differently by learning new choreographies, by inventing or improvising choreographies of its own, by jamming together disparate choreographies, or by layering two or three choreographies on top of one another. Rearticulating the terms of gender, as Jenkinson has discovered, is partly a project of expanding the range of motion and the directions of flexion that bodies can undertake without being damaged. This is why drag can apparently help get you through high school, and why faux drag might allow you to gain some autonomy as gender codes are continually being set on your body. If gender is choreography, as Foster proposes, then drag dance is the potential for something like autobiochoreography.

Before Monique Jenkinson was even in high school, Diane Torr was trying to make it in New York, working out her own autobiochoreographic survival strategy of drag and dance. Taking class at the Cunningham Studios and working in feminist theater in the early 1980s, Torr was earning very little money; her J1 visa had just expired, making her an undocumented immigrant. "With my dancing ability," a fellow artist suggested "that I try working as a go-go dancer" in New Jersey (Torr and Bottoms 2010, 49). "By watching other dancers," Torr explains, "I quickly discovered that the go-go formula basically consists of ten moves" (49). This knowledge was fortunate, because, as Torr reflects, "I couldn't have survived in go-go dancing without it because my body did not, in itself, match the curvaceous stereotypes that men in bars want to see" (75). In other words, once Diane Torr had understood that her modern dancer's body—"I was muscular, and I didn't have much of a waist" (75)—was not at all the body demanded by the choreographies of gender and sexuality practiced in New Jersey go-go bars, she immediately began to work in the space that Ann Cooper Albright calls the "slippage between the lived body and its cultural representation" (1997, 4). Drawing on insights from her training in dance and martial arts, and particularly from classes in Release Technique, Torr was able to stratify her body, its present gestural vocabulary, and the unfamiliar choreography of explicit, objectified, heteronormatively feminine sexuality.

With this distinction between performer and choreographies clear in her mind, Torr managed to set aside the problem of having the 'wrong' body and to take up instead the task of learning choreographic phrases *that would presuppose, and thereby perform, the body she didn't have.* "I was able to assume different gestures, different behaviors, by choice," she writes. "I can sway my hips from side to side, for example, because I know what that 'sexy,' 'feminine' vocabulary is" (Torr and Bottoms 2010, 75). Diane Torr thought of herself as a woman struggling to get by in "a culture in which women are still taught to think of themselves in two dimensions rather than three" (45).[13] Approaching topless go-go dancing as simply a kind of choreography—there are only ten moves, after all—is a way to shift the burden of proper gender expression from the body of the performer to the codified movements it is supposed to perform. From this perspective, it is not the body that is 'wrong'; the real problem is that the choreography only has ten moves, and you have to repeat them over and over for half an hour to make any money. In other words, Diane Torr figured out that in order to be a successful go-go dancer in New Jersey, she would have to treat its gendered choreography as a denaturalized series of gestures to be studied, rehearsed, and performed onstage.

One day, though, Diane Torr got into a big argument with the virulent antiporn feminist Andrea Dworkin, who called her up and berated her hotly for daring to call herself a feminist when she was participating in a form of sexual exploitation that was more or less equivalent to rape (Torr and Bottoms 2010, 50). Torr had been reading Dworkin's *Pornography: Men Possessing Women* (1981) on her breaks at the go-go bar and thought this was more than a bit unfair; here she was, making just enough money to keep her artistic practice alive, trying to organize the other dancers into a union, finding autonomy in a country that had just declared her an 'illegal alien,' and now she was being accused of abetting rapists. When

Dworkin told her that she should at the very least seek work as a waitress, Torr responded, "Whether in the role of buttoned-up secretary or go-go dancer, I was performing different kinds of feminine drag in exchange for money" (Torr and Bottoms 2010, 51). As a female-bodied dancer whose living depended on two-dimensional codes for embodiment, Torr came to see femininity as kinesthetically manageable from a critical distance—as if it were faux drag dance. She wasn't using drag femininity to 'feel real,' like Monique Jenkinson would, but she was at least able to instrumentalize the difference between felt gender and performed gender to project the outlines of a body she temporarily needed.

Shortly thereafter, Diane Torr quit go-go dancing and became a drag king.


*Back to the Shoes*

Pinning a black tiara askew in her hair, Monique Jenkinson stands still for a minute while a tall, slim man, dressed in a black tuxedo shirt and black pants that are hemmed a little high on the ankles to reveal dangerously pointy black heels—Mica Sigourney, known in the drag community as VivvyAnne ForeverMORE, appearing tonight as a butch queen up in pumps in the role of Jenkinson's adept assistant—fastens her into a feathered black bustier. "Ballet . . . ," Jenkinson muses, "my mother tongue." She draws on long black gloves that fan out in feathered cuffs on her upper arms. "The shoes: my first love affair." She does two or three quick *relevées* in her toe shoes; her black tutu rustles. Mica gives it an approving fluff and hands her a brunette fall, shaped into a messy ballerina bun, which she fastens into the circlet of the tiara.

Although she loves the physicality and theatricality of ballet as much as its shoe fetish, and despite the fact that she could earn a spot in the elite North Carolina School of the Arts summer program in ballet, Jenkinson insists, "I always feel like a charlatan saying I've been a ballerina" (2013). "Growing up taller than most of the other dancers in suburban Colorado in the 1980s, Jenkinson was handed the strong character roles—the Spanish dancer in *The Nutcracker*—and was told she couldn't get any bigger" (Smiley 2012). In particular, auditions seemed to be judging her body *itself*, rather than her technique or presence:

> My turnout is pretty good, and my toes point pretty, and, through
> my diligent fourteen-year-old efforts at starvation, I've gotten my-

self to a place where I still hate myself in a powder-blue leotard, but I can stand there . . . and then you're standing next to the girl who looks like a daddy longlegs, and she's effortless, and you think, "Oh, that's what they're looking for." My body's never going to be that. (Jenkinson 2013)

This realization propelled Jenkinson away from ballet and toward an undergraduate degree in modern and contemporary dance. At Bennington, though, she found that the storied dance department that had nurtured the diverse styles of Martha Graham and Doris Humphrey, Merce Cunningham and José Limon, and Trisha Brown and Yvonne Rainer, was currently devoted solely to Serious Art. "No camp! No spectacle! No facial expression!," Jenkinson declares with mock sternness, remembering her first semester. Unfortunately, these were exactly the qualities "which I had always been told were my strengths. In ballet, well: 'your thighs are a little big, you're too tall, but boy, you have *ardor*.'" Trapped between one form of dance that told her she was too big, too tall, and not anorexic enough, and another form of dance that forbade her theatrical sensibility, Jenkinson—very much like Katy Pyle of Ballez—felt that the qualities of her performing body she most valued were precisely the ones shutting her out of the choreography. When she relates her autobiography as a dancer, especially as a ballet dancer, she ends by remembering the stinging realization "that this is going to be a life of trying to please a culture that will never accept who I really am." And, she concludes with a sigh that seems to come all the way from her childhood, this feeling "is something I've had in common with gay men."

It is impossible to know how many gay men are in the audience at the Climate Theater tonight, but there are certainly a lot of men shouting, "Work, girl!" In fact, what they are probably shouting—"there are codes, there is a language" to queer subcultures, Jenkinson points out—is what she feels viscerally as "'I get you! You get me!'" which she classifies as "werq-with-a-q." "Werq" is a queer verbal recognition that "realness comes from some acknowledged, shared struggle," as Jenkinson defines it.[14] So if the audience recognizes a bit raucously that she is werqing tonight, the feeling is mutual: "In my realest moments," Jenkinson reflects, "there's been a kinship around trying to fit into a society that didn't value what you had to offer." This is why Jenkinson thinks of herself as having been "hoisted" back up on pointe by the drag community. This is why she uses words like "honor" and "pay tribute" in *Faux Real* to describe what she wants the piece to do. After all, "finding a home in this tribe of drag queens," she says tenderly to the audience, "brought me back to the shoes after all these years."

As the proto-goth Bauhaus song "St. Vitus Dance" slams through the speakers, Jenkinson is on pointe, her back to the audience. She's dressed like a punk version of the Black Swan, but instead of launching into Odile's thirty-two fouettés, she begins with a different tribute. She bourrées in place, still facing upstage, waving each arm up and down ferociously in turn: it's a cracked version of the *Dying Swan*, one of ballet's most famous solos. But Monique Jenkinson isn't just rechoreographing Pavlova's Dying Swan: her *échappés changés* are undertaken with the gymnastic exuberance of jumping jacks, she screams through a series of crazed turns, and, halfway through, she starts pecking at the air like a maddened bird, pumping her neck in and out. On the one hand, she is injecting ballet with the ragged, edgy punk-rock ethos that she feels its cloying ethereality has always lacked. On the other, she is paying tribute to the melodramatic high-camp *Dying Swan* solo of Les Ballets Trockadero de Monte Carlo—a ballerina doing a drag version of a drag version of a ballerina. Jenkinson has come to realize that for her, as for the Ballets Trockadero, an affinity for ballet may entail rechoreographing gender codes to accommodate the real body she has in the art form she loves. She recognizes in the Trockadero her proud forebearers, and colors her Dying Swan with some of their movement qualities: big, bitchy extensions; needle-sharp pointe work; drastically aerobic jumps; an *épaulement* straight from the Bolshoi; and wickedly expressive eyebrows.

She drops to the iconic Pavlova swan bow—sitting with one leg extended and the other tucked under the tutu, torso bent down so that the arms are feathery and long along the leg—but pops back up to howl soundlessly, along with the end of the Bauhaus song, the words "Do it!" When she sinks back to the ballerina bow, the theater erupts in whoops and applause. This is one important function of drag autobiochoreography: to take damaging lived experiences of gender normativity and re-dance them differently in public—to dance those learned choreographies again, but queerly, and in queer company.[15] To recuperate ballet for her body, Jenkinson returns to an origin story in dance (ballet as "mother tongue") and restages it through drag. Kareem Khubchandani, explaining how he has transformed the dances of his childhood into the "radical-feminist-bicurious-Bollywood drag queen" LaWhore Vagistan, underlines both the importance of origin stories—"they matter to us as queer people," he writes, and they "matter to us as dancers"—and that to "continue to dance queerly is not just a matter of individual resilience" (2017, 199, 203). As Jenkinson puts it, "It takes a village to make a solo!" (Huston 2009).

Monique Jenkinson has turned to the San Francisco drag community as a place of "deep kinship" where, she makes clear, "my body is valued, which helped heal some of the psychic wounds of ballet" (2013). "What was so freeing about drag is, if I'm standing next to Heklina, I look like Suzanne Farrell! Next to a real ballerina"—she grins and pauses for effect—"I sort of look like a moose." Not only has drag—as a practice and as a community—given her back a sense of humor about the relative position of her particular body to ballet; it has also incited a mischievous desire to bring a drag perspective to the chilled pink world of Western classical dance. In fact, standing onstage just before the Bauhaus song comes on, with one set of eyelashes drooping slightly, she gives her feathered elbow gloves a final tug. "I have to say," she remarks with studied innocence, "when I saw *Swan Lake* recently, after hanging out in drag clubs for so long, when she does those thirty-two fouetté turns, it was all I could do not to jump out of my comfy opera house seat and yell, '*Work! Get it, Odile! Get it, girl!*'" This is a queer intervention in ballet, but it is also the moment when Jenkinson becomes the drag audience that she believes every ballerina should have had.

### Autobiochoreography

"Do you all know what a drag mother is?" Monique Jenkinson asks us pointedly, walking across the stage in a black bra and a pair of gold-lamé boy-shorts over nude dance tights. She's telling us the history of coming to Trannyshack—an autobiographical account that has all the fervor of coming to Jesus, but all the irreverence of the Sisters of Perpetual Indulgence's "Hunky Jesus" Easter pageant—and how, one night in 1998, she went to a show that featured "a big drag queen named after an Icelandic volcano pretending to be PJ Harvey." Obviously, she concludes, "I was home." And that home came with its own family: sisters, aunties, and so forth. But a drag mother is special: "a drag mother is the person—usually a drag queen—who first put you up in drag, who teaches you how to do your eyebrows, how to walk in heels."

"Now my *true* drag mother," Jenkinson pronounces, slowing her words for emphasis, "is my own real biological mother, Mitzi." She pauses for an instant while we absorb this information and then adds, "How's that for a drag name?" It's a pretty good drag name, but it radically redefines what we might understand from the terms "true," "drag," "own," "real," and "biological." If Mitzi is Monique's drag mother, and if *Faux Real* is, as *San Francisco Magazine* described it, "an autobiographical sketch of her path to becoming a faux queen," then what is autobiography? (Smiley 2012). Is it, as choreographer Miguel Gutierrez says of his frankly queer, apparently self-revelatory pieces like *Age & Beauty Part I: Mid-Career Artist/ Suicide Note or &:-/* (2014), a way to "exploit the architecture of truth" by constructing an exposé of the construction of self? (2016).[16] As a queer rechoreographing of autobiography, *Faux Real* allows for a confusion of truth, self-invention, outright lies, family secrets, and bio-narrative that isn't based on biology.

Monique's offstage family includes not only Mitzi, and all of her drag sisters and aunties, but also her husband of many years. "'I don't claim queer. I consider myself culturally queer,' she says, while rolling a fake eyelash in the palm of her hand. Culturally queer, she explains, is about existing outside of the normal heteronormative structure" (K. Smith 2011). This is a complex identification, further complicated by the fact that the prerecorded track currently rolling in the Climate Theater is Jenkinson's voice, listing "the 20 albums that made me gay." When she gets to Sinéad O'Connor, she mentions that some of her earliest sex happened to the album, then hesitates. "Might best be filed under 'albums that made my boyfriend a lesbian,'" she concludes thoughtfully. In interviews, Jenkinson has repeatedly tried to explain that although she feels a strong cultural affinity with queerness, she really, really does not believe she is a gay man 'trapped in a woman's body.' Instead, "Monique Jenkinson claims that her parents have been grooming her to be a gay man since birth" (Labong 2009). Her queer sensibility may be due in large part to "five of the books that Mitzi put into my hands"—the first one is the anthem of 1970s feminism, *Free to Be You and Me*; the last one is the autobiography of Diana Vreeland. But Monique's queerness, like Mitzi's, happens in an ostensibly heterosexual context. Does that make *Faux Real* not queer, or does it make what is queer about *Faux Real* not autobiographical?

Before making these kinds of judgments, it is helpful to remember something Judith Butler marks as the indisputable claim of queer theory: "to be opposed to the unwanted legislation of identity" (2004a, 7). Furthermore, Butler states unequivocally that queer theory "seeks not only to expand the community base of antihomophobic activism, but, rather, to insist that sexuality is not easily summarized or unified through categorization."[17] Perhaps queer autobiography—especially if it is a theatrical, politically charged kind of self-narrative—can in fact be undertaken by someone who is only queer by affinity. Perhaps performing yourself in a queer mode, as Miguel Gutierrez said to me, queers the genre of autobiography itself: "I'm not attempting to pass as anything other than this fictive thing—or than multiple fictive things" (2016). The question of whether 'passing' as a real fiction—or a collection of real fictions—is autobiographical is like the question of whether Mitzi is a good drag name: it is, but that means we have to redefine the terms of realness, embodiment, and selfhood.

In that case, following the logic of Kareem Khubchandani's conviction that "I have queer politics because of my aunties," perhaps your true drag mother can actually be your own biological mother (2017, 203). After all, as Jenkinson tells us with a meaningful look, this condition is potentially a collective one: "A lot of people have drag mothers and don't even know it. I think you'll find you might." This vision of queerness as a kind of cultural layering that can happen regardless of biology, morphology, gender identity, sexual orientation, or kinship structure brings us back to the questions that Jenkinson posed at the beginning of *Faux Real*—questions of feeling. If she 'feels real' and she feels culturally queer, then queer faux realness is close to David Halperin's definition of "gayness" as "not a state or condition" but rather "a mode of perception, an attitude, an ethos: in short, it is a practice" linked to a "queer way of feeling" that "expresses itself through a peculiar, dissident *way of relating* to cultural objects" (2012, 13, 12).[18] Jenkinson thinks this feeling comes from a shared understanding of trying to achieve realness in a world that doesn't value you as real. "To be called a copy, to be called unreal," Butler writes, "is one way in which one can be oppressed, but consider that it is more fundamental than that . . . [It] is to find that you have not achieved access to the human" (2004a, 30). To call yourself "faux real," then, and to call your alter ego "Fauxnique," is both a way of marking the feeling of being barred from the real and, somewhat rebelliously, to take "realness" as a cultural form to which you have "a peculiar, dissident *way of relating*."

Gayle Salamon makes this claim poignantly in her account of the "boys of the Lex," the regulars of San Francisco's longtime main lesbian bar and the stars of its annual calendar.[19] To anyone who would call out these boys as not 'really' boys, Salamon demands, "What is served by insisting that their bodies make these boys women . . . other than the most rigidly deterministic and conservative notions of proper categories of sex and gender?" (2010, 93). Pointedly, she concludes, "Those who understand bodily morphology to be constitutive of a truth that exceeds ideologies of gender would do well to take seriously some of the ways in which gender is currently being lived." Both the boys of the Lex and the faux queens of the Stud contend with claims made on their bodies: claims about 'women,' claims about who is 'real,' claims about what is 'enough' to count as gender. It is not an accident that there is a long-standing San Francisco drag party called Daytime Realness.[20]

The Lexington was five blocks from Monique Jenkinson's house in the Mission District; many of its boys are her neighbors. In August 2013 the *San Francisco Examiner* ran an article titled "San Francisco Transgendered Community Reports Uptick in Targeted Violence" (Aldax 2013). Six months earlier, two transwomen had been brutally assaulted outside a bar in the Mission; in 2008 a woman was gang-raped in San Francisco by men who taunted her for being a lesbian; in the "Hate Violence in 2012" report issued by the National Coalition of Anti-Violence Programs, there were "documented 95 incidents of anti-LGBTQ violence" in the city that year (NCAVP 2013, 75). The term "hate violence" recognizes that these are all attacks on perceived forms of embodiment and desire that the perpetrators cannot stand to imagine as real, viable, and equal to their own. It is a violence that attempts to foreclose the possibilities for these bodies—these clothes, these faces, these ways of moving, these lives—in urban public space. But just as homophobia, transphobia, and misogyny are fundamentally interrelated, so too are the members of a coalitional "neighborhood" that can reject and repel them. In this geography the vulnerability of certain bodies to violence is very real, but also, hopefully, so are the queer kinships that might help to protect them from those kinds of violence.

"You," Jenkinson says suddenly to someone in the third row, "yeah, you've seen the show before!" She peers farther into the darkness of the theater, studying faces. "Remember when I said you might become involved?" she demands cheerfully. "This is it." She fixes the hot-roller curls of her honey-blond wig and paints a black stripe between her two front teeth. Fanning the paint with one hand, she holds her lips open in an exaggerated *O* while it dries. Undaunted by the prospect of speaking without moving her lips, Jenkinson runs through some members of her community who should now join her onstage: "Do we have any bears in the house? Butches? Amazons? Gym queens? Butch queens? Dykes? Yoga people, contact improv girls, strong women, strong men? I need your assistance." The house comes to life; people begin to maneuver around one another's knees to get to the aisle, and there is lively banter as they urge each other up on stage. "C'mon, Precious!" several voices call to Precious Moments, a fellow queen in Jenkinson's drag tribe. Obligingly, Precious sashays up the aisle to the stage, joining four or five other people already huddled around Mica, who is giving them whispered instructions.

This moment of community—and of an explicit call for the community to show themselves in solidarity by participating in the performance— echoes the scene earlier in the evening when Jenkinson asks for the house lights to come up. "It's a way of admitting what's going on," she explains—a moment that calls out the realness of being together while something potentially transformative is happening (2013). "You don't get to sit in the dark. Let's not pretend that it's this perfect anonymity, because we're connected." For Jenkinson, the house lights come up and the mic gets set down in the first ten minutes of the show precisely because "acknowledging our shared experience as performer and audience is a moment of real." Gutierrez, who shares Jenkinson's approach to "audience configurations that are more intimate than the architecture of the room would suggest," links this to choreographer Deborah Hay's idea that dancers can negotiate a relationship with the audience, choosing to "invite being seen" (2016).

Miguel Gutierrez doesn't use the word "realness" in relation to his work, but he does talk about the "disruptive authenticity" of queer autobiographical performance; there are moments when the risks taken by the bodies onstage have to be acknowledged and shared out in some way. *Age & Beauty Part I*, for example, begins by asking us to mark our own bodies with a slash of glossy pink nail polish, and includes a sequence in which the dancers—one of whom is the mid-career choreographer himself, in a snug one-piece swimsuit printed with alarmingly tropical palm fronds— ask the audience, "Do you wanna fuck us?" The disruptively authentic moments of Gutierrez's and Jenkinson's performances are not only about talking back or lighting the house; they are about distributing the vulnerability of performing yourself in the body that you have. They are saying to the audience: We know that you are reading our bodies; we know that you are judging; we know that you perceive our gender, race, age, sexuality, weight, height, and anatomy to be constitutive of our identities and the quality of our performances. But you are not separate from us in this way. If we admit that we need you to show up and to witness, to respond to our performances, to hold us up sometimes, to participate in our tellings of truth and lies, to recognize our claims to be real—well, we are only doing in this little queer theatrical space what we all have to do, and often at much greater risk, in the world.[21]

What does this have to do with drag mothers? Jenkinson answers this by enumerating the people she sees in the audience when the house lights go up: "One of you is my mother, one of you is my cousin, and one of you is Juanita MORE!"—who is Glamamore's drag daughter and VivvyAnne ForeverMORE's drag sister—"sitting next to my dad" (Jenkinson 2013). In other words, *Faux Real* pretends about many things, but it insists on acknowledging the real community that fills the theater. The lights that flood the audience when Jenkinson wants to find out who is there are a theatrical recognition that we are always "acting in concert," as Butler says at the beginning of *Undoing Gender*, "always 'doing' with or for another" (2004a, 1). In this context it is not a saccharine California truism to say that *Faux Real* is about having a real family. A real family can include a drag mother who is your biological mother, and your biological dad who is sitting next to your drag sister, Juanita MORE!

In the next dance number, Jenkinson slinks out onstage in head-to-toe, late-period Madonna drag—sex-kitten gap between her front teeth, plasticine blond hair veiled by a purple sari—lip-synching to the bizarre ashtanga-pop song "Shanti/Ashtangi." In the middle of the sequence, when she unfurls from her sari in a disco turn and vogues her way downstage, the bears, butches, gym bunnies, dykes, butch queens, contact improv girls, strong women, strong men, amazons, sisters, mothers, fathers, aunties, and Trannyshack veterans who have volunteered to participate take out a large mirrored platform that Mica has given them to hold. Encircling the platform, they hold it up together, and when Jenkinson crawls up onto it with a sultry pout, they hold her up too, bearing her full weight among them. As she balances on a yoga mat she has unrolled across the platform, suspending her legs precariously sideways on her elbows, she carefully avoids kicking anyone in the head: that's family.

## In Repertoire

On World AIDS Day in December 1997, and for many World AIDS Days thereafter, Diane Torr organized something called "Brother for a Day" (Torr and Bottoms 2010, 183). Torr's brother Donald died of AIDS in 1992, the same year that her close friend Charles Barber died of AIDS, and in the same few years that most of the people listed in Monique Jenkinson's artist statement as inspirations died too: Jack Smith, Leigh Bowery, more than half of the dancers in Les Ballets Trockadero. Torr felt shattered by those years, and Jenkinson is retrospectively haunted by them.

Every year on World AIDS Day, Torr performs as her brother Donald, "in remembrance of his inspirational life" (Torr and Bottoms 2010, 183). Her favorite way to do this is to reenact a memory she has of his teenage years, when he used to lip-synch to Dusty Springfield songs accompanied by a "very particular" version of her kinetic style:

> She had a gesture, for example, which involved throwing her hands up in the air and then letting them float down, as if on a feather. Her moves were specific, so you could reproduce them quite accurately if you were as dedicated as Donald was to his idol. Because he didn't have the life experience that lay behind the gestures, his version was a weirdly exaggerated copy; it wasn't Dusty Springfield's gesture, it was Donald's adaptation of it (184).

Torr's tribute to her brother takes the form of faux drag because he seemed most himself when he was being Dusty Springfield, especially in terms of movement quality. "Donald doing Dusty" had a style that was marked by Donald's unique bodily capacity but still managed "to capture a certain dramatic, dignified quality in the way she moved" (184). And Torr's performance of Donald doing Dusty is a rechoreographing of the trauma of his death, a way of reimagining him as he was for her when he was most real, alive and dancing—so she performs him like that, fabulously alive and dancing, "in a spirit of joy and affirmation" (183). Through a drag performance of a drag performance, Torr reembodies her brother and works toward healing her own ragged sense of grief. "Performing as a loved one is a way to confront loss that is much more positive and creative, it seems to me, than just sitting and mourning," she observes (183). By performing her brother as she remembered him, Torr found, she could transform the meaning of death for herself, and eventually for the many other women who participated in the drag tribute of "Brother for a Day." Being your brother for a day—a brother you have lost but whose memory is always alive in you—is one very specific way of utilizing drag as autobiography. "I would give up a day of being myself, Diane Torr, in order to embody the memory" of Donald or Charles, Torr writes feelingly (182). There is an almost overwhelming generosity in this act, an emptying out of your autobiographical self to make space for the biography of someone else.

A kinetic narrative of a life, done through drag, makes the 'bio' of both 'biography' and 'biology' mean differently.[22] What is biotic about the self— its materiality, its kinetic and haptic potential, and also its livability—can be given over temporarily to a self that is no longer in possession of its own life. Biotic embodiment is categorized not by an ontology of gender or sexuality but by the kind of living and moving it can sustain. Seen from this perspective, drag puts biotic potential at the service of biographic narrative, bypassing some of the alleged 'biological truths' of gender binaries and the finality that divides life from death. For deeply autobiographical endeavors such as grieving and honoring—acts of affective labor in which the self pays tribute to someone who has shaped its selfhood—drag offers a space in the body. The self gives over its materiality and kinetic capacity to someone it has lost, temporarily renouncing its right to self-representation in order to transmit an embodied biography that would otherwise disappear. Abdicating interiority, evacuating selfhood, this mode of mourning recenters the live body around the dead; in performing the biographic as if it were the autobiographic, it enacts a 'faux real' bio-narrative.

This biochoreography, as Torr's "Brother for a Day" performances might be called, takes gesture as a primary mode of doing selfhood. Through the process of dancing in drag as Donald, Torr rearticulates the ontology of her brother's selfhood *as kinetic*, and thereby identifies a mode of transmission that can activate and animate its essence. "For if choreography knows something," André Lepecki declares, "it is that an archive does not store: it acts" (2010, 38). If drag autobiochoreography offers the possibility of reimagining traumas of the body as the bases for new dances, drag biochoreography can be a way of grieving that is not only about acknowledging loss—not "just sitting and mourning," as Torr says—but also about drawing together the processes of 'making a piece on yourself' and 'having a piece set on you' until you can dance someone else as intimately as you would dance yourself. Like autobiochoreography, then, drag biochoreography draws on a collective intimacy to initiate healing, rather than on the "truthful revelation of a singular inner and private self" that traditional autobiography presupposes (Albright 1997, 120).

Both biochoreography and autobiochoreography conceive of bodies as permeable and interdependent, as capacious but marked, as tactical and almost infinitely layered. In drag forms of bio-narrative, bodies might be seen, in Deleuzian terms, as "an arrangement of coexistent, tiered, mobile planes, a 'disparateness' within an original depth" (1994, 51). Laurence Senelick notes that complex drag can be "multi-planar: it layers and interfoliates the different signs of gender to destabilize categorical perceptions of male or female. Watching such a figure in action is like looking through a stacked set of photographic plates or film-frames through which a multiplicity of images is superimposed on the eye" (2000, 11). Watching Diane Torr doing Donald doing Dusty is like watching the transposition of a unique and beloved essence, a singular prized choreography, as it is moved between bodies *and within those bodies*, sliding between planes of selfhood. To set biochoreography on your body is to see your body as a space of collage: always unfinished, always contingent, something built up and patched over with other bodies.

In treating her body as a biotic archive, as a theater that can house the performance of her brother being most himself, Torr gives us a sense of how drag fits into Diana Taylor's concept of "repertoire" as "embodied memory" (2003, 20). The etymology of "repertoire," Taylor notes, encompasses both "treasury" and "to find out": it both conserves and discovers. In the alteration of biographical gestures as they pass between bodies, a self is actively kept in memory but also fitted into a new self, fastened into a new body: "the repertoire both keeps and transforms choreographies of meaning," in Taylor's words.[23] Rehearsing someone else's biography as though it were autobiographical allows the drag "Brother for a Day" to feel again, *in herself*, the particular and beloved details of someone she has cherished, and to transform them into her own bodily repertoire. Each year, the "Brother" re-performs the movement phrases she has rehearsed as an active form of mourning; each year, then, instead of fading into vagueness, the memory of the body she has lost grows more deeply into her own body.

The final number in *Faux Real* is melancholy and melodic, lip-synched to Rufus Wainwright's "Poses." Languid and doleful, Jenkinson barely moves at all; as Mica swiftly and expertly wraps and unwraps her from a series of magazine-collaged costumes, she tilts her head like a starlet with a paper stole twined over one arm, accepts a papier-mâché beach ball and then throws it down sulkily, has a cigarette lit and placed between the fingers of one outstretched hand, and buries her hands in a fringed paper muff while shivering in a paper bikini. Rainbow confetti blows about her like snow; fall leaves twirl down to her collaged platform shoes while Wainwright sings of "green autumnal parks," where "all these poses, such beautiful poses / make any boy feel as pretty as princes," reminiscing about being "drunk and wearing flip-flops on Fifth Avenue" until he is "no longer boyish." As the seasons pass onstage in a whirlwind that evokes Busby

Berkeley's "Pettin' in the Park" from *Gold Diggers of 1933*, Jenkinson preens and postures, letting time fall all around her. At the end of the song, Wainwright croons "all these poses . . . made me a man," and then concludes "but who cares what that is?"

While Jenkinson alludes again here to the question of what 'makes me a man,' she is also using this sequence to pay tribute to someone she loves and very nearly lost. In the last scene in which she speaks directly to the audience, she summarizes "what I've learned from this tribe who has welcomed me as one of their own. That the moment is precious"—a nod to Precious Moments, who held her up one night onstage during "Shanti/ Ashtangi"—and "that when life is glamourless, just add more!," a reference to other members of her drag tribe, Glamamore and Juanita MORE! In other words, this song is for her whole drag family, whom she calls "these survivors among whom I am so honored to walk." But it is especially for Juanita MORE!, who survived three bouts with stage four Hodgkin's lymphoma (Soehnlein 2013). Juanita was born as a queen in 1991, after spending one part of the 1980s volunteering for hospice in the Castro ("'I'd go there to cook breakfast, but no one was eating. Everyone was dying'") and another part of the '80s frequenting Boy Bar in the East Village (Soehnlein 2013). "The inside of Juanita's drag closet is collaged with magazines, and this was a tribute to Juanita, to honor her," Jenkinson explains (2013). Of all of the work she's made, "Poses" is one of Jenkinson's favorites; it exemplifies the beliefs with which she ends *Faux Real*.

The first of these—"Whatever the moment throws at us, we are to meet it with guts and glamour"—has a rich backstage history, as Jenkinson relates:

> One of my drag mentors, Juanita MORE!, was joyously back after battling cancer, and the show theme was "Guts and Glamour." And she said, "I want everyone to wear this makeup—everyone has to wear the same face." It was from a Galliano Dior show in 2003, inspired by the Cockettes. Juanita, being Juanita, sent us all a packet: a picture of the model, the cut-out eyebrows, the size eyelashes we needed, this great big beauty mark. A bunch of the other queens were like, "She's such a fucking control freak!" And I was like, "I love that Juanita has a vision!" (2013)

The Cockettes are plundered by the fashion industry; Juanita MORE! salvages performance elements and returns them to a new generation of drag queens, meanwhile plastering the inside of her closet with a history that fashion itself quickly forgets. A cyclical, seasonal temporality of performance keeps a "face" in repertoire as it emerges from radical queer drag, is recycled by fashion, and then literally incorporated by a drag queen choreographing for her community. "Guts and glamour" itself suggests an autobiographical reading of Juanita's body: on the inside, the visceral stuff of the body, with all its terrible mortality, but also its courage and determination; on the outside, the enchantment of drag selfhood, the ethos of confronting tragedy with "just add more!"

Jeanne Vaccaro, writing about queer craft and texture, hypothesizes that "the politics of the handmade is a way to explore alternate modes of identity production, and to resist institutional and institutionally sanctioned gender formation" (2010, 254).[24] This model of homemade, erratically textured aesthetics as "politics" is at work in Jenkinson's homage to Juanita MORE![25] "Paper tears," Jenkinson explains; "it's stiff and noisy, it does not move with the body, it begins to disintegrate with the sweat of performance" (Sigourney and Jenkinson 2013).[26] In this fragile autobiographical endeavor somewhere between text and textile, Jenkinson notes, "the homemade-ness applies to the family structures" as well as the costumes: drag kinship is a form of queer craft (2013). In layering her body with the materials that line Juanita's closet, Jenkinson is collaging their histories together, acknowledging that their bodies are bound by kinship, by repertoire, and by a shared "vision" that encompasses the Cockettes and Galliano. If Juanita carries within her all of the shards of people she knew who died in hospice in the Castro in 1983, and all of the madcap cabaret creatures who pranced through Boy Bar in 1987, Jenkinson seems to say, this repertoire will not be lost. She will layer it into her body in *Faux Real*, just as she was willing to paste on the cutout eyebrows and gargantuan beauty mark Juanita sent her in the mail for "Guts and Glamour." And if Juanita were not, by a grim slip of fate, now one of "those survivors," as Jenkinson says, "among whom I am so honored to walk," *Faux Real* would keep her in repertoire, as best it could, the way Diane Torr keeps her brother: alive, and dancing.

Autobiography, in drag, is never only about one self. The most intimate acts of selfhood—grieving the dead, developing an identity, loving a family, acknowledging a shared history, desiring and being desired, belonging to a community—are things that we do in concert. Torr and Jenkinson show us how the biochoreography of others is layered into the autobiochoreography of the self, deepening and reshaping its repertoire; in these drag dances of memory and mourning, there is agency but never autonomy.

Figure 22. Monique Jenkinson (Fauxnique) in her collage costume during "Poses," at the end of *Faux Real*. Photo by Arturo Cosenza, courtesy of Monique Jenkinson and Marc Kate.

"One's life is always in some sense in the hands of others," Butler writes. "Even when I extend my own hand, it is as one who has been handled and sustained that I may offer something sustaining" (2011b, 386). When Jenkinson allows herself to be clad and disrobed, handled and equipped, given things and then dispossessed of them, over the course of "Poses," she is performing this process literally: she puts herself in the hands of others, in the last scene of *Faux Real*, because she is already bearing others inside of her.

## The Afterlives of Drag Queens

One night at the Stud, the club was nearly solid with bodies, overhung by a miasma of sweat, vodka, and music so loud it rippled in the air. The hostess was fierce, the bartenders were pouring hand over fist to keep up, and the crowd kept surging forward and pressing up against the tiny stage—except one, Jenkinson says to the audience, yanking the pink ribbons of her pointe shoes off her ankles with a sudden snap, just this one guy

> who was kind of not with us. Right in front of the stage, but kind of with his back to the show. And he was yapping and yelling (over the music at the Stud, which is a bit of a feat). And so I watched him ignore the hostess's number, and I was peeved. I got onstage and began my bit. And there he was yakking and yakking right up against the stage but ignoring the show.

She plucks the black rhinestone tiara from her hair with one brisk, barely controlled gesture. Her red silk dressing gown seems to flame of its own accord in the dimness of the stage. The only other light in the theater comes from the round bulbs of her mirror, casting dark shadows from her lashes that blot out the blue of her pearlized eye shadow. Her eyebrows are painted at drag height, brash and righteous.

> And I thought: "You're free. You're not at the opera house. When you come to a nightclub you're free to come and stand against the stage with your back to it and talk over the performance. Well, with freedom comes possibility. Something could . . . something could happen."

Jenkinson pauses mid-powder, brush upraised, eyebrows raised unto vertiginous disbelief. All at once it looks like she might cry, or throw something, or smash her makeup mirror. Then she gets ahold of herself. She believes in peace, she assures us, really she does. It's an important part of her spiritual practice. She would never *do* anything.

But with her dancer's precision, she could position herself exactly at the lip of the stage at exactly the right moment to just . . . *remind* him of the nature of live performance. Live performance, like live experience, is unpredictable. It's full of biotic potential. And that means that it's also always teetering on the verge of loss, of mortality, of being forgotten, of an empty seat next to your dad where Juanita MORE! should have been. Or an empty spot in the circle where Precious Moments should have been holding up her side of the platform while you balanced on your hands, carefully keeping the spikes of your heels to one side of Presh's head. What would you do?

She kicked him in the face.

"I just grazed his forehead!" she reassures us right away. "Just to keep him on his toes." And when he started shrieking and yelping and holding his nose piteously in both hands, "I just kept dancing. Oh girl, please! Do you know what some of these people have gone through to drag their asses onstage and perform for you? *Do you?*" she demands, her voice rising. Her eyebrows are at their full and furious height, and she enunciates each word distinctly in her rage. "*Do you think people threw bricks at the Stonewall so you could come here and ignore their daughters and granddaughters?*"

This is the dramatically kinesthetic version of a question posed by David Eng, Jack Halberstam, and José Muñoz in 2005: "What's queer about queer studies now?" When some people who might be identified as queer—in this case, mostly affluent white gay cis men in cities like San Francisco—no longer perceive themselves as belonging to a political history of queer bodies, it is a problem of temporality as well as ethics. We are brutally not post-racial; we have not gotten past homophobia, misogyny, femmephobia, transphobia, and patriarchy; and now, even more urgently than in 2005, the fact that "queer liberalism comes at a historical moment of extreme right-wing nationalist politics should give us immediate pause" (11). The perception that a history is distant, or pertains only to distant others, is what allows someone to turn their back on a stage of drag queens. But what's queer about queer studies now is that drag queens at the Stud, like the boys of the Lex, remember why people threw bricks at Stonewall. From Fauxnique to the Sisters of Perpetual Indulgence, from Drag Queen

Story Hour to the #MyNameIs campaign, and from *Stilettos for Shanghai* for Chechnya at the Castro to the 'drag bloc' glitter squads organized by Juanita MORE! to protest white supremacists gathering at Crissy Field, the San Francisco drag community is summoning an activist history and translating it for the twenty-first century.[27]

In an article about trans policy, Paisley Currah and Dean Spade recount the history of how "people who identified as drag queens" were crucial to "the initial incendiary moments of gay liberation" (2008, 1). Despite the valuable activism of these drag queens, Currah and Spade relate, mainstream gay and lesbian groups soon "aimed to distance themselves from cultural images of drag queens, transsexuals, and other gender outsiders so they could articulate an emerging vision of gay and lesbian Americans seeking a set of law and policy reforms focused on same-sex partnerships and eliminating sexual orientation discrimination" (1). Among the "gender outsiders" excluded from the steady march toward gay respectability were Sylvia Rivera and Marsha P. Johnson, two self-identified drag queens who cofounded STAR (Street Transvestite Action Revolutionaries) in 1970 and spent their lives fighting for the rights of people in their queer and trans communities, especially street youth, homeless people, people of color, and sex workers.[28] Sylvia Rivera, a working-class Latina queen whose fierceness was legendary[29]—when someone threw a Molotov cocktail at the Stonewall, she screamed, "Freedom! We're free at last!"—was finally recognized, toward the end of her life, as a trans icon (Gossett 2012).[30]

But in the middle of Rivera's life, which was messy and sometimes despairing, she took pride in the political implications of her drag: "I like to dress up and pretend, and let the world think about what I am," she said (Duberman 1993, 125). There is no more frivolous formulation for drag than "dress up and pretend," but Rivera took it to be a self-expressive practice of gender that was part of her activism as well as her identity.[31] Drag was deliberately provocative and thought-provoking, a rejection of pathologies and an affirmation of playfulness, a retort to all of those people who wanted to tell her just what she was and why that was wrong: let the *world* think about what I am! The drag daughters and granddaughters of the people who fought at Stonewall—and before that, at Compton's Cafeteria in San Francisco—are a testament to the fact that Sylvia Rivera and Marsha P. Johnson were not simply misguided or antiquated when they called themselves "drag queens." Rather, they were recognizing a potential that inheres in drag: a politics of calling out the assumptions of knowing and being that are brought to bear on gender expression.

To turn your back on a stage of drag queens, then, is to disavow the very people whose vision and activism has made LGBTQI life more possible. It is to assert that your life is inviolably separate, nonchalantly ahistorical, and untouched by the lives of others. But Monique Jenkinson tells the story of that guy at the Stud precisely because *Faux Real* demands that we rethink our sense of safety from the charges of unrealness that can be leveled at other people: people in drag, people on stage, people who ask to be called by names or pronouns that are not on their birth certificates. It asks that we consider the *relationality* of realness—how we are implicated, and how we are responsible, and how close we are to the histories that have shaped our bodies, names, spaces, families, and dances. And although the ethics of drag dance don't generally condone kicking people in the face, they do entail connecting with other bodies in the room: lost bodies, desired bodies, familiar bodies, ghostly bodies, queer bodies, and bodies that have forgotten that they, too, are subject to the politics of embodiment.

To be faux real is to be willing to undertake, in public, the process of assuming a body that people generally assume you should already have. It is to acknowledge, as Gayle Salamon says, that the "body is always *subtended by its history*" (2010, 78), that it bears the marks of those hideous powder-blue leotards as well as the discipline instilled by years of dancing. But to be faux real is also to envision a queer utopian future in which a faux queen is not called out for being 'not a real drag queen' or too much a 'real girl,' and—someday—in which transphobic violence cannot claim recourse to any "epistemological certainty" of gender, and homophobia cannot shelter under a rhetoric of 'natural' acts (1). "To be real, in this sense, is to hold one's own self open to the possibilities of what one *cannot* know or anticipate in advance," Salamon concludes. "It is to be situated at materiality's threshold of possibility rather than caught within a materiality that is at its core constricted, constrictive, and determining" (92). At this threshold, the biotic body is open to what lies at its limits: the dead and their repertoires, biography beyond biology, jammed choreographies of gender, genealogies of gesture.

In *Faux Real* autobiochoreography is a collaged and collective process, an account of selfhood staged through "multiple fictive things," as Miguel Gutierrez put it. Like Trajal Harrell's projects of "fictional archiving," *Faux Real* incorporates histories that might be deemed unworthy, impossible, disposable, scattered, past, foreign, false, unreal. In the practice of opening their bodies to embodied histories that are markedly different from their own, these artists do not merely *cross* gender; they expand its repertoire. Their dances are not travesties; they are not mockeries of women; they are not fantasies of icy autonomous veridicality. Instead, these drag dances illuminate what it is like when bodies do not stop at their borders or insist on their exclusive selfhood—when kinship is a haunted sociality of moving bodies, rather than an authorized genealogy of 'pure lines.' It is not merely from camp affection that drag dancers cherish things on the verge of disappearing: this is a generous and even tender way of imagining embodiment. They are performing what it would be like if we were all necessarily inhabited by others, if selfhood were not something we could do alone.

# Notes

## Introduction

1. This framework for seeing gender as a coded bodily action—the idea that genders are more like acts that we perform and less like something we 'are' or even 'have'—was most fully developed in Butler's *Gender Trouble* (1990), which drew on the "performative speech-acts" theorized by the linguist J. L. Austin in his 1962 book *How to Do Things with Words* (edited by J. O. Urmson and Marina Sbisà [Cambridge: Harvard University Press]). Dance scholars have long recognized the potential of Butler's work; for example, Gay Morris, in "Styles of the Flesh: Gender in the Dances of Mark Morris" (1996), insightfully adapted Butler's framework for movement analysis, while Susan Foster set out to reclaim Butler's theory of bodily action and gendered performance for dance studies in her article "Choreographies of Gender" (1998). Other examples of dance scholarship drawing on Butler's work include David Gere's "29 Effeminate Gestures: Choreographer Joe Goode and the Heroism of Effeminacy" (2001); Jonathan Bollen's "Queer Kinesthesia: Performativity on the Dance Floor" (2001); Susan Foster's "Walking and Other Choreographic Tactics: Danced Inventions of Theatricality and Performativity" (2002); Ramsay Burt's "Performing Unmarked Masculinity" (2009); Carrie Noland's *Agency and Embodiment: Performing Gestures/Producing Culture* (2009); Thomas DeFrantz's "Switch: Queer Social Dance, Political Leadership, and Black Popular Culture" (2017b); and Clare Croft's introduction to *Queer Dance: Meanings and Makings* (2017).

2. As Jane C. Desmond observes in her introduction to *Dancing Desires: Choreographing Sexualities On and Off the Stage*, "The 'swish' of a male wrist or the strong strides of a female can, in certain contexts and for certain viewers, be kinesthetic 'speech-acts' that declare antinormative sexuality" (2001, 6).

3. The history of the Women's One World Café Theater has been chronicled by Kate Davy in *Lady Dicks and Lesbian Brothers: Staging the Unimaginable at the WOW Café Theatre* (Ann Arbor: University of Michigan Press, 2010); and in *Memories of the Revolution: The First Ten Years of the WOW Café Theater*, edited

by Holly Hughes, Carmelita Tropicana, and Jill Dolan (Ann Arbor: University of Michigan Press, 2015). See also Jill Dolan, *The Feminist Spectator as Critic* (Ann Arbor: University of Michigan Press, 1991), and Sara Warner, *Acts of Gaiety: LGBT Performance and the Politics of Pleasure* (Ann Arbor: University of Michigan Press, 2012).

4. For example, see Jill Dolan's 1985 article "Gender Impersonation Onstage: Destroying or Maintaining the Mirror of Gender Roles?" (*Women and Performance* 2, no. 2: 5–11), and Alisa Solomon's 1993 essay "It's Never Too Late to Switch: Crossing toward Power," in the anthology *Crossing the Stage*, edited by Lesley Ferris (London: Routledge, 144–54). More generally, see Sue-Ellen Case, *Feminism and Theatre* (New York: Routledge, 1988), and the edited anthology *Performing Feminisms* (Baltimore: Johns Hopkins University Press, 1990); Elin Diamond, *Unmaking Mimesis* (New York: Routledge, 1997); Jill Dolan, *Feminist Spectator as Critic* (Ann Arbor: University of Michigan Press, 1991) and *Presence and Desire: Essays on Gender, Sexuality, Performance* (Ann Arbor: University of Michigan Press, 1993); and Carol Martin, ed., *On and Beyond the Stage: A Sourcebook of Feminist Theatre and Performance* (New York: Routledge, 1996). In *Performance and Cultural Politics*, Elin Diamond observes, "When performativity materializes as performance in that risky and dangerous negotiation between a doing (a reiteration of norms) and a thing done (discursive conventions that frame our interpretations), between somebody's body and the conventions of embodiment, we have access to cultural meanings and critique" (1996, 5).

5. Foster, following Michel de Certeau, identifies a political potential for dance as a "tactic," explaining that if we understand "theater as strategy and theatricality as a possible tactic," we will realize that "resistive action . . . can only be formulated while in motion" (2002, 131). Although Foster laments that "there is little room for the body to move" in Judith Butler's framework of gender performativity (2002, 137), Ramsay Burt posits that "Foster's account of the process of learning a dance style and Butler's account of the social construction of embodied experience both therefore locate the body in an intermediary position between the individual and society" (2009, 151).

6. This piece premiered at the Joyce Theater in New York and was subsequently presented in places like Chicago's Harold Washington Library Auditorium and Philadelphia's Annenberg Center.

7. Avery Gordon writes of historical trauma, especially racial oppression, as a spectral presence that refuses to relinquish its hold on contemporary cultural life: there is an ethics to this kind of ghostliness. "To be haunted," Gordon states, "is to be tied to historical and social effects" (2008, 190). Performance studies scholars Joseph Roach (1996) and Diana Taylor (2003) have explored how live performance

can express this necessary haunting of the present by its pasts. As Taylor writes, a "transitive notion of embodied memory" is crucial to remembering what might not be preserved by fixed, official archives; through performance, a charged moment of "repertoire" transmitted through staged bodies, "forms handed down from the past are experienced as present" (191, 24).

8. This phrase is indebted to the "Bring Your Own Body: Transgender between Archives and Aesthetics" exhibition, curated by Jeanne Vaccaro with Stamatina Gregory in fall 2016 at Cooper Union, New York. I am differentiating here between *feeling* wrong-bodied (i.e., claiming the right to alter or reinterpret your own body so that it better fits you) and being *judged* as wrong-bodied (i.e., being prohibited from spaces or opportunities because your body does not fit a normative category). In her book *Assuming a Body: Transgender and the Rhetorics of Materiality*, Gayle Salamon notes that the former experience—in which "the body of which one has a 'felt sense' is not necessarily contiguous with the physical body as it is perceived from the outside"—is shared by trans and cisgender people (2010, 14).

9. The website for the National Center for Transgender Equality reports that anti-trans bills have been proposed in more than twenty states.

10. Books on drag in this vein include Roger Baker's *Drag: A History of Female Impersonation in the Performing Arts* (New York: New York University Press, 1994)—which includes sections titled "Squalling Cats," "Enter Pursued by Laughter," and "All Legs and Limelight"—and James Hicks's coffee-table book *Drag Dolls, Dames, and Divas* (Drag Dolls Publishing, 2014). From another direction, drag has been attacked by feminist critics as misogynist caricature and yet another "weapon" of patriarchy, as Erika Munk wrote in the *Village Voice*, calling "most men in drag . . . no more subversive than whites in blackface" (1985, 89). Munk's argument was taken up by lawyer and journalist Kelly Kleiman in 2000, in an article titled, "Drag = Blackface" (*Chicago-Kent Law Review* 75, no. 3: 669–86). Sociologist Steven P. Schacht, coeditor of *The Drag Queen Anthology: The Absolutely Fabulous but Flawlessly Customary World of Female Impersonators* (New York: Routledge, 2004) and author of several articles on drag, continues to assert that what drag queens "are really paying homage to is male superiority, however men might choose to express it" (2002, 167).

11. Analyzing choreographer Trajal Harrell's use of Harlem ball culture alongside postmodern dance, Moore explains that "in black queer spaces, *werk!* is as much a compliment of a job well done as it is the labor of transgressive, interdisciplinary creative forms" (2014, 20). I follow Moore's definition—laid out in his dissertation, "Fierce: Performance, Creativity and the Theory of the Fabulous Class"—of *werk* as "the creative labor of fierceness," which revises Marxist ideas of alienation in favor of the possibility of "reclaimed labor because of both its proximity to the body and

to one's own creativity and sense of expression" (2012b, 77). Notably, Moore characterizes the work of embodied queer performance as "a labor not of distance but of closeness, a labor not as a loss of the self but as the seizing of selfness" (179).

12. Similarly, Judith Butler has emphasized how bodily action functions as bodily activism, identifying the theoretical work that is done by "forms of gender that break with mechanical patterns of repetition, deviating from, resignifying, and sometimes quite emphatically breaking those citational chains of gender normativity, making room for new forms of gendered life" (2014).

13. The "devaluation of performance in Western intellectual traditions," performance scholar E. Patrick Johnson notes pointedly, "coincides with the devaluation of black people" (2003, 7). Thomas DeFrantz traces queer-of-color "creative aesthetic social dissent" back to voguing, which he sees as a vital form of "physically enlightened gestural life" (2017b, 478–79). See also David Román's critique of "antitheatrical biases that trivialize the performing arts and their audiences" (2005, 16), and Diana Taylor's call to revalorize performance as necessary to the project of decolonizing scholarship (2003).

14. This kind of "undoing" is not a destruction of gender, but rather what Salamon calls "a disruption of its taken-for-granted signifying practices" (2014, 19).

15. Following this logic, Ramsay Burt applies Butler's framework to dance history in *The Male Dancer*. "If the traditions and conventions, through which gender is represented in dance, are a set of corporeal styles that have sedimented over time," Burt posits, then logically "it is possible to correlate changing ideas about the nature of gendered bodies with ideas about theatre dance" (2007, 17).

16. As dance scholar Ann Daly suggested in 1989, "Dance is an ideal laboratory for the study of gender, because its essential medium—the body—is where sex and gender are said to originate; it is where the discourses of the 'natural' and the 'cultural' thrash it out" (23). And Muñoz, who wasn't strictly a dance scholar, saw queer dance as "utterly necessary" to queer politics (2009, 81). "Queer dance, after the live act, does not just expire," he wrote; its moves enter into "vast storehouses of queer history and futurity."

17. Muñoz also connects the special materiality of ephemera (which he sees as a queer form of evidence) to Raymond Williams's insight in *Marxism and Literature* (Oxford: Oxford University Press, 1977) that "structures of feeling" are especially relevant for the arts. "For Williams, a structure of feeling is a *process* of relating the continuity of social formations within a work of art," Muñoz explains (2008, 10). For dance—whose ephemerality has long been debated—we could see social structures as a residue, materializing both within present bodies as they dance (and witness dance), and in the lingering effects of a dance after the bodies have gone.

18. Jack Halberstam notes wryly, "I know at least three people who like to claim

that *they*, and they alone, coined the name 'drag king,'" citing Esther Newton's testimony of a "'drag king' competition" she had witnessed in Chicago in the late 1960s to show that drag kings were not only a phenomenon of the 1990s (Halberstam 1998, 233, 301).

19. The line of thinking set up in *Reading Dancing*, the title of a 1986 book by Susan Foster (Berkeley: University of California Press), which was carried on by scholars like Sally Ann Ness—"I am assuming," Ness begins, that "the gesture of dancing was a kind of *linguistic* or quasi-linguistic mark-making" (2008, 1)—and Carrie Noland (2009), is still going strong, as evinced by Henrietta Bannerman's 2014 article "Is Dance a Language? Movement, Meaning, and Communication" (*Dance Research* 32, no. 1: 65–80). Of course, dance scholars who explore the idea of dance as being like language are also deeply invested in the body's agency and materiality. It is Foster who coins the term "bodily theorics" (1995, 8) and who recognizes the "tactical" potential of moving bodies (2002), while Carrie Noland identifies the capacity for a "gestural performative," a way of moving with agency that is informed by kinesthesia (2009, 190). When we "shift our imagination away from thinking that dance is inscrutable," Sima Belmar points out, we see how dancers demonstrate their "agency-in-movement" within the constraints of choreography and cultural conventions (2015, xi).

20. Undoubtedly, this consciousness is racialized as well as gendered; Marlon Bailey finds that "because the black body is read through and within a visual epistemology in which race, gender, and sexual hierarchies are corporeal, Ballroom members refashion themselves by manipulating their embodiments and performances" with heightened self-awareness (2013, 57).

21. This idea is indebted to Judith Butler's formulation of embodied relational politics in *Precarious Life*: "Loss and vulnerability seem to follow from our being socially constituted bodies, attached to others," she writes (2004b, 20). "Perhaps mourning has to do with agreeing to undergo a transformation . . . the full result of which one cannot know in advance" (21).

22. As Laurence Senelick notes, stripping acts as a reassuringly "emblematic" moment when a performer, "purporting to reveal his or her essential" nature, shows the naked "real" body under the drag artifice, much as "the revelation of the female breast was a climatic plot device in baroque drama" (2000, 494). It is for this reason, as Marjorie Garber details, "that bed scenes occur so frequently as moments of discovery" for "'truths' about gender and sexuality in cross-dressing narratives" (1992, 202). In *Female Masculinity* Jack Halberstam describes the category of "femme pretender" who often deliberately "blows her cover by exposing her breasts or ripping off her suit" (1998, 249).

23. Both Harrell and Miguel Gutierrez, another choreographer making queer

dance-based performance work, have been presented at American Realness, a dance festival founded in 2010 by Gutierrez's manager/producer, Ben Pryor, in collaboration with Abrons Arts Center. Pryor traces the festival's title to the history of drag balls but notes that it also alludes to the very real lack of funding for American performing artists.

24. In *Cities of the Dead* Joseph Roach proposes that "audiences may come to regard the performer as an eccentric but meticulous curator of cultural memory, a medium for speaking with the dead" (1996, 78). In the case of Richard Move's drag performance of Martha Graham, for example, David Román writes of "Archival Drag; or, the Afterlife of Performance" (2005), André Lepecki analyzes "The Body as Archive: Will to Re-Enact and the Afterlives of Dances" (2010), and Victoria Thoms devotes a chapter of her book *Martha Graham: Gender and the Haunting of a Dance Pioneer* (2013) to "Ways of Speaking with the Dead: Graham and Queer Resurrection."

25. A parallel might be drawn with the queer-of-color critique of passing that C. Riley Snorton undertakes as a transman in black social spaces (2009). Rejecting the charges of 'failure' or 'deceit' in passing, Snorton argues that the frequent "productive misrecognition" of his gender is actually "transforming the scripts of gendered embodiment" (88–89). In calling for more work on "the interstitial relationships among articulation (we are who we say we are), performance (we are what we do), and practice (we are routinized bodily actions)," Snorton sets up a useful framework for analyzing drag dances as more than illusions, parodies, appropriations, or tropes of the 'wrong' body (79).

26. Ballet scholar Carrie Gaiser Casey notes that Balanchine choreographed his own *Ballet of the Elephants* (1942), which was meant to feature "'fifty elephants and fifty beautiful girls'" (2009, 121). Arguably, this conceit for a dance was doing less to burnish the shining history of ballet than Jones and Zane's choreography for the Ailey company, but, Casey reports, the Balanchine Foundation went right on to hail *Ballet of the Elephants* as an "'original choreographic tour de force.'" "It seems vital," Casey writes in her feminist critique of Balanchine's inviolable status, "to illuminate the structures of thought and historical habits by which one choreographer's silliness renders him irrelevant and another's merely demonstrates his range."

27. For histories of drag in clubs and on theatrical stages, a reader might begin with Esther Newton's seminal ethnography, *Mother Camp: Female Impersonators in America* (1972), or with Laurence Senelick's monumental overview, *The Changing Room: Sex, Drag, and Theatre* (2000). Other important accounts of drag history include Marjorie Garber's *Vested Interests: Cross-Dressing and Cultural Anxiety* (1992), Jack Halberstam's *Female Masculinity* (1998), Del LaGrace Volcano and Jack Halberstam's *The Drag King Book* (1999), José Muñoz's *Disidentification:*

*Queers of Color and the Performance of Politics* (Minneapolis: University of Minnesota Press, 1999), Carole-Anne Tyler's *Female Impersonators* (New York: Routledge, 2003), Leila Rupp and Verta Taylor's *Drag Queens at the 801 Cabaret* (Chicago: University of Chicago Press, 2003), Diane Torr and Stephen Bottoms's *Sex, Drag, and Male Roles: Investigating Gender as Performance* (2010), and Maite Escudero-Alías's *Long Live the King: A Genealogy of Performative Genders* (Newcastle-upon-Tyne: Cambridge Scholars Publishing, 2009). Anthologies addressing drag history include *Crossing the Stage: Controversies on Cross-Dressing* (London: Routledge, 1993), edited by Lesley Ferris; *The Drag Queen Anthology: The Absolutely Fabulous but Flawlessly Customary World of Female Impersonators* (2004), edited by Steven P. Schacht and Lisa Underwood (Binghampton: The Haworth Press, 2004); *The Drag King Anthology* (New York: Harrington Park Press, 2003), edited by Donna Jean Troka, Kathleen LeBesco, and Jean Bobby Noble; *Camp: Queer Aesthetics and the Performing Subject: A Reader* (Ann Arbor: University of Michigan Press, 1999), edited by Fabio Cleto; and *Queer Dance: Meanings and Makings*, edited by Clare Croft (2017). In the last decade or so, critical intersectional work has been done on race and class in drag; see, for example, Ragan Rhyne's 2004 article "Racializing White Drag" (*Journal of Homosexuality* 46, no. 3–4: 181–94); Jana Evans Braziel's "Dréd's Drag Kinging of Race, Sex, and the Queering of the American Racial Machine-Désirante" (2005); Naomi Bragin's 2014 article "Techniques of Black Male Re/Dress: Corporeal Drag and Kinesthetic Politics in the Rebirth of Waacking/Punkin'" (*Women and Performance* 24, no. 1: 61–78); and Kareem Khubchandani's 2016 article "Snakes on the Dance Floor: Bollywood, Gesture, and Gender" (*Velvet Light Trap* 77: 69–85). There are also dissertations on drag from intersectional perspectives; for example, Loran Renee Marsan's "Critical Crossings: Intersections of Passing and Drag in Popular Culture" (2012, UCLA), and Katie Horowitz's "The Trouble with 'Queerness': Drag and the Making of Two Cultures" (2012, UC Berkeley).

28. In December 2015, at 80WSE Gallery in New York City, Vaginal Davis did stage what she described as an adaptation of *The Magic Flute* as "living sculpture," in collaboration with the German group CHEAP Kollectiv (Davis and Sachsse 2015).

29. There are drag Marthas performed by John Kelly, who also appeared with the Trockadero Gloxinia Ballet Company as Dagmar Onassova (god-daughter to Rrose Sélavy), Mark Dendy (who used to dance with Jane Comfort and Company and whose first drag persona, Sandy Sheets, was developed under the guidance of Andre Shoals), and Roy Fialkow (a former Trockadero dancer who choreographed a Graham-esque piece called *Lamentations of Jane Eyre* for the company in 1984).

30. After it premiered in Tokyo, this piece toured extensively and came to the Joyce Theater in New York in November 1985.

Chapter One

1. Purcell's *Dido and Aeneas* (1689) recounts the tragic romance between Dido, Queen of Carthage, and Aeneas, who sails into Carthage and then leaves her to found Rome; Purcell's version features an evil Sorceress who orchestrates the plot. In addition to the Barbara Sweete film version (1995), I have watched video footage of a performance in Brussels (1989), the Mark Morris Dance Group (MMDG) twenty-fifth anniversary season at the Brooklyn Academy of Music (BAM) in New York City (2006), and a 2015 performance at the Irvine Barclay Theatre. (My thanks go to the New York Public Library's Jerome Robbins collection, to the BAM archives, and to Jenefer Johnson at UC Berkeley.) I also attended two live performances at Cal Performances (one in 2000, the last time that Mark Morris danced the lead, and the other in 2011, with Amber Star Merkens as Dido/Sorceress). Currently, Laurel Lynch dances both female lead roles, partnered by Domingo Estrada Jr. as Aeneas. For the libretto, see http://markmorrisdancegroup. org/the-dance-group/works/2016-17-season/dido-and-aeneas. A number of dance and opera scholars as well as journalists have written about this ballet; a reader could begin with Joan Acocella's lively and affectionate biography (1993), with Gay Morris's insightful "Styles of the Flesh: Gender in the Dances of Mark Morris" (1996), or with Stephanie Jordan's recent book of "choreo-musical analysis," *Mark Morris: Musician-Choreographer* (2015), which includes archival clips hosted on the MMDG website. Other useful sources include a dissertation by Hwan Jung Jae (2012, Temple University) and a number of articles focused on *Dido and Aeneas* (e.g. Carol Martin 1999, Sophia Preston 2000, Stephanie Jordan 2011, and Duerden and Rowell 2013). Lynn Garafola's "Mark Morris and the Feminine Mystique" (in her 2005 book, *Legacies of Twentieth-Century Dance* [Middletown, CT: Wesleyan University Press, 205–209]) and a section of Ramsay Burt's *The Male Dancer: Bodies, Spectacle, Sexualities* (2nd ed., 2007), like Gay Morris's piece, take up questions of gender in Mark Morris's choreography.

2. In general, as Randy Martin writes, "dance is unlike language," because "movement lacks the discrete equivalents of sound-images that words provide" (1995, 109). However, Martin notes, certain dance forms that employ an established vocabulary of gestures and movement phrases—Indian *kathak*, mime sections in nineteenth-century story ballets, Ghanaian dancing, Balinese classical dance, etc.— can be interpreted reliably by audiences who are literate in their conventions. *Dido and Aeneas* goes beyond these forms: as Sophia Preston (1998; 2000) and Stephanie Jordan (2011; 2015) have demonstrated, Morris's *Dido and Aeneas* displays an "almost semaphoric matching of gesture for word" (Preston 2014, 25). In fact, its "dance words" are so tightly bound to the text that a disjunction between the two

can convey the nuances of irony, foreshadowing, metonymy, or analogy (Jordan 2015, 229). When the gesture for "love" is used to illustrate the word "hate" by the evil Sorceress, for example, its ironic effect depends on the audience having already learned the first meaning of the gesture. Dance scholarship has commonly turned to linguistic analysis in treating *Dido*; Ellen W. Goellner and Jacqueline Shea Murphy recognize "Morris's verbal movement punning" (1995, 2), and Mark Franko analyzes how "lexicons and syntaxes" in *Dido* relate both to citations of gender and to quotations of "baroque and modernist vocabularies" of movement (2006, 7). Morris himself explains, "Whenever you hear that word and you see that action you learn it that way, and you identify it," laying out his pedagogical vision for this piece (Jae 2012, 186). Similarly, in tracing the history of "mimomania" in opera, Mary Ann Smart reports that Johann Jakob Engel's treatise *Ideen zu einer Mimik* (1783) made an early argument that "if the 'language' of gesture is to be understood, it needs to be just as formalized as any verbal language" (2004, 13). In classical ballet, Susan Foster observes, mime traditionally operates in staccato bursts of narrative, halting the technical and aesthetic pleasures of the dance while it does the work of communication (1996, 8). In *Dido and Aeneas*, by contrast, the whole dance is imbued with signifying gestures, creating a continuous kinetic narrative. In *Dido* "the gestures are exactly—much to some people's dismay—*exactly* what the text is doing," Morris emphasized in an interview with his biographer Joan Acocella (2009). In her dissertation, Jae points out that Morris may be exaggerating, since there are probably fewer than 100 gesture words, while there are 1,555 words in the libretto (2012, 188).

3. Acocella explains how this gesture illuminates the nuances of its referent: "The gesture has so much fateful poetry of its own—the long, outward stretch of the arms (fate controls the whole world), the raising of the arms (fate is directed by heaven), the muscular tension in the shoulders (fate is powerful), the spidery splay of the fingers (fate is terrible, or will be for Dido)—that the body can carry the weight of that meaning without our having to hear the word" (1993, 143). Jordan points out that the fingers thereby form a shape "like a mudra" (2011, 179), and Preston asserts that this gesture is a meta-reference to the narrative technique of Indian classical dance: "Morris almost certainly does *not* include the 'lotus' hand position as a reference to the flower," she writes, "but instead for its association with a dance form that has such potential as a story-telling vehicle" (1998, 10).

4. For a table of gestures and their various uses in *Dido*, see Duerden and Rowell (2013, 150–52) and Preston (2000, 348). An early list of "iconic or symbolic movements" keyed to words was compiled by Preston (1998, 9); in 2011 Jordan added several terms, noting, for example, that "desire" is linked kinetically to "fire/flame" (213). The choreographic lexicon of *Dido and Aeneas* subscribes to a 'melting pot'

idea of inclusiveness, straining to speak to everyone who might be in its audience. Various scholars and critics have cataloged the sources for its movement vocabulary: Acocella pointed out the use of American Sign Language and the "beautiful hand-languages of Indian and Indonesian dance" (1993, 143); Gay Morris saw quotations from Nijinsky's risqué, hieratic ballet *L'Après midi d'un faune* (1996, 148). Anna Kisselgoff observed "hornpipe dances" and a "modern-dance sensibility" (1989). Carol Martin picked out, among other things, references to Martha Graham's *Lamentation*, Mary Wigman's seminal German Expressionist solo *Witch Dance*, the *mudras* (hand gestures) and *abhinaya* (mime acting) of classical Indian dances, the dichotomy of Odette/Odile from Marius Petipa's *Swan Lake*, and the choreography used in the film version of *The Sound of Music* to accompany the song "I am sixteen going on seventeen" (1999). Noting that the "vamp free-hip and -shoulder style of the Sorceress was based partly on the Cruella De Vil villainess of Disney's *101 Dalmations*," Jordan concluded, "Morris's movement vocabulary is pan-cultural and trans-historical, both in terms of gesture and larger body movement" (2011, 174).

5. For a cultural analysis of AIDS and theater, see David Román's *Acts of Intervention: Performance, Gay Culture, and AIDS* (1998); both Gere and Román draw on *AIDS: Cultural Analysis/Cultural Activism* (Cambridge: MIT Press, 1987), edited by Douglas Crimp. In an article titled "Remembering AIDS" that questions practices of memorializing and disappearance, Román singles out "gay male culture in the late 1980s and early 1990s, the years when AIDS fatalities and new infections were rising at alarming rates" as the moment "when AIDS activism was at its most visible and effective" (2006, 238).

6. In fact, costumes for all male and female dancers in *Dido* are the same— simple, long, black, unisex sleeveless tunics or sarongs that fall to mid-calf, referencing the chitons worn by both genders in ancient Greece and also, Morris added, the look of early Martha Graham pieces and Indonesian dance (Jae 2012, 56)—and the whole cast wears red lipstick, small gold hoop earrings, and red fingernail polish. The sole exception is the role of the hero Aeneas, which is danced bare-chested. In addition, Aeneas wears black nail polish (and no lipstick), while Dido's nails are painted gold. For the premiere, Morris persuaded everyone to go on "fierce diets," as Jordan reports, and to dye their hair jet-black, which they reprised for the film version (2011, 173–74).

7. It's not an accident that gendered style is at the forefront of these gestural descriptions of identity. Western concert dance has traditionally been a place where these gendered binaries are reinforced onstage; it was easy for Morris to find a gesture for a "fair" woman, for example, because he could derive it from the classical ballet mime for a "beautiful" female character (Duerden and Rowell 2013,

148). This codification of how the bodies of female dancers should signify, most pronounced in ballet but present in other dance forms as well, narrows the range of dancers in terms of morphology, race, age, and ability. In the wings, suspicions about "the trouble with the male dancer" (Burt 2007) have historically led to a policing of gender boundaries, bound up with homophobia, effeminophobia, and choreophobia (Fisher and Shay 2009).

8. Acocella proposes that his "big male body gives [Dido] the quality of monumentality that is so essential to her pathos" (1993, 101). She argues that because Morris doesn't attempt to perfect his representation of femininity when he plays Dido, "the violation of sexual identity depersonalizes the portrait, just as masks presumably did in Attic tragedy." It's true that Morris draws himself up to a full and imperious height when he dances the role, and he uses the squared bulk of his shoulders to mark off an untouchable space, a royal presence. The imposing effect of Morris's size and masculine body is felt most fully at the moment when Dido confronts Aeneas, ablaze in a righteous rage at the knowledge that Aeneas has chosen to leave her and set sail for Italy. As the line "For 'tis enough, what e'er you now decree / That you had once a thought of leaving me" is sung, Dido towers over Aeneas, menacing him with her sheer physical mass. However, the effect of producing Dido's queenliness through Morris's decidedly masculine body is not exactly one of "depersonalization." Rather than striving for androgyny or mask-like neutrality, Morris cultivates a state in which he can stack gender markers on his body.

9. Gay Morris, following Butler's early work on drag and performative "styles" of the body, states that Mark Morris's choreography demonstrates how "dance (which can incorporate drag) offers far more subtle and wide-ranging possibilities for attacking rigid gender categories than does drag alone" (1996, 142). Addressing how gender performativity overlaps with performative speech-acts in this ballet, Ramsay Burt writes, "In [J. L.] Austin's terms, one could say that Morris's performance of femininity was not used seriously, but in ways parasitic upon its normal use" (2007, 40). Burt sees Morris as staging failed or "infelicitous" speech-acts, an approach that makes room for "parasitic" acts of theatrical gender performance.

10. For example, dance critic Alastair Macaulay writes in a review from 2000, "His Dido and her court move in two dimensions, like antique bas-reliefs. The style is ancient, Eastern, tragic, and noble. His Sorceress and her retinue are three-dimensional, modern. Their style is Western, funny, rude" (816).

11. In their choreomusical and Labanotation-based analysis of this scene, Duerden and Rowell find the gesture accompanying "torment" to be especially significant, describing how Dido's "deeply melting" way of "softly placing her hands in front of her" adds meaning to the musical appoggiatura (2013, 148). Gender style, then, is an important factor in their conclusion that "Dido's precise articulation of a

minor detail in the music seems to embody something of her inescapable tragedy."

12. As David Gere writes of Joe Goode's *29 Effeminate Gestures* (1987), which begins with a list of ways a man might appear to be effeminately "too much," it is possible that a dancer does "not 'cross-dress' but rather 'cross-gestures'" (2001, 375–76). In *29 Subversive Gestures* (2012), Shyamala Moorty and Cynthia Ling Lee respond to Goode's piece (and to Butler and Gere's scholarship) by interrogating "ethno-cultural nationalism" and idealized femininity in *kathak abhinaya*; they turn the "too much" in the direction of 'not enough,' highlighting tactics of "queer failure" and layered embodiment (Chatterjee and Lee 2017, 51, 53).

13. For an account of musical parallelism (and counterpoint) in this scene, see Rachael Riggs-Leyva, "Reading Music, Gesture, and Dualism in Mark Morris' *Dido and Aeneas.*" "It is fitting," she concludes, "and slightly humorous, that they climax on a phrase-ending chord" (2013, 402).

14. Nijinsky choreographed *Faune* so that the dancers' bodies were always posed in two-dimensional space, moving in flattened and angular lines that imparted a sense of anachronistic, almost hieroglyphic poses. Bronislava Nijinska described how Nijinsky insisted on a "bas-relief form" in which dancers would "align their bodies so as to keep their feet, arms, hips, shoulders, and heads in the same choreographic form inspired by archaic Greece" (1981, 405). Dido's hieratic movements, therefore, also claim a heritage in Nijinsky's Greek-inspired piece. On the surface this citation reads as archaic, noble, and classicizing, but for those who are attuned to the connotations, as Gay Morris observes (1996, 130), it also links Dido's sexuality to that of Nijinsky's notorious Faun. For a discussion of *Faune*'s flatness as a mode of distinguishing between composition and choreographer, see Hanna Järvinen's 2009 article "Dancing without Space—On Nijinsky's *L'Après-midi d'un Faune* (1912)" (*Dance Research* 27, no. 1: 28–64).

15. This led Shawn to a project titled *An American Ballet* (1926)—in which he intended to appear as the virile white "Messiah" and "the flame of Liberty's Torch" who would guide the jazz-addled masses—and to a problematic identity as the "Father of American Dance" (Scolieri 2013). Whereas Shawn was suspiciously emphatic about the heterosexual manliness of his choreography and dancers, Morris made *Dido and Aeneas* a shining example of his artistic capacity to dance two opposing female lead roles. Between the Sorceress's camp hyperbole and Dido's insistence on the bodily nature of her sorrow—epitomized by the spread-legged "press'd with torment" gesture—the ballet runs the gamut of gestural codes for femininity and effeminacy.

16. Classicist Froma I. Zeitlin characterized Pentheus as an emblem of cross-dressing and femininity in Greek theater generally (1985, 63–94). Laurence Senelick notes, however, that although "the destruction of Pentheus was a popular motif

in Greek art . . . the scene of his transformation into a man in drag" was not often represented (2000, 43). Kirk Ormand, another classicist, cautions against an anachronistic tendency to read Pentheus's effeminacy as indicating homosexuality—some forms of pederasty were normative in classical Athens—and emphasizes that "social shaming" happens because Pentheus becomes a passive, emotionally suggestible figure instead of the strong masculine ruler he had once been (2003, 13). Seen from this perspective, Pentheus's tragedy has the same structure as Dido's dilemma: femininity and embodiment are seen as posing a problem for rational, decisive, self-possessed leadership.

17. Writing on "Dido's Otherness," Susan Foster notes that Tate and Purcell's Dido is as shrewd as she is amorous, since she is at least partly motivated by the "strong and hence fortuitous political alliance" she could make with Aeneas (2007, 126). By comparison, Foster finds, Jean Georges Noverre's 1766 *ballet d'action* version of *Dido and Aeneas* (which did not use Purcell's score) presents an exoticized and helplessly enamored Dido, conflating her body with her realm only in order to "feminize Carthage . . . [and] make it available for subsequent colonization" (125).

18. In Purcell's opera, the codes for Dido—her substantial, poignant arias, for example—indicate that our sympathies should lie with the tragically betrayed queen. "Purcell compounds the elevation of Dido as the focus of the tragedy," Duerden and Rowell elaborate, both "in the weight that he gives to her arias and their placement within the opera: at the beginning and at the end" (2013, 156).

19. Camp is a contested terrain. Following Susan Sontag's famous "Notes on 'Camp'" (1964), it has often been defined in terms of an appreciation of "style." In this vein, for example, Ramsay Burt describes camp as "a metropolitan, gay, subcultural style that assumes a common appreciation of the value of artifice and subversion, or surface rather than depth" (2007, 169). In *Mother Camp* (1979), an ethnography of mid-'60s urban club drag queens in the United States, Esther Newton characterized the essential qualities of camp as "*incongruity, theatricality*, and *humor*" (106), associating it (as Sontag had done) with a gay male sensibility. In later writings—responding in part to Sue-Ellen Case's assertion that the "butch-femme couple" in performance could take up "the camp space of irony and wit" (1988/1989, 305)—Newton explored how lesbians might make use of camp and drag "to destabilize male monopolies" (1996, 165), an analysis extended by Jack Halberstam's *Female Masculinity* (1998). For an overview of histories and theories of camp, see *Camp: Queer Aesthetics and the Performing Subject: A Reader* (1999), edited by Fabio Cleto.

20. In Newton's example, a butch lesbian appears as a drag queen to win the Homecoming Queen Contest of Cherry Grove, in memory of "her *sister* Martin, who had died of AIDS two years before" (1996, 170). When "she *became* Martin" by

putting on his gown and inhabiting his form of drag, she takes up a mode of queer mourning that affirms non-genealogical kinships (189).

21. Jordan explains that the witches' "overt 'mickey-mousing'" may well be Morris's own "little stylistic self-mockery" (2015, 248), since critics tend to harp on his matching of music and movement, which can, as Acocella says wryly, sometimes come "very close to that of 'I'm a Little Teapot'" (1993, 142).

22. Duerden and Rowell observe that this scene is "the only time the dance breaks quite free of the musical rhythms," emphasizing this as an example of how "Morris uses the potential of dance-music relationships to deepen the complexity of meaning in the choreography" (2013, 147). Another aspect of this relationship, Jordan points out, is that the audience hears all of the smashing of bodies and crashing to the floor, entailing that "gross fleshly spillage projects itself between us and the music" (2011, 194).

23. I owe this formulation and many other insights to Sima Belmar, whose feedback on this chapter has been invaluable to me.

24. Preston affirms this understanding and emphasizes that it is both gestural and musical: "It is only at the end of the dance that we can understand the subtleties of the beginning, just as, in Purcell's music, the tonality of Dido's death is pre-echoed time and again in earlier sections. The resulting almost cyclical structure that is engendered in the audience's understanding of the work, taking them back to the beginning each time they see and hear the end, leads to a feeling of inevitability in the unfolding of the tragedy" (2000, 12).

25. One of the significant differences between the film version and live performances, as Stephanie Jordan notes, is that the moment of Dido's death is visible in the film from the perspective of an overhead camera but obscured in live performance by dancers placed upstage (2011, 176). "No one's ever seen it happen!" Mark Morris crowed in one interview. "It's like Santa Claus!" (Morris and Acocella 2009).

26. "A walk can be a dangerous thing," Judith Butler remarked, reflecting upon the murder of a young man in Maine who walked with "a distinct swish" (Butler and Taylor 2009, 205). In Gayle Salamon's essay "Passing Period" (2015), the justification given for the murder of gender-nonconforming teenager Leticia King by one of her classmates is the perception of gendered gestures done 'wrong'—a swishy walk, a dramatic way of entering a space, the act of applying lip gloss. In fact, Salamon makes clear, it is the *visibility* of "gender transgression" and "violating gender roles," made manifest through gesture and posture, that sparked a phobic hatred into physical violence (201–202).

27. Acocella also cites the influence of "unisex group works" by Laura Dean and Lucinda Childs (1993, 104). Although in traditional Balkan dancing there are some separate "women's dances" and "men's dances," it is also worth noting that in parts

of Serbia, Croatia, and Bulgaria, many of the folk dances include both men and women (Leibman 1992, 126). Furthermore, in groups like Koleda—whose members had a "great range of sexual habits" and valued tolerance, utopian collectivity, and the occasional slivovitz-fueled all-nighter—no one was excluded from the dancing because of their sexuality or gender identity (Acocella 1993, 31). In a chapter of *Dancing across Borders* on "Kolomania: Balkan Dance as American Expression," Anthony Shay affirms Acocella's assessment of "the intensity of this community feeling" in Koleda as typical of American Balkan dance groups, emphasizing people's attraction to the ensemble (over solo or couples' dances like belly dance or tango), as a way "to obtain the warmth they thought characterized village life" (2008, 121, 119).

28. A good example of this is the casting history of the role of the lead sailor. As Acocella notes, first "Teri Weksler, the tiny 'paper cup,' was given the role of the lead sailor in *Dido and Aeneas*, a role full of big, heavy hops and big, squatty *pliés*, a role, in other words, that called for size and weight" (1993, 80–81.) Besides Teri Weksler, who originated the role, the lead sailor was also performed by Kraig Paterson, a tall, thin, male dancer, who went on to originate the high-camp drag role of the maid in Morris's *Hard Nut* (1991)—and to dance it inimitably for the next twenty-five years—by "fashion[ing] her after Naomi Campbell," as he recalled (Acocella 2016, 19). In the early 2000s, the lead sailor role was given to Lauren Grant, the "smallest, earthiest member of the company," as Marcia B. Siegel described her (2008). A small, solid woman who looks even smaller and more solid in the heavy pliés, Grant can be seen in the 2006 BAM performance blustering about in a big cocky swagger, wiping her nose with her arm. By the time she was performing in 2011 at Cal Performances in Berkeley, Grant was making a conspicuous gesture of scratching her balls.

29. When asked on the occasion of the company's thirtieth anniversary what he *does* particularly notice about his current dancers, Mark Morris said, "Watching them dance in London recently, I realized that you can't knock them over" (Ulrich 2010, 28). He seems impressed above all by the collective weightedness of their bodies rather than by their virtuosity—or by any gendered qualities they might possess, such as delicate grace or vigorous command of space.

30. "My company is an eighth the size of New York City Ballet, and twice the age of those dancers," Morris boasts, but MMDG dancers "menstruate, they don't have stress fractures, they read books . . . they're not kept like veal" (2003, 242).

31. Gay Morris links this "role reversal" to other works by Morris, including *New Love Song Waltzes* (1982), in which "a man carries a woman tenderly onto the stage in his arms, and then a man carries another man in exactly the same fashion" (1996, 130).

Chapter Two

1. The subtitle of *Blood Memory* is "An Autobiography," but most scholars are skeptical of its status in the genre. As Victoria Thoms points out, the coherence of the book founders as Graham "struggles to represent the autobiographical significance of the embodied performance yet is haunted by the inability to fully articulate in writing its significance for her" (2008, 3). Following feminist theories of life-writing, Thoms sees Graham's fifty years of choreographing "a strong and determined female character" as an attempt to evade this inadequate, flat, danceless genre of written autobiography, proposing instead that we understand "Graham's danced oeuvre as an alternative form of autobiography" (4). Earlier scholars such as Marian Horosko and Lynn Garafola had also raised concerns about the authorship of *Blood Memory*; Garafola judged it "cobbled together by hands other than the author's" (Garafola 1993, 167). Victoria Phillips's archival research has turned up evidence to support this: a manuscript given to Doubleday, for example, bore the inscription (from Graham's companion Ron Protas to editor Jacqueline Kennedy Onassis), "'JACKIE THIS IS A MIXTURE OF MARTHA AND ME TALKING'" (2013, 63).

2. There are conflicting reports of Graham's age at her retirement, compounded by her habit of lying about her age and the fact that she resisted the finality of leaving the stage. Agnes de Mille reports in her biography that Graham last performed in 1968, and this is corroborated by longtime Graham dancer Bertram Ross, who dates Graham's last appearances onstage to *Time of Snow* and *Lady of the House of Sleep* in 1968 (Franko 2012, 13) However, Arlene Croce, writing in 1991, gives the year of Graham's retirement as 1969 (2000, 677), as does Mark Franko's recent in-depth study of the relationship between her biography and choreography (2012, 3); *Blood Memory* states that Graham's last performance was in *Cortege of Eagles* (1967) in 1970.

3. I am grateful to Victoria Thoms both for her insightful analysis and for her helpful comments on an early draft of this chapter.

4. The role was Jocasta in *Night Journey* (stage premiere 1947, film 1961).

5. As Henrietta Bannerman points out, Graham did create a few ballets with comic aspects, perhaps most notably *Every Soul Is a Circus*, *Acrobats of God*, and *Maple Leaf Rag* (Bannerman 2003). However, not one of these dances is straightforwardly humorous; for example, dancer Ethel Winter reveals that the comic aspect of *Acrobats of God* is somewhat of an accident, as it "wasn't going to be such a comedy when Martha started choreographing it. We were told the first night not to play it for laughs. But it started to come off that way, and Martha went with it, so everyone went with it" (Horosko 2002, 119).

6. "She didn't double-cast her roles and share them with young women . . . until her sixties," dance critic Arlene Croce noted, "or parcel out the bulk of her personal repertory until her seventies" (2000, 676).

7. "From at least 1935 onwards," Victoria Thoms notes, "with Graham's burgeoning interest in Jungian psychology, the phrase 'blood memory' was a key touchstone in Graham's dance philosophy: the idea of a transhistorical bodily inheritance" (Thoms 2008, 6). Mark Franko adds that psychoanalysts Otto Rank and Erich Fromm were "equally, if not more, influential" on Graham than Jung (2012, 11).

8. I am not suggesting that Graham's writings do not reveal important facets of her choreography and philosophy; for example, see Mark Franko's examination of the written "geno-choreography" that undergirds Graham's danced "pheno-choreography" (2012). My point is that Graham understood her autobiography as an inadequate portrayal of her life, spirit, and dancing. We see this illustrated in Victoria Phillips's reconstruction of Graham's fragmentary, poetic verbal musings on "blood memory," which "*Blood Memory* sanitized—or did not include" (2013, 71).

9. Dance scholar Helen Thomas, who called "the history of western theatre dance . . . a history of lost dances," was joining a chorus of critics and theorists who worried that dance was dangerously evanescent (Thomas 2003, 121). "Dance exists at a perpetual vanishing point," dance critic Marcia Siegel wrote in 1968; in 1993 performance studies scholar Peggy Phelan declared that, since "performance's only life is in the present," it followed ontologically that "performance's being . . . becomes itself through disappearance" (Siegel 1968, 1; Phelan 1993, 146). By 2004, dance theorist André Lepecki observed, dance studies as a field tended to define its subject "as that which continuously plunges into pastness—even as the dance presents itself to visibility," capturing the simultaneous dread of impending loss and the fascination with the flickering present (2004, 4).

10. The *New York Times* cites "the average retirement age for dancers to be just short of 34," based on a Teachers College report from 2004 (Aguirre 2007.) Alex Dube, director of Career Transitions for Dancers, states even more pessimistically, "An average dancer career ends at 29 years of age or can end much earlier with a debilitating injury or illness" (Orellana 2007). Nancy Upper estimates in *Ballet Dancers in Career Transition: Sixteen Success Stories* (2004) that a professional dancer's career lasts ten to fifteen years.

11. Graham's grandiose, transhistorical claims to "blood memory" contrast sharply with Alvin Ailey's use of the same term, highlighting the way that whiteness allowed Graham to universalize her perspective. When Ailey describes the role of "blood memory" in his work, as Thomas DeFrantz explains in *Dancing Revelations:*

*Alvin Ailey's Embodiment of African American Culture*, he means the bloodiest, most traumatic memories of the antiblack violence of his childhood in southeast Texas, including lynching and rape (2004, 27).

12. Bertram Ross, Graham's dance partner for many years, wrote an unpublished biography of Graham in which he characterized her as "the great image maker. She makes an image to fit, to suit the particular situation and time" (Phillips 2013, 65).

13. Sally Ness evokes this idea when she writes, "The dancer's body can be seen to form the 'host material,' a living tissue for dance's gestural inscriptions. Its anatomy provides the 'sites' or 'places' where gesture can leave its mark in the rendering of a 'final form'—that is in a structure that bears an enduring and permanent signifying character" (2008, 1). While I appreciate Ness's vision of the dancer's body as a ghostly organism that invites gestures, the idea of an "enduring and permanent" mark seems to foreclose the evolution of corporeal signification.

14. When Jackie 60 moved from Nell's to 432 W. Fourteenth Street in March 1991, "we didn't even miss a week," Valenti notes. "Mother's End" was the last party at Mother, which closed after costs had tripled in the span of four years (Valenti 2016).

15. The inaugural drag artist at the Pyramid Club had been John Kelly (Lawrence 2016, 258); as Dagmar Onassis, "the love child of Maria Callas and Aristotle Onassis," Kelly went on not only to dance with the Original Trockadero Gloxinia—Russianizing her name to Dagmar Onassova for the occasion—but also to sing at Carnegie Hall (Kelly 2001, 45, 25).

16. According to Christopher Reardon, who interviewed Move for his 2001 article in the *Village Voice*, that "someone" doing Nijinsky was Robert LaFosse, former New York City Ballet principal dancer and choreographer; the "someone else" doing Ruth St. Denis was Maxine Sherman, a former lead dancer with Alvin Ailey and Martha Graham.

17. This prologue serves two distinct but equally postmodern purposes: on the one hand, it evokes the pastiche aesthetic of the show. Images flash by as we see "Martha, in her waning years, going through the motions of *Acrobats of God*" interspersed with clips of Groucho Marx doing the Lindy Hop, Barbara Stanwyck starring in the noir film *The Strange Love of Martha Ivers*, and Jerry Lewis pretending he's Carmen Miranda (Perron 2000). On the other hand, for the many people in the audience who couldn't pick Martha Graham out of a police lineup (or, as a recent advertisement by Americans for the Arts warns, think she is a "Snack Cracker"), the video actually identifies the original so that they can recognize the impersonation.

18. In 2011 Richard Move explored this moment more explicitly, creating a piece at Dance Theater Workshop called *Martha @ . . . The 1963 Interview*, in which he appears as Martha, conversing with the dance critic Walter Terry (played by

the playwright Lisa Kron in drag), at the 92$^{nd}$ Street Y. Describing his interest in performing Martha at sixty-nine, Move explained, "Martha's about to die her first death. . . . It is the next year or two where the feet and hands start to be crippled. Within the next year Sontag uses her as one of her examples of camp. And by 1965 or so critics were basically saying, 'Get her off the stage'" (Kourlas 2011).

19.  A 1998 *New York Times* article on Move opens with the following line: "Despite forensic evidence, the modern-dance pioneer Martha Graham did not die in 1991. . . . Oh, she also grew 16 inches and is often mistaken for a soft-spoken, witty man named Richard Move" (Harris 1998). Similarly, a *New York Times* review from 2004 begins, "Richard Move plays Martha Graham big. At 6-foot-4, he is at least a foot taller than the diminutive Graham (and his mountainous bun adds even more inches)" (Kourlas 2004b). Deborah Jowitt recalled fondly that when *Martha @* played Town Hall, on a respectably-size dance stage on W. Forty-Third Street, "the cramped little dive where the series originated had a certain je ne sais quoi, but it was nice to see our cabaret hostess, a soft-voiced, soignée six-foot-five Martha Graham (Move), in a space where her imposing chignon doesn't practically brush the ceiling" (Jowitt 2001).

20.  Like the show of stripping to some anatomical "token of authenticity" (Senelick 2000, 495), "when the wig is doffed, ceremonially, at the end of a transvestic stage performance . . . the 'answer' . . . is disclosed" (Garber 1992, 389).

21.  As I discuss in the chapter on Les Ballets Trockadero, the function of body hair for the company has a different logic, inherited from Charles Ludlam's stage aesthetics.

22.  Richard Move has gone on to channel other female performing artists; in 2011, reflecting on his interest in Ana Mendieta (the subject of his 2009 film, *Bloodwork*, and an exhibition he curated at New York University in 2010, culminating in a symposium called "Where Is Ana Mendieta?—25 Years Later"), he wrote, "My metakinetic response grew increasingly more powerful and evoked a corporal and spectral presence. . . . I persistently felt from her a sense of what I may best describe as haunting, which became further intensified through an alarming, yet intuitively supportive series of synchronicities" (2011, 167–68).

23.  This idea is explored in André Lepecki's *Exhausting Dance*, whose last chapter is subtitled "to be done with the vanishing point." Arguing for a "political ontology of choreography," Lepecki proposes that a melancholic attachment to the past can be part of an antiracist and queer effort "with generative potential" (2006, 128).

24.  It was perhaps inevitable that the Graham company lawyers, immune to the charms of Move's drag veneration of Martha, would send him a hand-delivered cease-and-desist order. Retorting hotly that he "had every right to impersonate a public figure like her," Move replaced the publicity photo of her with one of his own

and printed a little disclaimer on his flyers (Reardon 2001). As it turned out, the short-lived scandal was a good advertisement for the show, and, as the company had its own serious internal problems with the rights to Martha's legacy, *Martha @ Mother* was left to its own devices, which suited Richard Move perfectly.

25.  My argument here is indebted to Judith's Butler's "'Remarks on Queer Bonds,'" especially to her call to "return to a reflection on embodied life" as a way of understanding "this way of being bound up with one another, of being implicated in each other's lives, a mode of interdependency that is hardly chosen and never precisely easy" (2011b, 384). In thinking about drag dance as an ethics of the inhabited body, I am partly responding to Butler's question "Can responsibility be thought on the basis of this socially ecstatic structure of the body?"

26.  On that *Martha @* night in 1998, the audience at Mother would see work by John Jasperse; there was also John Kelly 'doing' Pina Bausch, in a long pink satin gown, by throwing himself whackingly into the wall stage left. Moreover, alongside the serious contemporary dance and the satirical impersonation, Robert Tracy, the author of *Goddess: Martha Graham's Dancers Remember* (1996), gave a lecture, complete with slide show, on Graham's collaborations with Isamu Noguchi and Alexander Calder. This was dance history done live—a historiography of pearlescent eye shadow and risky lifts, not just videotapes and print clippings. In 2001 *Martha @ Town Hall* featured performances by Bill Shannon, Meredith Monk, and Mark Morris (in a world premiere called *From Old Seville*), as well as Richard Move dancing as Graham in *Phaedra*, *Mary's Episode*, and *Lament* (Lamentation). When Move wasn't dancing or ceding the stage to other choreographers, he read aloud from *Blood Memory* while dancer Deborah Goodman—who was on faculty at the Martha Graham School and served as Yuriko's assistant— gave a technique demonstration.

27.  For an analysis of this case in terms of race, gender, and copyright law, see Anthea Kraut's incisive chapter, "Copyright and the Death/Life of the Choreographer," in *Choreographing Copyright: Race, Gender, and Intellectual Property Rights in American Dance* (2015). Marian Horosko recounts the drama surrounding this bizarre legal situation from a dancer's perspective: "Ron Protas, a long-time 'friend' (as designated in Graham's 1989 will), former photographer, and her companion for twenty years, filed suit in Federal Court for the Southern District of New York, claiming that the school did not have the right to use the Graham name without obtaining a license from the Martha Graham Trust, which he directs" (2002, 178). Horosko (whose pedigree includes a debut with the Ballet Russe de Monte Carlo and subsequent stints with the Metropolitan Ballet and New York City Ballet) notes pointedly that although Protas was named as the principal beneficiary of the Graham estate, he has never danced. To summarize briefly: in 2000, nine

years after Martha Graham's death, Ronald Protas created the Martha Graham School and Dance Foundation, to which belonged (he claimed) the trademark and copyright of Martha Graham's name, technique, and ballets. In 2001 Protas filed a suit against the Martha Graham Center of Contemporary Dance and the Martha Graham School of Contemporary Dance, charging them with the infringement of those rights; the center and school promptly filed a countersuit that alleged Protas's mismanagement of Graham's legacy and claimed ownership of her work, technique, props, and costumes. In 2002 the center was awarded the rights to forty-five of Graham's dances (not all of which were deemed "reproducible," since some dances had been lost and some had entered public domain), while Protas owned seven works. Malcontent, Protas appealed in 2004, only to lose the rights to those seven dances as well; when he asked for a new trial in 2005, the court ruled this idea "meritless." It was not until July 11, 2006, that a third ruling—decidedly in favor of the rights of the school and the center to carry on Martha Graham's tradition, and with barely concealed irritation for Protas's many appeals—was issued, apparently providing a permanent resolution to the conflict. Leaving aside Protas's personal motives, Kraut points out the complexity of categorizing choreography as "work-for-hire": "the assertion of intellectual property rights in dance simultaneously rests on the notion of an inalienable right to one's personhood and enacts an alienation of artist from work by turning the artist into a subject of property and the work into an object of property" (2015, 261).

28. For Richard Move's own Deleuzian theorizing of the artistic process of listening, absorbing Graham's voice, and what he calls "becoming sound bodies" in *Martha @ . . . The 1963 Interview*," see Move 2018.

29. I am grateful to Richard Move and to Catherine Cabeen for sharing their artistry and theoretical insights with me. I first saw *Martha @* in 2007, in San Francisco, and have been fortunate since then to see more of Move's work, including live choreography—his piece *The Show (Achilles Heels)* (2002) was performed by the Martha Graham Dance Company at the Joyce in 2013—as well as footage of *Martha @* performances from 1998 and 2001.

30. In 2017, for example, Move celebrated the twentieth anniversary of *Martha @* by opening the New York Live Arts "Live Ideas" festival with two pieces—a new work about gender multiplicity called *XXYY* and a special performance of *Martha @*—featuring Crockett and Cabeen in both.

31. In *The Independent* Jenny Gilbert noted that "he's got the voice to a T," encouraging her readers to imagine its qualities for themselves: "think steely virago doing an ad for room fragrances" (2001). Wendy Perron of *Dance Magazine* described how, "in perfect mimicry of Graham, he . . . pulled back his lips in elegant disdain, and finished each sentence with a sensual guttural trail" (2001). "Move has

her throaty patrician inflection down pat," the dance critic Marcia B. Siegel concurred, reviewing for the *Boston Phoenix* (2003). In the *New York Times* William Harris praised the show's "cornucopia of Martha Graham anecdotes and pontifications, delivered by Mr. Move with deliciously exaggerated diction" (1998). The dance critic of the *San Diego Union Tribune*, sensing that the show was a kind of séance, stated her conviction that "Move absolutely nails it; close your eyes, and it's easy to imagine those slow, dreamy, carefully enunciated words coming from Graham's own mouth" (de Poyen 2005).

32. Mark Dendy, after a number of unsuccessful attempts to get into the main Graham company, went on to create his own drag version of Martha. In addition to occasional public performances impersonating Martha Graham in her diva mode (e.g., the 1996 Bessie Awards and a 1997 appearance at Jacob's Pillow), Dendy wrote and choreographed an evening-length piece, *Dream Analysis* (1998), in which he and Richard Move appeared as double Marthas (Bory 2008).

33. When Move moved to New York in 1989, he decided that he "didn't want to be one of those two-dimensional, cartoonlike men" in Graham's company, as he told dance journalist Joseph Carman, even if he appreciated the feminist point in making "the man the sex object—not the woman" (Carman 2000). As Arlene Croce noted, Move's perspective was shared by some of Graham's male dancers: "Paul Taylor, Graham's Theseus [in *Phaedra* (1962)], later wrote, 'Sometimes I think she views us men onstage as giant dildos'" (Croce 2000, 679).

34. See, for example, Jeffrey Henderson's 1991 article "Women and the Athenian Dramatic Festivals" (*Transactions of the American Philological Association* 121: 133–47) and Marilyn A. Katz's slightly ironic 1998 piece, "Did the Women of Classical Athens Attend the Theater in the Eighteenth Century?" (*Classical Philology* 93, no. 2: 105–124).

35. Sue-Ellen Case concludes her article on "Classic Drag: The Greek Creation of Female Parts" by proposing that contemporary performers retaliate in the same terms: "feminist practitioners and scholars may decide that such plays [e.g., *Medea*] do not belong in the canon" (1985, 327).

36. Henrietta Bannerman, a specialist in Graham technique, gives a specific example of Graham's gender reversal of the 'universal' body: "The contraction is housed in the pelvic area, which for Graham dancers, male and female alike, is the well-spring or core of physical energy" (2010, 41). Bannerman concludes, "For women this is the center of femaleness, and for Graham it was both the source of all genuine movement and bodily gesture."

37. As Ramsay Burt points out, Graham was particularly attached to the role of Jocasta, even allowing herself to be filmed while dancing it (1998, 34–53). In her close reading of *Night Journey* through the lens of Bourdieu, Gay Morris points out

that "in her previous use of Greek myth, Graham had abstracted the characters," whereas her choreography for Jocasta not only uses gesture more mimetically but also shifts "the focus of the Oedipus myth from man to woman" (2001, 74). Mark Franko called the process of choreographing and performing this role an "autobiographical rite" for Graham, a ritual of realizing that "a misguided belief in her own immortality" could no longer be sustained (2012, 125). Even though she was still a tremendously gifted dancer in the late 1940s—Robert Cohan remarked that when he joined the company in 1946, he took her to be in her thirties, misjudging her age by twenty years—she was keenly aware of the state of her body, reflexively subtracting fifteen years whenever someone inquired about her age (Tracy 1996, 147).

38. In the chapter of *Female Masculinity* titled "Drag Kings," for example, Jack Halberstam writes, "The history of public recognition of female masculinity is most frequently characterized by its stunning absences," an issue reflected in drag king cultures (1998, 231). If masculinities "present themselves in the register of the real, eschewing the performative and the artificial," then femininities are relegated to the additive, superficial, glittery realm of theatricality and excess (266).

39. Cabeen notes that Move was the first person ever to list her as an "Artist" in the program. "Richard's work is incredibly respectful of Martha Graham," she says, but at the same time, "I have always felt that I can dance at my full stature within it" (2016).

40. In the last scene of *Into the Void*, Klein is unbuttoned, unpinned, untucked, unbound, unpacked, and finally pressed, body to naked body, against a woman covered in his signature blue paint. Klein is embodied by Cabeen, who strips him down to her body and makes him bear, on her breasts and belly, the blue that marked his models. The male artist does not hover in lordly, aesthetic abstraction above the visceral life of his female subjects; the body that is at the universalized base of creative practice is a woman's body, 'dressed up' in the elaborate trappings of masculinity.

41. Moreover, the teachers Cabeen most admired happened to be gay black men: Peter London in Graham technique and then Bill T. Jones, whom she describes as "the idol I looked up to" and for whom she continues to set work as an official *repetiteur* and teaching artist (2016). In turn, Cabeen's role models rewarded her for the way she took up space, made eye contact, took speaking roles (including Jones's famous solo *Floating the Tongue*, from 1978), and partnered women with strength and confidence.

42. In 2007 the Martha Graham company commissioned Richard Move, along with two other choreographers, to make a piece for company repertoire in response to *Lamentation*. The "queer kinship" of Move's piece, *Bardo*, is discussed at length by Victoria Thoms (2013).

43. Mark Franko said that the piece conveyed "emotion only after reducing it

to formal design. . . . The choreographic material of *Lamentation* is the physical material of grief" (1995, 46). Julia L. Foulkes describes how "a solitary dancer sat on a bench enshrouded in a tubular costume that restricted the arms and legs and covered the head so that only the feet and face were visible. . . . This dance distilled one emotion—grief—into the strained, yearning movement of a confined body" (2002, 18). Helen McGehee, the dancer who taught Richard Move's first Graham technique class, describes the costume as "the dance itself" (Thoms 2013, 150). Russell Freedman, one of Graham's biographers, practically got into the costume and writhed around with Martha's ghost in his synopsis: "this mummylike figure began to rock with anguish from side to side, plunging her hands deep into the stretching fabric, writhing and twisting as if trying to break out of her shroud . . . and as her body moved, so did the stretch jersey of the costume she wore, folding in upon itself, forming frightening contours and shadows" (1998, 61).

44. Gay Morris notes that Graham's heavy makeup abstracted her face in a way that presaged her tragic Greek heroine years: "Her face is painted a dead white with cavernous dark eyes and red lips; her expression throughout the dance is mask-like" (2001, 72–73).

45. In 2006 Janet Eilber, the current director of the Graham company, made a controversial decision to invite Move to perform during the company's eightieth-anniversary season. Calling Move's participation "a flagrant sign that we want to add context" to Martha Graham's legacy, Eilber asked Move to perform both a spoken routine and a pas de deux with dancer Desmond Richardson during the evening (Kourlas 2006). It was upon the occasion of this invitation that Richard Move pointed out, "You know, the irony isn't lost on anyone, that my relationship with the official Graham enterprise began with cease-and-desist orders." Move's pas de deux, which Graham had choreographed in 1965 and which was very rarely performed by the company, was called *Part Real—Part Dream*.

46. Victoria Thoms writes feelingly of the way age "is the blind spot for a theoretical discipline [dance studies] that has done robust and superb work considering the dynamics of race, gender, and class," and suggests that dance scholars examine "the effects of 'age' as a performative identity" through the work of Judith Butler (2013, 122, 123). One response to this call is Nanako Nakajima and Gabriele Brandstetter's 2017 anthology, *The Aging Body in Dance: A Cross-Cultural Perspective* (New York: Routledge).

Chapter Three

1. Among Kazuo Ohno's teachers were modern dancer Ishii Baku (in 1933) and Wigman acolytes Eguchi Takaya and Miya Misako (in 1936); he was also impressed

by seeing Harald Kreutzberg (who studied with Wigman) dance in 1934 (Fraleigh and Nakamura 2006, 14).

2. Although they collaborated closely for many years, Hijikata was more interested in the dark, decaying, anarchic, self-excoriating, and perverse, while Ohno tended to be drawn to spirituality, the mysteries of life and death, and the natural world. See Hijikata's "Inner Material/Material" (2000); Nanako Kurihara's 2000 introduction to "Hijikata Tatsumi: The Words of Butoh" (*Drama Review* 44, no. 1: 12–28); Fraleigh and Nakamura's *Hijikata Tatsumi and Ohno Kazuo* (2006), Bruce Baird's *Hijikata Tatsumi and Butoh: Dancing in a Pool of Gray Grits* (New York: Palgrave Macmillan, 2011); and Miryam Sas's *Experimental Arts in Postwar Japan: Moments of Encounter, Engagement, and Imagined Return* (2011).

3. I am indebted to Megan Nicely for sharing her butoh knowledge and suggestions for this chapter, and grateful to Judy Halebsky for advice on an early version.

4. My thanks go to Elena Cervellati at the Università di Bologna for her help with research in the Archivio Kazuo Ohno, where I was able to view performance videos from 1977 and 1994, and to Yoko Shioya and Lara Mones of the Japan Society in New York, who granted me access to the September 2016 exhibition honoring the 110th anniversary of Kazuo Ohno's birth. This exhibition featured footage and ephemera from the Kazuo Ohno Archives, including costumes; the films *Portrait of Mr. O* (Chiaki Nagano, 1970), *Kazuo Ohno* (Daniel Schmid, 1995), and *Three Films for Kazuo Ohno's La Argentina* (Yasumasa Morimura, 2010); Takao Kawaguchi's "Body Sculpting" workshop; and Takao Kawaguchi's performance of *About Kazuo Ohno—Reliving the Butoh Diva's Masterpieces* (2013). Like Takao Kawaguchi, I have never seen Kazuo Ohno perform live.

5. Ninotchka Bennahum, author of *Antonia Mercé "La Argentina": Flamenco and the Spanish Avant Garde* (2000), concludes that, in her opinion, "Only in the dancing body, a body fully trained in musical, Spanish classical, and flamenco techniques, can the memory of La Argentina be brought to life onstage again" (178). Bennahum's book mentions Kazuo Ohno only in a footnote: "Perhaps Argentina's use of flamenco offered material to an Eastern ally of the dance, Kazhuo Ono. Ono, an ex-Kabuki actor, specializing in female roles, constructed his most famous persona in 1986 out of souvenir programs and press clippings given to him by Argentina's family" (225).

6. *Admiring La Argentina* "is Bergsonian in its conception," Mark Franko notes, because of the way that it "embeds memory within itself as a choreographic trope" (2011, 108,115). In *Matter and Memory* (1912), Henri Bergson explains memory as an active, haunting force—a territory that does not fully reveal its population to our consciousness: "when a memory reappears in consciousness, it produces on us the effect of a ghost whose mysterious apparition must be explained by special causes," Bergson writes. "In truth, the adherence of this memory to our present condition is

exactly comparable to the adherence of unperceived objects to those objects which we perceive" (2004, 186–87). Bergson's model of memory proposes that it is *the memory that moves into us*, not we who intentionally select and summon a memory at will. Furthermore, for Bergson, just as objects have shadowy, unperceived multitudes of other objects that cling to them, unseen, so do memories; when these memories arrive and announce their presence in our consciousness, they are faintly trailed by other translucent memories of the past.

7. "Even if I have danced perfectly," Ohno said, "I cannot repeat it. . . . For this reason I am always careful to give birth to new lives" (D'Orazi 2001, 133; translation mine).

8. Repetition involves sinking into layers of past time that undulate within the surface of a perceived present; Deleuze characterizes this as the "noumenal character" of the present, which entails "*the ever-increasing coexistence of levels of the past*" (1994, 83). Kazuo Ohno describes the past as an accretion in the present body: "A body can be understood as a memory of the universe, a memory that has accumulated over billions of years, and we wear this history of the universe" (D'Orazi 1997, 90; translation mine).

9. "I was in a terrible state," Ohno remembers, "because I hadn't neither the strength to reply nor the resolve to perform" (Ohno and Ohno 2004, 266). It is only when all of the bodies move together as *one*—when, in a subsequent vision, La Argentina resolves Ohno's anxiety by inviting him to move with her, saying, "'Ohno-san, I'm going to dance, so please let's dance together'"—that he has the strength to emerge from retirement. In *Fault Lines: Cultural Memory and Japanese Surrealism*, Sas argues that this "foreclosure of access" is central to butoh as a form; butoh, she writes, "is structured around an iteration and a citation based on longing or a complex structure of nostalgia" (1999, 168).

10. This is an essential distinction: the butoh dancer must be receptive and responsive to these active memories—to "remember the dance inside their mother's womb, not to think about it, but to move from 'the feeling of it,'" as Ohno told the students in his workshop—but cannot be passive or absent (Fraleigh 1999, 61).

11. Both Hijikata and Ohno identified butoh in terms of the dancing body's relation to the dead; Yoshito Ohno noted that "Ohno uses the Japanese term for ghost, *yūrei*, which generally refers to . . . the departed soul of a dead person, which appears as a shadowy resemblance of the deceased. It is thought to have a specific purpose for coming back to the world of the living and reveals itself only to a particular few" (Ohno and Ohno 2004, 174). Hijikata characterized butoh as "a corpse standing desperately upright" (Fraleigh and Nakamura 2006, 18), explaining, "To make gestures of the dead, to die again, to make the dead re-enact their deaths; this

is what I want to experience" (Velez and Velez 1990). Kazuo Ohno said that successful butoh dance expresses the moment when "the dead begin to run" (Holborn and Hoffman 1987). Performance as a mode of channeling the dead is a concept familiar from Noh theater, as Stanca Scholz-Cionca observes: "To the early *nō* masters conscious of their *hinin* status . . . the contact with numinous forces . . . produced a theater of spectres, haunting memories, and transformations" (2010, 162). Miryam Sas links Ohno's "strongly antitechnical, anti-intentional idea of movement" to Zeami's theory of "*senu tokoro*" (time or space of not doing) as a goal for Noh actors (1999, 174).

12. In the 1960s Hijikata also began a phase of exploring drag as a dual strategy for creating dance and mourning the loss of his older sister, whom he felt he carried "inside my body" (2000, 79). Ohno also explored his relation to his beloved mother through drag, most notably in *My Mother* (1981).

13. These terms tend to find their way into the lexicons of critics and scholars. Fraleigh and Nakamura write, "*Admiring La Argentina* serves as a rebirth for Ohno from the introspective 'death' during his ten-year absence from dance and the stage" (2006, 90); Jennifer Dunning characterized the piece as feeling "too long buried in some curve of flesh" (1981); Franko refers to "the memory image that had gestated within him" (2011, 109); and Scholz-Cionca notes that by "referring to the 'listening body, well-attuned and waiting,' Ōno even sets up a sort of womb idolatry" (2010, 166).

14. Noh and Kabuki in Japan, like classical Greek drama and Elizabethan theater, have traditionally employed cross-dressed men to act all female roles. In classical Noh theater, female roles are played by masked male actors, with the demanding "crone" roles reserved for the most experienced performers. After 1629, when women were banned from the Japanese stage, Kabuki developed the category of the *onnagata*, a highly specialized male actor who represents an idealized, mannered femininity that Japanese dance scholar Katherine Mezur calls "female-likeness," emphasizing the constructedness of this gender performance (2005). "In all my interviews," Mezur reports, "not one onnagata said he imitated real women, but every onnagata commented on how he manipulated his body in particular ways to fit onnagata *kata* [forms]" (182).

15. In an analysis of *Suiren* (Water Lilies), another piece Kazuo Ohno dances in a dress, Franko proposes that "he performs a through- rather than a cross-dressing, abandoning the lateral model in which dressing 'across' still confirms the old hermeneutics of the self at its terminal points" (1992, 604).

16. In fact, Ohno did make one direct foray into the realm of the onnagata: he confided to Richard Schechner that he wanted to restage Mary Wigman's *Witch-*

*dance* in a custom-designed onnagata cherry-blossom kimono and wig, thus casting the Orientalist aspirations of Ausdruckstanz into an echo chamber of citation, appropriation, and multilayered drag (Schechner 1986, 168–69).

17. "Anyone who has seen this Japanese artist perform, often in elaborate female dresses . . . will never forget his dancing," the Japanese choreographer and dancer Eiko wrote in eulogy upon Kazuo Ohno's death in 2010. "Wearing white pancake, blue eye shadow, and red lipstick on his wrinkled face, Ohno moved many viewers to tears at every concert—me and Koma included" (2010, 67–68). Eiko, who had once been Ohno's student and remained close to him all his life, connects Ohno's power as a dancer in his later years to his "elaborate female dresses," corroborating Hijikata's visceral impression that Ohno dancing in a dress was dangerously compelling.

18. Mark Franko's nuanced description of Ohno as a drag performer, for example, echoes Miyabi Ichikawa's seminal article, "A Preface to Buto," written in 1983. Ichikawa called "Ohno Kazuo's female impersonation" an expression of "the negation of the body itself through powerful metamorphosis" (Klein 1998, 70). Drawing on Franko's insight that Ohno's drag "speaks of disparate sexes in one body without invoking paradox or inviting us to delude ourselves about the 'truth'" (Franko 1995, 105), Vida Midgelow argues that Ohno "avoids the effects of neo-conservative drag, in which the enacted presentation of the opposite sex reinforces gender binaries" (Midgelow 2007, 178). This idea of drag shows how one body may host "disparate sexes," without recourse to a grounding truth about gender; fragments of gendered identities can cohabitate in it, enflesh themselves, and then perform together. In this vein, Katherine Mezur—arguing for the potential of "transcultural feminist theories" in analyzing Kabuki—emphasizes the "male body beneath [the female costume] as integral and/or essential to onnagata performance" in a way that produces "complexities, differences, and multiplicities of possible 'other' meanings and genders" (2005, 240). Mezur's approach to bodies and roles as "an unstable composite" counters the easy trope of drag as parodic inversion (137).

19. Fraleigh observes, "In the beginning of butoh, metamorphosis of the fetus in the womb was a major theme for Ohno, and it continues still in the butoh of today" (2010, 45). In an article on gender roles in butoh, Kinneret Noy links Ohno's feminine costumes to "Buddhist concepts of *henshin* (metamorphosis), and its related concept of *henja nanshi* (the transformation of a female body into a male body)" (2009, 196).

20. Marisa C. Hayes, a workshop participant at the Ohno studio, relates, "Yoshito speaks of the body as a vessel that must be emptied before it can take form through dance" (2010, 131).

21. In the second half of the piece, there are more sections set to Callas singing Puccini, including the final scene.

22. Takao Kawaguchi also took part in the *Dance Archive Box* project (2014–2015), as Nanako Nakajima mentions in her essay "The Archiving Body in Dance" (2017, 197–98).

23. Takao Kawaguchi's own perspective on Ohno and drag is that "he had to throw away his gender, to get rid of his maleness, to be free," as he explained in the Japan Society workshop; Ohno is "becoming woman so that he can do more."

24. I am grateful to Trajal Harrell for a generous interview, ongoing correspondence, and video footage of *The Return of La Argentina* from ImPulsTanz 2016. I have not seen that piece live, but I attended the UC Berkeley performance of *The Ghost of Montpellier Meets the Samurai* (2016).

25. Tavia Nyong'o describes eloquently what Harrell draws from ball culture: the sense of "a black and brown queer avant-garde: a popular, underground, often criminalized space of utopian counter-positions" to white heteronormativity (2017, 255).

26. Jansen identifies this dress as Comme des Garçons in her article "Activating the Archive: On Trajal Harrell's *The Return of La Argentina*" (n.d.), written as part of Harrell's residency at the New York Museum of Modern Art. (This piece was commissioned by MoMA but premiered at Centre National de la Danse in Paris, on October 3, 2015.) In an interview with Gia Kourlas (2013), Harrell discussed what he sees as unexplored connections between butoh and Rei Kawakubo: "I haven't seen anyone say, Let's really look at the performativity between Butoh and Comme des Garçons."

27. In "Trajal Harrell and the Art of Conscientious Hosting" (2016), performance studies scholar Debra Levine proposes that a third ghost joins their party—Ellen Stewart of La MaMa.

28. As Nyong'o writes of Harrell's own practice, "Critical fabulation as both textual practice and performative enactment works reparatively beyond repair; its intent and (where achieved) its effect is to render temporarily inoperative the narrative machinery by which the status quo continuously reproduces the past as an image of itself, shutting down possibilities of living or feeling otherwise" (2017, 257).

29. "In *butō* dance it is the soul that 'wears the body as a glove,'" Eugenia Casini Ropa writes, an image that conveys the close, embedded fit of costume over body over soul (2010, 109).

30. This conception of the hosting body, shaken by tremblings and passages of warm, live image-memories, is indebted to Bergson: "It is from the present that

comes the appeal to which memory responds," he writes, "and it is from the sensori-motor elements of present actions that a memory borrows the warmth that gives it life" (2004, 197). As Tavia Nyong'o remarks, Trajal Harrell is "an instinctive Bergso-nian" (n.d., 1).

31. When Eungie Joo of the New Museum asked Trajal Harrell about "the pres-ence and absence of the black male body" in *Twenty Looks*, Harrell replied that he had chosen to cast himself as the only dancer of color as a deliberate strategy of anti-representation (Harrell et al. 2017, 302). "I knew that if I and other brown skin bodies were onstage, all the imaginative strategies would go out the window for 85% or more of the audience," he elaborated, because "that's just how people shorthand with race." Nyong'o calls this position "an edgy contact improvisation with and against the color line in art and aesthetics," in contrast to the limits of casting "bodies [that] bear only the expressive possibilities to which ascriptive race-thinking demands" (2017, 256). "Through sharing out the unshareable," Nyong'o concludes, "Harrell asks whether the transgression of racial boundaries in expres-sive movement can ever be ethical, and has the courage not to impose a didactic answer to this quandary."


Chapter Four

1. I first saw the Trockadero perform at UC Berkeley in 2005. Since then I have attended dozens of rehearsals and performances, been on tour with the company, watched footage of past shows as well as documentaries, and spoken extensively with the dancers, ballet masters, and company staff. Without them—and especially without the generosity and wisdom of Tory Dobrin—this book would not exist.

2. The specific qualities of this ideal form, of course, change over time and vary within the field (for example, Theophile Gautier's division between the sensuous 'pagan' vivacity of Fanny Elssler and the elevated 'Christian' grace of Marie Ta-glioni). Though paradigms for dancers' turnout, height, muscularity, speed, and so forth undergo shifts that reflect broader cultural values regarding gender roles, sexuality, race, and athleticism, at any given time and place there *are* ideal bodily forms that govern the training, selection, and public reception of dancers.

3. On the courtly body, see Jennifer Nevile's *Eloquent Body: Dance and Human-ist Culture in Fifteenth-Century Italy* (Bloomington: Indiana University Press, 2004) and Sandra Schmidt's 2010 essay "'Sauter et voltiger en l'air': The Art of Movement in Late Renaissance Italy and France" (in *The Body in Early Modern Italy*, edited by Julia L. Hairston and Walter Stephens [Baltimore: Johns Hopkins University Press: 213–25]). For the monarchical body, see Mark Franko's *The Dancing Body in Re-*

*naissance Choreography* (Birmingham, AL: Summa Publications, 1986) and 2003 article "Majestic Drag: Monarchical Performativity and the King's Body Theatrical" (*Drama Review* 47, no. 2: 71–87). For an overview from Romanticism to modern dance of images of the ballerina's "perpetual virginity, an idealised and ethereal femininity that reaches for the sky," see Leslie Sayers's 1993 essay "'She might pirouette on a daisy and it would not bend': Images of Femininity and Dance Appreciation" (166), and for a counterpoint to the Romantic ideal of femininity, see Lynn Garafola's 1986 article "The Travesty Dancer in Nineteenth-Century Ballet" (*Dance Research Journal* 17, no. 2/18, no. 1: 35–40).

4. The bodily theorizing of dance, Susan Foster proposes, can refract and challenge "other systems of representation that together constitute the cultural moment within which all bodies circulate," including practices of gender, sexuality, and historiography (2011, 5). By expanding the definition of choreography "to encompass all manner of human movement including the operations of gender in constructing masculine and feminine roles," Foster envisions dance as "a slowly changing constellation of representational conventions"—as if dances moved in elliptical orbits, with their own gravity and luminosity, and could gradually pull other cultural practices into new trajectories (5). This view of dance reminds us that dancers are not merely bodies to be inscribed upon, but also actors in the public sphere of bodily practices.

5. "The Trocs remind us of things about ballet and our relationship to it that we may have forgotten," dance scholars Rachel Duerden and Neil Fisher write in their analysis of *Go for Barocco*, a parody of Balanchine's 1940 piece *Concerto Barocco*, choreographed in 1974 by Peter Anastos (2004, 112).

6. The emergence of "queer theater . . . runs parallel to the gay liberation movement," Don Shewey suggests, because it "grew from communities of people for whom theater was more than a career—it was a way to live" (2002, 128). "To oppose the theatrical to the political within contemporary queer politics is, I would argue, an impossibility," Judith Butler declared in her 1993 essay "Critically Queer," citing the need for "a set of histories" that would account for the rise of queer theatrical activism, including "traditions of cross-dressing, drag balls," and "drag performance benefits" (1993b, 23).

7. In *Charles Ludlam Lives!*, Sean Edgecomb emphasizes that "Ludlam saw his theater as a catalyst for communality," noting his influence on contemporary artists like Taylor Mac (2017, 15).

8. "'Trockadero' was a reference from Proust," Kaufman explains, "and 'Gloxinia,' a type of flower, referred to Ludlam's abiding love of plants" (2002b, 94).

9. The Gloxinia aesthetic cleaved to an old idea about cross-dressing in ballet, an unthreatening inversion of gender stereotypes. Drag roles for men in ballet

dated at least back to Enrico Cecchetti's portrayal of Carabosse (in *The Sleeping Beauty*, 1890) and were, like the 'dame' roles in the English pantomime tradition, a form of light theatrical entertainment. Tracing this role to the long French theatrical tradition of *soties* and *duègnes*—male actors who played "the terrifying hag [as] comical"—Senelick emphasizes that pantomime dames are caricatured creations of pure farce, prone to slapstick physical comedy (2000, 229–30, 242). These drag characters could be evil fairies, ugly stepsisters, old widows, or comic 'mothers' in huge skirts, harried by their broods of scampering children: they were mostly misogynist caricatures rather than roles with any emotional depth or character development. French theater historian Julia Prest concurs, noting that even in the "twenty-first century, a male actor may dress as a woman (the pantomime dame) if s/he is made to be grotesque through the exaggeration of feminine signifiers," since this "neutralizes any potential for transgression contained within the figure of the theatrical cross-dresser" (2006, 158).

10. Charles Ludlam was citing a book he had read in college, *The Art of Acting*, "by the French actor Coquelin, who originated the role of Cyrano" (Tomkins 1976, 96).

11. This trope affects both drag queens and kings; in *The Drag King Book*, Del LaGrace Volcano, Jack Halberstam, and Maureen Fischer/Mo B. Dick discuss the pressure on kings to disrobe in order to reveal themselves to be "pretty girls," as Fischer says disparagingly (Volcano and Halberstam 1999, 111).

12. Ludlam maintained that his *Camille* was "a totally legitimate interpretation of the original," emphasizing its emotional depth (Ludlam and Dasgupta 1978, 71). He claimed to have "pioneered the idea that female impersonation could be serious acting" (Kaufman 2002a).

13. As queer theorists like Heather Love have noted, camp and other forms of "backwardness" are "a key feature of queer culture" that manifest "in celebrations of perversion . . . in explorations of haunting and memory, and in stubborn attachments to lost objects" (2007, 7).

14. Jennifer Dunning described the same quality in Bassae: "there was an inevitable suspension of disbelief when he danced, for, without a trace of wistfulness or irony, he became the essence of a ballerina before one's eyes—as believably beautiful, glamorous and poetic as a Pavlova or an Alonso" (1990).

15. For an analysis of Mallarmé's views on performance, see May Lewis Shaw's *Performance in the Texts of Mallarmé: The Passage from Art to Ritual* (1993).

16. For an overview of the image of the ballerina and an ethnographic inquiry into its effects on contemporary dancers, see Jennifer Fisher's "Tulle as Tool: Embracing the Conflict of the Ballerina as Powerhouse" (2007). For an argument "in defense of ballet" as a form of pleasure and play for the amateur ballerina, see Alex-

andra Kolb and Sophia Kalogeropoulu's 2012 article "In Defense of Ballet: Women, Agency, and the Philosophy of Pleasure" (*Dance Research* 30, no. 2: 107–125). For a related proposal of "a feminist potential inherent in the genealogical 'family tree' metaphor used by ballet practitioners" that addresses Balanchine specifically, see Carrie Gaiser Casey's dissertation, "Ballet's Feminisms: Genealogy and Gender in Twentieth-Century American Ballet History" (2009, 2).

17. "Since the advent of George Balanchine's company," Wendy Oliver notes, "the American female ballet dancer has been slimmer than ever before" (2005, 46–47). Dance educator Heather Margaret Ritenburg corroborates this in her study of the effect of the "Balanchine ballerina body" image on young female dancers: "Several bodies and body shapes are made impossible through being selected as a Balanchine ballerina: the old body and the disabled body appear to have no place as well as the racialized body" (2010, 75).

18. Suzanne Farrell did say, for an interview in *Balanchine's Ballerinas*, "Balanchine idolized women" (Tracy and DeLano 1983, 154)—and this was from a woman who at eighteen years old had received a letter from Balanchine stating, "I hope by now you are thin and beautiful and light to lift" (Ritenburg 2010, 71). From a sociological perspective, Stephanie Jordan and Helen Thomas conclude, "Balanchine's comments, often chauvinistic comments, about women are famous . . . [and] ballet culture as a whole supports them" (1994, 12).

19. Gelsey Kirkland's experience of having Balanchine prod at her ribcage is the example that Steven P. Wainwright and his coauthors give to explain why Pierre Bourdieu's framework of habitus and field should be applied more often to ballet. Ann Daly, reflecting on the evolution of her methodology since her anti-Balanchine article, states, "Drawing upon Pierre Bourdieu's theory of habitus, I [have] called for a more complex understanding and analysis of how culture operates in constructing the gendered dancing body" (2000, 39–40). "Bourdieu's concept of bodily intelligence, enhanced by Foster's idea of bodily theorising, is important for a sociological analysis of dance because it makes it possible," Gay Morris writes, "to see the social as imbedded in the practice of dance" (2001, 58). For many dance scholars, then, Bourdieu's theory of habitus (an acquired set of naturalized bodily practices) and field (the various social spaces of interactions in which the values of habitus are negotiated) presents a useful model for exploring dance as a cultural phenomenon.

20. DeFrantz cites Keith Hennessy's rendition of the maiden's solo from Nijinsky's *Rite of Spring* (in *Bear/Skin*, 2015) as one example of "doing queer as the extended failure of a performance" of ballet history (2017a, 173); this raises larger questions about what constitutes re-performances of ballets or histories. Although the Trockadero repertoire might be categorized as "reconstructions," Vida Midgelow's book on ballet's "counter-narratives and alternative bodies" does not analyze

the Trockadero ballets as "reworkings," because she sees the company as undertaking a "reconceptualising and rechoreographing of the movement language" (2007, 3).

21. In an interview in 2012, Paul Ghiselin indicated the extent to which the Trockadero view "ballerina" as a role that can be learned by any dancer who is willing to participate wholeheartedly in the company's project: "Right now we have one guy" who can't do pointe work at all, Ghiselin told me earnestly, "and I'm teaching him to go on pointe. I'm giving him little ballerina classes. But every class, every rehearsal, he's 100 percent there, he's cheerful, he's friendly, he's ready to learn."

22. Examples of 'character' pointe roles for men include Bottom in Frederick Ashton's *The Dream* (1964) and the L'Elegant in Bronislava Nijinska's *Les Fâcheux* (1924): both were danced by Anton Dolin. More common are minor comic travesty roles on pointe, such as the 'dame' parts in versions of *Cinderella* (1948) choreographed by Ashton, Rudolf Nureyev, and Stanton Welch, and in Mark Morris's *The Hard Nut* (1991). Principal male roles are almost never danced on pointe, except in rare situations where a plot-based drag role calls for dancing, as is the case for the Ballet Dancer in Alexei Ratmansky's *Bright Stream* (2003). For historical examples of men dancing briefly on pointe, see Sandra Noll Hammond's 1987–1988 article, "Searching for the Sylph: Documentation of Early Developments in Pointe Technique" (*Dance Research Journal* 19, no. 2: 27–31).

23. Robert Carter is aware that he is part of the shift in what ballet can be: there was a time when "boys would be kicked out of ballet school for being so bold" as to try training on pointe, he notes, and now "there are pointe classes for men at Stuttgart [Ballet's] Academy" (2012). In his opinion, the Trockadero have "greatly" affected the field of ballet, in terms of both training and professional opportunities.

24. While Raven Wilkinson was telling Gia Kourlas that mainstream ballet was still toxic for black women, Robert Carter was finishing a successful three-week season with the Trockadero at the Joyce Theater in Manhattan, where he performed as Odette, the principal role in *Swan Lake*. Jennifer Dunning crowned him "one of the company's most skillful and poignant ballerinas" in her *New York Times* review (2006). The *Financial Times* claimed that Odette's solo was "danced so expertly one forgot this was a travestie troupe" (Ostlere 2006), and Deborah Jowitt of the *Village Voice* commented that Robert Carter could whip "off scads of immaculate fouettés and pirouettes" without batting a false eyelash (2006).

25. Carter joined the Trockadero in the same year as Paul Ghiselin, but while Ghiselin, who is older, had only "a crash course" from "the girls at Ohio Ballet" before attempting pointe work with the Trockadero (Kourlas 2004a), Carter started training on pointe at age twelve (Straus 2008, 84). "I am first an artist and the expression of my art is truly without gender," Carter states (2011, 12). "Dancing roles

conventionally created for and danced by women has never been a strange concept for me." As someone who has been immersed in the Trockadero since he was ten years old, he explains his artistry in non-identitarian terms: "I've never thought about it," he replies when asked about race. "It's never been an issue for me" (2012).

26. This part of Trockadero history is not well documented, so this account relies on Bertram Coleman's dissertation (1993) and the Trockadero archive in the New York Public Library's Jerome Robbins Dance Division.

27. More recently, choreographer Sean Dorsey's *The Missing Generation* (2015) sets out to explicitly "investigate the contemporary impact of the loss of so much of an entire generation of gay and transgender people to AIDS in the 1980s."

28. It is undeniable that ballet has a queer history (not only because Lincoln Kirstein, the *other* man who brought ballet to America, was gay), as detailed by Peter Stoneley (2007). As Joseph Carman notes, it is difficult to distinguish exactly which factors make ballet a welcoming field for queer men but much less so for queer women (2006, 56). Writing of "The Gay Elephant in the Room," Jennifer Fisher observes that "relatively little has been written about homosexuality and ballet until recent years," despite the general sense that ballet has traditionally been a haven for gay men (2009, 39). Ramsay Burt, who traces the association between ballet and homosexuality to Diaghilev and the Ballets Russes years, wonders if the "reason why the taboo still persists is the need for dance and ballet companies to raise funding and attract sponsorship" (2007, 29).

29. Named for Cervantes's portrait of a man who believes he is a knight-errant undertaking chivalric quests, despite the fact that the age of chivalry has long passed, the Don Quixote effect occurs when a habitus becomes affixed to the past, remaining "attuned" to outdated conditions, and thereby pulls away from the field (Bourdieu 1984, 109). This disjunction creates a tension that can eventually snap, wresting field and habitus into a sudden new alignment. When bodies mobilize a past in this way, they create a future for a different bodily habitus, an unforeseen swerve in the development of the field as a whole (Bourdieu and Wacquant 1992, 138). Sociologist Nicos Mouzelis observes that the Don Quixote effect is a rare moment when Bourdieu recognizes that "reflexivity and rational strategizing" occur at an individual level (2007). In fact, Mouzelis argues, reflexive accounting and self-conscious strategizing are part of people's actions in a much more consistent way than Bourdieu acknowledges. In this framework, agency can emerge from embodied dispositions that anticipate change because—perhaps in a delusional way—they are still nostalgically attached to a history.

30. At the choreographic level, at the biographical level, and at the level of technique—several ballets have been staged for the company by Elena Kunikova, who trained at the Vaganova Choreographic School—the Trockadero channel

"those great Imperial Russian ballets that you don't see so often nowadays," as Paul Ghiselin says. "What we try to bring back is that connection with the spirit, the grandeur of emotions—a little bit of that awe from yesteryear" (Brennan n.d.). "The truth is, we're doing a lot of hard-core classical ballets that just aren't done that much anymore," Dobrin told journalist Sid Smith (2012).

31.  Ballet is even more restrictive in its bodily ideal than other dance forms: "The habitus of classical ballet produces dispositions (or tastes) toward the body that emphasize beauty, youthfulness, and athleticism, and hence aging, injury, and re- tirement are aspects of the ballet career that are deeply problematic within the field of classical ballet" (Wainwright and Turner 2004, 101). For ballerinas, the prob- lem is exacerbated, as dance sociologist Pirkko Markula points out, citing a list of dance scholars who have demonstrated that the "image of the female dancer emphasizes the characteristics connected to the ideal Western femininity such as ethereal beauty, lightness, youthfulness and/or sexual attractiveness" (2006, 8). As the Trockadero enact their genealogy of ballet through the difference of their bod- ies, they grapple with the corporeal precariousness and gendered constraints that haunt their art form.

32.  "When I joined the company," Ghiselin relates, "that's exactly what I was go- ing for: I wanted to be the eccentric old dame, I wanted to be the Myrtha [Queen of the Wilis in *Giselle*], I wanted to be the Taglioni [the aging ballerina in *Pas de Quatre*], I wanted to be the Dying Swan" (2012). His commitment to dancing as an aged ballerina (in his own body, as a persona, and in stage roles) is true to the spirit of Trockadero founders Natch Taylor and Peter Anastos, who loved watching older ballerinas dancing.

33.  For a close reading of aging swan ballerinas and queer temporality, see Julian B. Carter's "Chasing Feathers: Jérôme Bel, *Swan Lake*, and the Alternative Futures of Re-Enacted Dance," which explores Bel's *Veronique Doisneau* (2004) at the Paris Opera Ballet through the "cygnine idiom's tendency to curve back on itself" (2017, 109).

34.  "We fall down; I think that's one of the reasons people love us," Ghiselin says (2012).

35.  Attached to the multiplicity of dramatic, decadent, outsize personae of ballet history, Trockadero dancers do not trace their origins to any single source. Instead, Robert Carter explains, when he dances Odette, he uses a bodily synthesis of past ballerinas: "Rather than imitate, I like to try and incorporate little parts from each of the ballerinas I use to bring something completely different to the role" (2011, 12). The Trockadero are dancing 'full-out' (to the best of their bodily abilities, as all dancers do) but within the particularities of the many ghostly bodies they have

imprinted on their own. "Olga [Supphozova] has a slightly different mind-set than I do," Carter muses. "She's more mature, more measured, more thoughtful. I take more time dancing her way than I do with my natural self, because I have a quick, fiery impulse" (2012). Carter calls this process "condensing," which captures the idea that he is not synthesizing differences into one smooth surface, but rather bundling them tightly into a variegated concentration.

36. Butler proposes that our responsibilities "are toward those we sometimes cannot name and do not know, and who may or may not bear perceivable traits of familiarity to an established sense of who 'we' are. Indeed, it may be that what this notion of ethics requires is that we no longer know precisely who 'we' are" (2011b, 386). This dissolution of identity, for Butler, is the condition of ethical queer bonds.

37. Dance Theater Workshop was a studio and theater space in Chelsea that supported numerous New York companies. It closed in 2011, plagued by funding issues, and became part of New York Live Arts.

38. "Even in the contemporary dance scene," Pyle relates, she was always being told that the "huge pleasure" of lifting other bodies couldn't be given to her, because "you're a woman—or, you're a girl, really: you're a girl" (2016).

39. In her analysis of *The Firebird* as a queer failure that succeeds on its own terms, Gretchen Alterowitz writes, "Pyle shifts the focus from virtuosity and perfection to styles and characteristics clearly coded as queer and, in so doing, suggests a way to circumvent dominant systems" (2014, 354).

40. By challenging the aesthetic boundaries that separate 'low' camp from 'high' art, artists like Move, Pyle, and the Trockadero dancers are taking up a venerable tradition in queer politics: "acts of gaiety," as Sara Warner calls them, that make a place in queer resistance for pleasure, melodrama, zaniness, and camp (2012).


Chapter Five


1. Marlon Bailey emphasizes that while "the theory of realness emerges from the Ballroom community itself," it "offers a way to understand, primarily, how, in society beyond the Ballroom scene, all gender and sexual identities are performed" (2013, 56).

2. In "She Is Not Acting, She Is" (2014), Sabrina Strings and Long T. Bui contrast the freedom of gender realness with the stereotypes of racialized femininity in *Ru-Paul's Drag Race*.

3. As music journalist Peter Shapiro notes in *Turn the Beat Around: The Secret History of Disco*, this song became "the cornerstone of gay disco," raising questions

about how realness functioned for black gay men in particular (2005, 78). In *Paris Is Burning* (1990), Cheryl Lynn's disco hit "Got to Be Real" (1978) plays over the long final sequence of credits and outtakes.

4. I have attended live performances of many versions of *Faux Real* in San Francisco and Berkeley, as well as watching video footage; this chapter focuses on the original (2009) version. I am grateful to Monique Jenkinson and Marc Kate for sharing materials and insights.

5. In "Female-Femmeing: A Gender-*Bent* Performance Practice," Meredith Heller argues for this practice as a "queer engagement with femininity" undervalued by drag scholars (2015, 3).

6. In January 2015, in response to growing discomfort in the community around the term "tranny," club founder Heklina changed the name to Mother—after, of course, consulting Chi Chi Valenti and Johnny Dynell (Heklina 2014).

7. It was Wayne Koestenbaum's ardently gay autobiography of "a post-Callas opera queen" (1993, 134), that inspired Jenkinson's very first piece, appropriately titled *Mimicry and Flaunting* (2000). The first two reasons Koestenbaum gives for the gay cult of Callas are a shared feeling of having been "opened up in public" and the fact that "she revised her body" (139). Koestenbaum specifically connects "the Medea style" of Callas's eyeliner to the labor of producing an image; it showed "that her face was a tablet on which she wrote her life, and that femininity was a lot of work" (140).

8. Elizabeth Schewe, writing about the autobiographical strategies of Kate Bornstein and RuPaul, affirms that they also use bio-narrative performance to involve their audiences; these two quite different actors "share an overwhelming desire to engage their readers as active participants in creating textual meaning and challenging repressive politics" (2009, 691).

9. José Muñoz has proposed that "the work of contemporary French philosopher Jean-Luc Nancy and his notion of 'being singular plural' seems especially important" for queer dance (2009, 10).

10. "The autobiographical is not the personal," Lauren Berlant declared in an interview with Jay Prosser; on the contrary, "all sorts of narratives are read as autobiographies of collective experience" (Berlant and Prosser 2011, 180).

11. The linguistic philosopher Mark Johnson follows a somewhat similar line of reasoning—"*that meaning is not just what is consciously entertained in acts of feeling and thought; instead, meaning reaches deep down into our corporeal encounter with our environment*" (2007, 25)—but his claim is distinct from Noë's in accepting the "image-schematic logic" of representation and simulation (181).

12. As bell hooks noted about *Paris Is Burning*, "The desire for stardom is an ex-

pression of the longing to realize the dream of autonomous stellar individualism," and that is a fantasy of isolation and inviolability (1996, 224).

13. When Torr articulates how she was able to survive this two-dimensionality without damaging her sense of self (as a person, as a woman, and as a feminist), she identifies the Release Technique classes in which "our attention was directed inward so that we developed a three-dimensional awareness of the body rather than simply thinking in terms of the studio mirror" (45).

14. The exact etymology of "werq" is unclear, but, like "werk," it evolved from black queer vocabularies that overlapped with backstage dance lexicons. One of Jenkinson's drag mentors, Mr. David (who performs as Glamamore, and is Viv-vyAnne ForeverMORE's drag mother), attests to hearing it in the late 1970s or very early '80s (Jenkinson 2013). On "werq" as a declarative that affirms "the sartorial, the expressive, the performed, and the embodied over the biologic, the state record, the birth certificate, the checkbox," see Treva Ellison, "The Labor of Werqing It: The Performance and Protest Strategies of Sir Lady Java," in *Trap Door: Trans Cultural Production and the Politics of Visibility*, ed. Reina Gosset, Eric A. Stanley, and Johanna Burton (Cambridge, MA: MIT Press, 2017: 1–22), 1.

15. In her analysis of Nora Chipaumire's *Dark Swan* (2005–2013), another "corporeal rewriting" of Fokine's *Dying Swan*, Ananya Chatterjea discusses how this dance "is at once a re-narrativization of history" and "Chipaumire's own revolution against systems that have sought to simultaneously hypersexualize and desexualize African women's bodies" (2017, 7, 9).

16. I saw *Age & Beauty Part I* at the Whitney in 2014; I am grateful to Miguel Gutierrez for sharing his thoughts with me during an interview in 2016. For close readings of Gutierrez's work, see Ryan M. Davis's 2015 article "All the Possible Variations and Positions: The Intimate Maximalism of Miguel Gutierrez" (*Theater* 45, no. 1: 10–31), and Amanda E. Hamp's 2016 article "I want to understand (what is happening to me!): Miguel Gutierrez Performs How to Be Okay in a Non-Utopia" (*Drama Review* 60, no. 2: 14–31).

17. This is part of a long conversation; for example, Cathy J. Cohen's 1997 essay "Punks, Bulldaggers, and Welfare Queens: The Radical Potential of Queer Politics," made the point that any "queer politics that simply pits the grand 'heterosexuals' against all those oppressed 'queers'" is missing the chance for a radically *intersectional* queer politics that recognizes how race and class, as well as gender and sexuality, shape marginalization and privilege (458).

18. This is clear in Jenkinson's artist statement: she gives her lineage as "radical queer performance (Jack Smith, John Kelly, Leigh Bowery) that uses glamour, excess, and drag to entertain, transcend, and horrify" in the tradition of "the Cock-

ettes, General Idea" and the Trockadero. The Cockettes's 1960s drag extravaganzas, which took "cock-" and "-ette" in entirely new directions, included one of San Francisco's earliest faux queen performances (Smiley 2012).

19. The Lexington closed in 2015, "because we can't run a sustainable business in the Mission anymore because of the economics of the neighborhood and the diminished presence of queer women living in it," founder and owner Lila Thirkield explained to journalist Marke B. of *48 Hills*, adding that general "economic gender inequality" also plays a role in the paucity of lesbian bars (B. 2014).

20. Daytime Realness, cohosted by Heklina (of Trannyshack/Mother) and DJ Carnita (of Hard French), has been held since 2011 at El Rio, a neighborhood bar in the Mission District established in 1978 that makes a point of welcoming queer and trans people. El Rio is also home to Hard French, a party that inspired Kelly Lovemonster to start Swagger Like Us—a "utopic moment," as he described it to Monique Jenkinson, "for people of color to congregate . . . to be carefree . . . a place to dance and move your body" (Lovemonster and Jenkinson 2018). "I think of us both as political creatures," Lovemonster told Jenkinson: "Your daily actions and work are shot through with political integrity, and you think about the political dimensions of live work, of bodies coming together in rooms, of the possibilities around spectacle, entertainment, and pleasure."

21. As Jill Dolan proposes, "Considering theater audiences as participatory publics might expand how the *communitas* they experience through utopian performatives might become a model for other social interactions" (2005, 11). Writing on Tim Miller's choice to sit down, naked, in the laps of audience members during his piece *My Queer Body*, Dolan makes the point that moments "of literal physical interaction and emotional intersubjectivity" work to diminish "the mystic gulf between stage and house" and emphasizing "the spectator's and the performer's mutual vulnerability" (32).

22. "Can we please get over the word 'bio'?" trans writer Julia Serano asked in frustration, after a keynote speaker at Femme 2006 referred to herself as a "bio-dyke." "I may be a trans woman, but the last time I checked, I was not inorganic or nonbiological in any way" (2012, 176).

23. In her analysis of the Peruvian performance collective Yuyachkani, Taylor points out that questions of "impersonation and appropriation" tend to rely on identity positions that have been "cemented into the social imaginary as biological fact" (2003, 194–95). She argues against this "to each their own" approach, positing instead that performance can be an ethical form of witnessing (195).

24. Vaccaro goes on to define "*trans*-corporeography"—following Vicky Kirby's idea of "corporeography" (1997)—as a way of seeing transgender embodiment in choreographic terms: "the body in composition with itself, engaged in an autonomous process and choreographic labor" (Vaccaro 2010, 255). I am grateful to Maxe

Crandall for suggesting Jeanne Vaccaro's work to me, and for uncountable other things in and beyond this chapter.

25. It might be more accurate here to speak of "texxture," the term Sedgwick borrows from Renu Bora: "Texxture is the kind of texture that is dense with offered information about how, substantively, historically, materially, it came into being" (Sedgwick 2003, 14).

26. This image of self-spun stuff as text is described as an autobiographical process of "perpetual interweaving" by Roland Barthes: "the subject unmakes himself, like a spider dissolving in the constructive secretions of his web" (1975, 64). One night, in fact, "Poses" was interrupted by the consequences of its own aesthetic; as the fragile paper cape draped around her shoulders began to tear, "Jenkinson whispered a two-word SOS to her assistant, Mica Phelan [*sic*]: 'Scotch tape.' 'Everything is tape and glue and smoke and mirrors,' Jenkinson said," describing both the touchingly handmade and the immanently entropic (Garchik 2009).

27. The Sisters of Perpetual Indulgence, who proudly claim on their website to have been "ruining it for everyone" with their outrageous drag activism since 1979, are a "21$^{st}$-century Order of queer nuns" committed to sex-positive, anti-homophobic social justice projects that support people with AIDS, queer and trans youth, and those targeted by hate crimes. The #MyNameIs campaign, organized in 2014 by queens like Lil Miss Hot Mess, is "a coalition of drag and other performers, transgender people, Native Americans, immigrants, domestic violence survivors, and our allies who advocate for the reformation of Facebook's dangerous and discriminatory 'real names' policy," as its website explains. Drag Queen Story Hour, produced by Michelle Tea and RADAR Productions, presents queer role models for children, making it a point to feature drag queens of color in predominantly gay white neighborhoods like the Castro. *Stilettos for Shanghai*, a documentary film about the Sisters traveling to the Shanghai Pride celebration in 2014, became Sister Roma Roma's way to fund-raise for LGBTQI people fleeing persecution in Chechnya in 2017. In the wake of white supremacist violence in Charlottesville, Virginia, in 2017, Juanita MORE! (in conjunction with fellow queen Honey Mahogany and NAMES Project founder Cleve Jones) organized a protest against a similar event planned for Crissy Field in San Francisco.

28. On Sylvia Rivera and Marsha P. Johnson, see Layli Phillips and Shomari Olugbala's 2006 essay "Sylvia Rivera: Fighting in Her Heels: Stonewall, Civil Rights, and Liberation," in *The Human Tradition in the Civil Rights Movement*, ed. Susan M. Glisson (Lanham, MD: Rowman and Littlefield: 309–334); Jessi Gan, "'Still at the Back of the Bus': Sylvia Rivera's Struggle" (2013); Susan Stryker's *Transgender History* (Berkeley: Seal Press, 2008); Reina Gossett's "The Spirit Was . . ." blog (2012); and *Happy Birthday, Marsha!* (2018) by Reina Gossett and Sasha Wortzel.

29. Jessi Gan argues that this exclusion was largely due to Rivera's race and class,

since "a working-class Puerto Rican/Venezuelan drag queen" was a difficult identity to lionize in the struggle for gay rights, unless it was put "in the service of a liberal multicultural logic of recognition" (2013, 292).

30. In 2002, when Rivera died, the tireless trans activist Dean Spade founded a legal nonprofit "to guarantee that all people are free to self-determine their gender identity and expression, regardless of income or race, and without facing harassment, discrimination, or violence," and named it after her, as the Sylvia Rivera Law Project website explains. And so her afterlife is unfolding under the banner of their hand-drawn logo, which reads "Liberation is a collective process."

31. As part of her archival research, Gossett has transcribed Sylvia Rivera's reflections on Stonewall from a 1989 NPR broadcast. "Today I'm a 38-year-old drag queen," Rivera declared. "I can keep my long hair, I can pluck my eyebrows, and I can work wherever the hell I want. And I'm not going to change for anybody. If I changed, then I feel that I'm losing what 1969 brought into my life, and that was to be totally free" (Gossett 2012). At the end of her "Ten Posts for Sylvia Rivera's Ten Year Memorial," Gossett cites a line from Adrienne Rich's essay "Resisting Amnesia: History and Personal Life" (1983): "Historical responsibility has, after all, to do with action—where we place the weight of our existences on the line, cast our lot with others, move from an individual consciousness to a collective one."

# Bibliography

Acocella, Joan. 1993. *Mark Morris*. New York: Harper Collins.

Acocella, Joan. 1996. "Evening of a Faun." *Village Voice*, December 31, 79–80.

Acocella, Joan. 2005. "Ladies and Gentleman: The Trocks." *New Yorker*, January 10, 82–84.

Acocella, Joan. 2006. "Queen for a Day." *New Yorker*, March 13, 14.

Acocella, Joan. 2015. "The Long Journey." *Opera Quarterly* 31, no. 3: 182–85.

Acocella, Joan. 2016. "The Not Too Hard Nut." *New Yorker*, December 12, 19.

*Admiring La Argentina*. 1977. Performance video of Kazuo Ohno from Dai-ichi Sei Mei Hall, Toyko. 70 min. DVD.

*Admiring La Argentina*. 1994. Performance video of Kazuo Ohno from September 1, directed by Yoshito Ohno, filmed by Izuru Mizutani at Teatro Fonte, Yokohama. 60 min. DVD.

Aguirre, Abby. 2007. "Tentative Steps into a Life after Dance." *New York Times*, October 21, 24.

Ahmed, Sara. 2012. "Queer Feelings." In *The Routledge Queer Studies Reader*, edited by Donald E. Hall and Annamarie Jagose. New York: Routledge, 422–41.

Albright, Ann Cooper. 1997. *Choreographing Difference: The Body and Identity in Contemporary Dance*. Middletown, CT: Wesleyan University Press.

Aldax, Mike. 2013. "San Francisco Transgender Community Reports Uptick in Targeted Violence. *San Francisco Examiner*, March 27. http://www.sfexaminer. com/sanfrancisco/san-francisco-transgender-community-reports-uptick-in-targeted-violence/Content?oid=2336149.

Alterowitz, Gretchen. 2014. "Embodying a Queer Worldview: The Contemporary Ballets of Katy Pyle and Deborah Lohse." *Dance Chronicle* 37, no. 3: 335–66.

Argelander, Ronald. 1974. "Charles Ludlam's Ridiculous Theatrical Co." *Drama Review* 18, no. 2: 81–86.

B., Marke. 2014. "Why SF's Iconic Dyke Bar, the Lexington Club, Is Closing." *48 Hills*, October 23. http://www.48hills.org/2014/10/23/lexington-club-closing-owner-says-higher-rent-gentrification-gender-inequality-hurt-iconic-lesbian-bar.

Bailey, Marlon M. 2011. "Gender/Racial Realness: Theorizing the Gender System in Ballroom Culture." *Feminist Studies* 37, no. 2: 365–86.

Bailey, Marlon M. 2013. *Butch Queens Up in Pumps: Gender, Performance, and Ballroom Culture in Detroit*. Ann Arbor: University of Michigan Press.

Bannerman, Henrietta. 2003. "Dancing for Laughs: Martha Graham and Comedy." *Critical Dance.com*, September 2003. http://www.criticaldance.com/features/2003/marthagrahamcomedy200309.html.

Bannerman, Henrietta. 2010. "Martha Graham's House of the Pelvic Truth: The Figuration of Sexual Identities and Female Empowerment." *Dance Research Journal* 42, no. 1: 30–45.

Barnes, Clive. 1974. "An Oddly Touching 'Camille.'" *New York Times*, May 14, 31.

Barthes, Roland. 1975. *The Pleasure of the Text*. Translated by R. Miller. New York: Hill and Wang.

BBC World Service. 2001. "Martha Graham: The Goddess of Dance," February 22. http://www.bbc.co.uk/worldservice/arts/highlights/010222_martha.shtml.

Bell, Biba, and Richard Move. 2017. "Richard Move in Conversation with Biba Bell." *Critical Correspondence*, April 21. https://movementresearch.org/publications/critical-correspondence/richard-move-in-conversation-with-biba-bell.

Belfiore, Elizabeth S. 1992. *Tragic Pleasures: Aristotle on Plot and Emotion*. Princeton, NJ: Princeton University Press.

Belmar, Sima. 2015. "Easier Said Than Done: Talking Identity in Late Twentieth-Century American Concert Dance." PhD diss., University of California, Berkeley.

Bennahum, Ninotchka Devorah. 2000. *Antonia Mercé "La Argentina": Flamenco and the Spanish Avant Garde*. Hanover, NH: Wesleyan University Press.

Berger, John. 1972. *Ways of Seeing*. London: Penguin Books.

Bergson, Henri. 2004. *Matter and Memory*. Translated by Nancy Margaret Paul and W. Scott Palmer. Mineola, NY: Dover Publications. First published 1912.

Berlant, Lauren, and Jay Prosser. 2011. "Life Writing and Intimate Publics: A Conversation with Lauren Berlant." *Biography* 34, no. 1: 180–87.

Bo, Justine. 2017. "Ballez: This LGBTQ Dance Company Wants to Change How We Think about Gender in Ballet." NBC *Left Field*, June 22. https://www.youtube.com/watch?v=MpfOjeWyupA.

Bollen, Jonathan. 2001. "Queer Kinesthesia: Performativity on the Dance Floor." In Desmond, *Dancing Desires*, 285–314.

Bory, Alison. 2008. "Dancing with My Self: Performing Autobiography in (Post) Modern Dance." PhD diss., University of California, Riverside.

Bourdieu, Pierre. 1984. *Distinction: A Social Critique of the Judgment of Taste*. London: Routledge.

Bourdieu, Pierre. 1990. *In Other Words: Essays toward a Reflexive Sociology*. Palo Alto, CA: Stanford University Press.

Bourdieu, Pierre, and Loïc J. D. Wacquant. 1992. *An Invitation to Reflexive Sociology*. Chicago: University of Chicago Press.

Boyce, Johanna, Ann Daly, Bill T. Jones, and Carol Martin. 1988. "Movement and Gender: A Roundtable Discussion." *Drama Review* 32, no. 4: 82–101.

Braziel, Jana Evans. 2005. "Dréd's Drag Kinging of Race, Sex, and the Queering of the American Racial Machine-Désirante." *Women and Performance* 15, no. 2: 161–88.

Brecht, Stefan. 1978. *Queer Theatre*. Frankfurt am Main: Suhrkamp.

Brennan, Mary. N.d. "Interview with Paul Ghiselin, Ballet Master: Bring Me My Swan Costume." *Dance Consortium*. http://www.danceconsortium.com/content.aspx?CategoryID=1839.

Brown, Ismene. 1996. "The Man Who Inherited a Legend." *Daily Telegraph*, August 16. http://www.telegraph.co.uk/culture/?xml=/arts/1996/08/17/bdron17.xml.

Brown, Ismene. 2013. "10 Questions for Les Ballets Trockadero de Monte Carlo's Leader Tory Dobrin." *The Arts Desk*, February 12. http://www.theartsdesk.com/dance/10-questions-les-ballets-trockadero-de-monte-carlos-leader-tory-dobrin.

Burt, Ramsay. 1998. "Dance, Gender, and Psychoanalysis: Martha Graham's Night Journey." *Dance Research Journal* 30, no. 1: 34-53.

Burt, Ramsay. 2000. "Dance Theory, Sociology, and Aesthetics." *Dance Research Journal* 32, no. 1: 125–31.

Burt, Ramsay. 2007. *The Male Dancer: Bodies, Spectacle, Sexualities*. 2nd ed. New York: Routledge.

Burt, Ramsay. 2009. "Performing Unmarked Masculinity." In Fisher and Shay, *When Men Dance*, 150–67.

Butcher, S. H., trans. N.d. *Poetics by Aristotle*. http://classics.mit.edu/Aristotle/poetics.html.

Butler, Judith. 1986. "Sex and Gender in Simone de Beauvoir's *Second Sex*." *Yale French Studies* 72: 36–49.

Butler, Judith. 1993a. *Bodies That Matter: On the Discursive Limits of "Sex."* New York: Routledge.

Butler, Judith. 1993b. "Critically Queer." *GLQ* 1: 17–32.

Butler, Judith. 1999. *Gender Trouble: Feminism and the Subversion of Identity*. London: Routledge. First published 1990.

Butler, Judith. 2004a. *Undoing Gender*. New York: Routledge.

Butler, Judith. 2004b. *Precarious Life: The Powers of Mourning and Violence*. London: Verso.

Butler, Judith. 2011a. "Bodies in Alliance and the Politics of the Street." *Transversal* (September). European Institute for Progressive Cultural Politics. http://www.eipcp.net/transversal/1011/butler/en.

Butler, Judith. 2011b. "Remarks on 'Queer Bonds.'" *GLQ* 17, nos. 2/3: 381–87.

Butler, Judith. 2014. "When Gesture Becomes Event." Théâtre Performance Philosophie Conference. June 27. Sorbonne University, Paris. Video by Sébastien Couston, Labo LAPS. http://labo-laps.com/videos-theatre-performance-philosophie-tpp-2014.

Butler, Judith, and Athena Athanasiou. 2013. *Dispossession: The Performative in the Political*. Cambridge, UK: Polity Press.

Butler, Judith, and Sunaura Taylor. 2009. "Interdependence." In *Examined Life: Excursions with Contemporary Thinkers*, edited by Astra Taylor. New York: New Press, 185–213.

Cabeen, Catherine. 2011. "Gender/Drag/Truth and Lies." *Catherine Cabeen* (blog), April 11. http://catherinecabeen.blogspot.fr/2011/04/genderdragtruth-and-lies.html.

Cabeen, Catherine. 2016. Personal interview. September 19.

Carman, Joseph. 2000. "Move Over, Martha." *The Advocate*, May 9: 70–73.

Carman, Joseph. 2006. "Gay Men & Dance: What's the Connection?" *Dance Magazine* 80, no. 11: 56–58.

Carman, Joseph, Steven Sucato, and Wendy Perron. 2005. "He Said/She Said: Dancers and Choreographers Talk about the Role of Gender in Their Lives and Work." *Dance Magazine* 79, no. 11: 60–64, 66–70.

Carter, Julian B. 2017. "Chasing Feathers: Jérôme Bel, *Swan Lake*, and the Alternative Futures of Re-Enacted Dance." In Croft, *Queer Dance*, 109–124.

Carter, Robert. 2011. "Talking Point." *Dancing Times* (March): 12.

Carter, Robert. 2012. Personal interview. March 21.

Case, Sue-Ellen. 1985. "Classic Drag: The Greek Creation of Female Parts." *Theatre Journal* 37, no. 3: 317–27.

Case, Sue-Ellen. 1985. 1988/1989. "Toward a Butch-Femme Aesthetic." *Discourse* 11, no. 1: 55–73.

Casey, Carrie Gaiser. 2009. "Ballet's Feminisms: Genealogy and Gender in Twentieth-Century American Ballet History." PhD diss., University of California, Berkeley.

Casini Ropa, Eugenia. 2010. "A Soul That 'Wears the body as a glove': German Ausdruckstanz and *Butō*." In *Avant-gardes in Japan. Anniversary of Futurism and Butō: Performing Arts and Cultural Practices between Contemporariness and*

*Tradition*, edited by Katja Centonze. Venice: Libreria Editrice Cafoscarina, 105–110.

Chatterjea, Ananya. 2017. "Of Corporeal Rewritings, Translations, and the Politics of Difference in Dancing." In *The Oxford Handbook of Dance and Politics*, edited by Rebekah J. Kowal, Gerald Siegmund, and Randy Martin. New York: Oxford University Press, 283–301.

Chatterjee, Sandra, and Cynthia Ling Lee. 2017. "Our Love Was Not Enough: Queering Gender, Cultural Belonging, and Desire in Contemporary *Abhinaya*." In Croft, *Queer Dance*, 45–65.

Christon, Lawrence. 1989. "The 15-Year Comic Art of Keeping Men on Their Toes." *Los Angeles Times*, April 21. http://articles.latimes.com/1989-04-21/entertainment/ca-2284_1_trocks-les-sylphides-swan-lake.

Chtcheglov, Ivan. 1953. "Formulary for a New Urbanism." In *Situationist International Anthology*, edited and translated by Ken Knabb. Berkeley: Bureau of Public Secrets. http://www.bopsecrets.org/SI/Chtcheglov.htm.

Cleto, Fabio, ed. 1999. *Camp: Queer Aesthetics and the Performing Subject: A Reader*. Ann Arbor: University of Michigan Press.

Coan, Jaime Shearn. 2016. "Copy Is Original: Takao Kawaguchi's *About Kazuo Ohno*: Reliving the Butoh Diva's Masterpieces." *Brooklyn Rail*, September 1. http://brooklynrail.org/2016/09/dance/copy-is-original-takao-kawaguchis-about-kazuo-ohno-reliving-the-butoh-divas-masterpieces.

Cohen, Cathy J. 1997. "Punks, Bulldaggers, and Welfare Queens: The Radical Potential of Queer Politics." *GLQ* 3: 437–65.

Coleman, Bertram. 1993. "Les Ballets Trockadero de Monte Carlo." PhD diss., University of Texas at Austin.

Comfort, Jane. "Repertory: *S/HE* (1995)." Jane Comfort and Company. http://janecomfortandcompany.org/portfolio/she-1995.

Conrad, Peter. 2000. "The Many Faces of Morris, Dancer." *The Guardian*, June 11. https://www.theguardian.com/theobserver/2000/jun/11/features.review47.

Crenshaw, Kimberlé. 1991. "Mapping the Margins: Intersectionality, Identity Politics, and Violence against Women of Color." *Stanford Law Review* 43, no. 6: 1241–99.

Crisp, Clement. 2006. "Review: Trockadero Ballets, Peacock Theatre, London." *Financial Times London*, March 23. http://www.trockadero.org/reviewfinancialt.html.

Croce, Arlene. 1974. "Dancing: The Two Trockaderos." *New Yorker*, October 14, 182–88.

Croce, Arlene. 2000. *Writing in the Dark, Dancing in the New Yorker*. New York: Farrar, Straus, and Giroux.

Croft, Clare. 2017. Introduction to *Queer Dance: Meanings and Makings*, edited by Clare Croft. New York: Oxford University Press, 1–33.

Currah, Paisley, and Dean Spade. 2008. "The State We're In: Locations of Coercion and Resistance in Trans Policy, Part 2." *Sexuality Research and Social Policy* 5, no. 1: 1–4.

Curtin, Catherine. 2011. "Rose-Coloured Dance: The Politics of Cross-Dressing in Hijikata Tatsumi's Ankoku Butoh." *Contemporary Theatre Review* 21, no. 4: 472–86.

Daly, Ann. 1987. "The Balanchine Woman: Of Hummingbirds and Channel Swimmers." *Drama Review* 31, no. 1: 8–21.

Daly, Ann. 1989. "To Dance Is 'Female.'" *Drama Review*, 33, no. 4: 23–27.

Daly, Ann. 2000. "Feminist Theory across the Millennial Divide." *Dance Research Journal* 32, no. 1: 39–42.

Dalva, Nancy. 2003. "Dido and Didi." *Dance Insider*, April 17. http://www.danceinsider.com/f2003/f0417_2.html.

David, Ceri. 2009. "Jocks of the Trocks." *(Daily Telegraph) Sunday Magazine*, September 20, 19–20.

Davis, Vaginal Creme, and Susanne Sachsse. 2015. "Vaginal Davis and Susanne Sachsse Talk about Their Restaging of *The Magic Flute*." *Artforum.com*. November. http://artforum.com/video/id=56441&mode=large.

DeFrantz, Thomas. 2004. *Dancing Revelations: Alvin Ailey's Embodiment of African American Culture*. Oxford: Oxford University Press.

DeFrantz, Thomas. 2017a. "Queer Dance in Three Acts." In Croft, *Queer Dance*, 169–79.

DeFrantz, Thomas. 2017b. "Switch: Queer Social Dance, Political Leadership, and Black Popular Culture." In *The Oxford Handbook of Dance and Politics*, edited by Rebekah J. Kowal, Gerald Siegmund, and Randy Martin: New York: Oxford University Press, 477–96.

DeLano, Sharon. 1976. "Boys in Tutus: An Interview with Peter Anastos a.k.a. Olga Tchikaboumskaya." *Christopher Street*, October.

Deleuze, Gilles. 1991. *Bergsonism*. Translated by Hugh Tomlinson and Barbara Habberjam. New York: Zone Books.

Deleuze, Gilles. 1994. *Difference and Repetition*. Translated by Paul Patton. New York: Columbia University Press.

de Mille, Agnes. 1991. *Martha: The Life and Work of Martha Graham*. New York: Random House.

de Poyen, Jennifer. 2005. "Move's 'Martha @' Odd Yet Moving," *San Diego Union Tribune*, March 5, E5.

Desmond, Jane C. 2001. "Introduction: Making the Invisible Visible: Staging Sexualities through Dance." In *Dancing Desires: Choreographing Sexualities On and Off the Stage*, edited by Jane Desmond. Madison: University of Wisconsin Press, 3–32.

Diamond, Elin. 1996. *Performance and Cultural Politics*. New York: Routledge.

Dobrin, Tory. 2012. Personal interview. March 21.

Dolan, Jill. 2005. *Utopia in Performance: Finding Hope at the Theater*. Ann Arbor: University of Michigan Press.

Dolven, Jeff. 2015. "Purcell's Dido and the Fate of Mark Morris." *Opera Quarterly* 31, no. 3: 186–89.

D'Orazi, Maria Pia. 1997. *Butō: La nuova danza giapponese*. Rome: Editori Associati.

D'Orazi, Maria Pia. 2001. *Kazuo Ōno*. Palermo: L'Epos.

Dorsey, Sean. 2015. "The Missing Generation." *Sean Dorsey Dance*. www.seandorseydance.com.

Duberman, Martin. 1993. *Stonewall*. New York: Dutton.

Duerden, Rachel, and Neil Fisher. 2004. "Balanchine, Wittgenstein, and Les Ballets Trockadero de Monte Carlo: Philosophical Insights through Artistic Parody." In *Dance, Identity, and Integration: Tributes to the late Carl Worz and Muriel Topaz: Conference Proceedings, Congress on Research in Dance; International Dance Conference, Taiwan, August 1-4, 2004*, edited by Janice LaPointe-Crump (New York: Congress on Research in Dance), 112–15.

Duerden, Rachel, and Bonnie Rowell. 2103. "Mark Morris's *Dido and Aeneas* (1989): A Critical Postmodern Sensibility." *Dance Chronicle* 36: 143–71.

Dunning, Jennifer. 1976. "An Off-Shoot of the Off-Shoot." *Soho Weekly News*, March 4.

Dunning, Jennifer. 1981. "The Dance: Kazuo Ohno." *New York Times*, July 31, 22.

Dunning, Jennifer. 1990. "Partners Change, Along with Attitudes." *New York Times*, February 4, 8.

Dunning, Jennifer. 2006. "Big-Foot Ballet, with All the Thrills and Spills." *New York Times*, December 21, E11.

Edgecomb, Sean F. 2017. *Charles Ludlam Lives! Charles Busch, Bradford Louryk, Taylor Mac, and the Queer Legacy of the Ridiculous Theatrical Company*. Ann Arbor: University of Michigan Press.

Eiko. 2010. "Kazuo Ohno, 1906–2010." *Dance Magazine* 84, no. 9: 67–68.

Elswit, Kate. 2008. "Petrified? Some Thoughts on Practical Research and Dance Historiography." *Performance Research* 13, no. 1: 61–69.

Eng, David L., Judith Halberstam, and José Muñoz. 2005. Introduction to "What's Queer about Queer Studies Now?" Special issue of *Social Text* 84/85: 1–17.

Estrada, Domingo, Jr. 2014. "Meet the MMDG Dancers: Domingo Estrada Jr." *Dance Motion USA*, October 8. http://dancemotionusa.tumblr.com/post/99510340850/meet-the-mmdg-dancers-domingo-estrada-jr.

Fehlandt, Tina. 2015. "Dancing Dido." *Opera Quarterly* 31, no. 3: 190–93.

Finch, Kirrin. 2016. "Jules Skloot: Exploring Gender Identity through Dance and Performance." Dapper Scouts. http://kirrinfinch.com/dapper-scouts/jules-skloot.

Fisher, Jennifer. 1999. "Moved by Martha." *Los Angeles Times*, July 25. http://articles.latimes.com/1999/jul/25/entertainment/ca-5924.1.

Fisher, Jennifer. 2007. "Tulle as Tool: Embracing the Conflict of the Ballerina as Powerhouse." *Dance Research Journal* 39, no. 1: 2–24.

Fisher, Jennifer. 2009. "Maverick Men in Ballet: Rethinking the 'Making it Macho' Strategy." In Fisher and Shay, *When Men Dance*, 31–48.

Fisher, Jennifer, and Anthony Shay, eds. 2009. *When Men Dance: Choreographing Masculinities across Borders*. New York: Oxford University Press.

Ford, Andrew. 1995. "Katharsis: The Ancient Problem." In *Performativity and Performance*, edited by Andrew Parker and Eve Kosofsky Sedgwick. New York: Routledge, 109–132.

Foster, Susan Leigh. 1995. "Choreographing History." In *Choreographing History*, ed. Susan Leigh Foster. Bloomington: University of Indiana Press, 3–24.

Foster, Susan Leigh. 1996. *Choreography and Narrative: Ballet's Staging of Story and Desire*. Bloomington: Indiana University Press.

Foster, Susan Leigh. 1998. "Choreographies of Gender." *Signs* 24, no. 1: 1–33.

Foster, Susan Leigh. 2001. "Closets Full of Dances: Modern Dance's Performance of Masculinity and Sexuality." In Desmond, *Dancing Desires*, 147–207.

Foster, Susan Leigh. 2002. "Walking and Other Choreographic Tactics: Danced Inventions of Theatricality and Performativity." *SubStance* 31, nos. 2/3, Issue 98/99: 125–46.

Foster, Susan Leigh. 2007. "Dido's Otherness: Choreographing Race and Gender in the *Ballet d'Action*." In *Dance Discourses: Keywords in Dance Research*, edited by Susanne Franco and Marina Nordera. London: Routledge, 121–30.

Foster, Susan Leigh. 2011. *Choreographing Empathy: Kinesthesia in Performance*. New York: Routledge.

Foucault, Michel. 1984. "Nietzsche, Genealogy, History." In *The Foucault Reader*, edited by Paul Rabinow. Originally translated 1977 by Donald F. Bouchard and Sherry Simon. New York: Pantheon Books, 76–100.

Foulkes, Julia L. 2001. "Dance Is for American Men: Ted Shawn and the Intersection of Gender, Sexuality, and Nationalism in the 1930s." In Desmond, *Dancing Desires*, 113–146.

Foulkes, Julia L. 2002. *Modern Bodies: Dance and American Modernism from Martha Graham to Alvin Ailey*. Chapel Hill: University of North Carolina Press.

Fraleigh, Sondra. 1999. *Dancing into Darkness: Butoh, Zen, and Japan*. Pittsburgh: University of Pittsburgh Press.

Fraleigh, Sondra. 2010. *Butoh: Metamorphic Dance and Global Alchemy*. Champaign: University of Illinois Press.

Fraleigh, Sondra, and Tamah Nakamura. 2006. *Hijikata Tatsumi and Ohno Kazuo*. London: Routledge.

Franko, Mark. 1992. "Where He Danced: Cocteau's Barbette and Ohno's *Water Lilies*." *PMLA* 107, no. 3: 594–607.

Franko, Mark. 1995. *Dancing Modernism/Performing Politics*. Bloomington: Indiana University Press.

Franko, Mark. 2006. "Dance and the Political: States of Exception." *Dance Research Journal* 38, nos. 1/2: 3–18.

Franko, Mark. 2011. "The Dancing Gaze across Cultures: Kazuo Ohno's *Admiring La Argentina*." *Dance Chronicle* 34, no. 1: 106–131.

Franko, Mark. 2012. *Martha Graham in Love and War: The Life in the Work*. New York: Oxford University Press.

Freedman, Russell. 1998. *Martha Graham: A Dancer's Life*. New York: Clarion Books.

Freeman, Elizabeth. 2010. *Time Binds: Queer Temporalities, Queer Histories*. Durham, NC: Duke University Press.

Friedman, Jeff. 2006. "Muscle Memory: Performing Embodied Knowledge." In *Text and Image: Art and the Performance of Memory*, edited by Richard Cándida Smith. New Brunswick, NJ: Transaction Publishers, 156–80.

Frye, Marilyn. 1983. *The Politics of Reality: Essays in Feminist Theory*. New York: Crossing Press.

Gan, Jessi. 2013. "'Still at the Back of the Bus': Sylvia Rivera's Struggle." In *The Transgender Studies Reader 2*, edited by Susan Stryker and Aren Z. Aizura. New York: Routledge, 291–301.

Garafola, Lynn. 1989. *Diaghilev's Ballets Russes*. New York: Oxford University Press.

Garafola, Lynn. 1993. Untitled review. *Drama Review* 37, no. 1: 167–73.

Garber, Marjorie. 1992. *Vested Interests: Cross-Dressing and Cultural Anxiety*. New York: Routledge.

Garchik, Leah. 2009. "Halt! Who Goes to Pacific Heights?" *San Francisco Chronicle*, July 22, E12.

Gere, David. 2001. "*29 Effeminate Gestures*: Choreographer Joe Goode and the Heroism of Effeminacy." In Desmond, *Dancing Desires*, 349–81.

Gere, David. 2004. *How to Make Dances in an Epidemic: Tracking Choreography in the Age of AIDS*. Madison: University of Wisconsin Press.

Ghiselin, Paul. 2012. Personal interview. March 21.

*Ghostlight.* 2003. Directed by Christopher Herrman. Written by Penny Fearon, Christopher Herrman, and Richard Move. Featuring Richard Move, Ann Magnuson, Deborah Harry, and Mark Morris.

Gilbert, Jenny. 2001. "Martha Graham: It's Such a Drag Being an Icon." *The Independent,* November 4. http://www.independent.co.uk/arts-entertainment/theatre-dance/features/martha-graham-its-such-a-drag-being-an-icon-9185684.html.

Goellner, Ellen W., and Jacqueline Shea Murphy. 1995. "Movement Movements." In *Bodies of the Text: Dance as Theory, Literature as Dance,* edited by Ellen W. Goellner and Jacqueline Shea Murphy. New Brunswick, NJ: Rutgers University Press, 1–18.

Goffman, Erving. 1956. *The Presentation of the Self in Everyday Life.* New York: Anchor Books. Reprinted 1959.

Goldberg, Marianne. 1997. "Homogenized Ballerinas." In *Meaning in Motion: New Cultural Studies of Dance,* edited by Jane C. Desmond. Durham, NC: Duke University Press, 305–20.

Goodwin, Joy. 2006. "A Choreographer Begins Shedding His Inner Martha." *New York Times,* December 17, A31.

Gordon, Avery F. (1997) 2008. *Ghostly Matters: Haunting and the Sociological Imagination.* 2nd ed. Minneapolis: University of Minnesota Press. Citations refer to the 2008 edition.

Gossett, Reina. 2012. "Sylvia Rivera & NYPD Reflect on Stonewall Rebellion" [Transcribed from Sound Portraits: NPR, 1989]. *"The Spirit Was . . .": Ten Posts for Sylvia Rivera's Ten Year Memorial.* http://thespiritwas.tumblr.com/post/18108920192/sylvia-rivera-nypd-reflect-on-stonewall.

Gottlieb, Robert. 2007. "The Tremendous Trocks Spoof, Stumble, and Soar." *New York Observer,* January 8. http://www.trockadero.org/new-york-observer.html.

Graham, Martha. c. 1953. "An Athlete of God." *National Public Radio.* January 4, 2006. http://www.npr.org/templates/story/story.php?storyId=5065006.

Graham, Martha. c. 1976. Documentary interview. Production of WNET Thirteen and the Martha Graham Dance Company.

Graham, Martha. c. 1991. *Blood Memory: An Autobiography.* New York: Doubleday.

Greskovic, Robert. 1974. "Trockadero." *Soho Weekly News,* September 19, 17.

Gutierrez, Miguel. N.d. "About." http://miguelgutierrez.org/project/about.

Gutierrez, Miguel. 2016. Personal interview. September 17.

Hafezi, L. N. 2014. "An Afternoon with the Ballez." The Helix Queen Performance Network, May 1. http://helixqpn.org/post/88567248392/an-afternoon-with-the-ballez.

Halberstam, Jack [Judith]. 1998. *Female Masculinity*. Durham, NC: Duke University Press.

Halberstam, Jack [Judith]. 2005. *In a Queer Time and Place: Transgender Bodies, Subcultural Lives*. New York: New York University Press.

Halberstam, Jack [Judith]. 2011. *The Queer Art of Failure*. Durham, NC: Duke University Press.

Halperin, David. 2012. *How to Be Gay*. Cambridge, MA: Harvard University Press.

Harrell, Trajal. N.d. "Works/Info." http://betatrajal.org/home.html.

Harrell, Trajal. 2015. Personal interview (Skype). September 23.

Harrell, Trajal, et al. 2017. "Questions for Trajal Harrell." *Not Vogue: Twenty Looks or Paris Is Burning at the Judson Church (XL) Finale*, edited by Trajal Harrell, 300–303.

Harris, William. 1998. "Dragging Martha Back from the Dead." *New York Times*, December 6, 79.

Harss, Marina. 2015. "Morris' Golden Girl." *Dance Magazine*, February 1. http://dancemagazine.com/inside-dm/morris-golden-girl.

Hayes, Marisa C. 2010. "Walking towards Authenticity: Butoh Workshops at the Kazuo Ohno Dance Studio." *Theatre, Dance, and Performance Training* 1, no. 1: 130–33.

Heklina. 2014. "'Trannygate.'" *Huffington Post*, June 29. http://www.huffingtonpost.com/heklina/trannygate_b_5539042.html.

Heller, Meredith. 2015. "Female-Femmeing: A Gender-*Bent* Performance Practice." *QED* 2, no. 3: 1–23.

Hijikata, Tatsumi. 2000. "Inner Material/Material." Translated by Nanako Kurihara. Originally published as *Naka no sozai/sozai* (Hijikata DANCE EXPERIENCE, July 1960). *Drama Review* 44, no. 1: 36–42.

Hinkson, Mary. 2001. *Essential Elements*. Martha Graham Legacy Project.

Holborn, Mark, and Ethan Hoffman. 1987. *Butoh: Dance of the Dark Soul*. Videocassette. New York: Aperture.

hooks, bell. 1996. *Reel to Real: Race, Sex, and Class at the Movies*. New York: Routledge.

Hoover, Lou Henry. 2017. "To Be a Showboy." In Croft, *Queer Dance*, 37–44.

Horosko, Marian. 2002. *Martha Graham: The Evolution of Her Dance Theory and Training* (revised edition). Gainesville: University of Florida Press.

Howe, David Everitt. 2015. "Dance in the Ruins: Trajal Harrell, Adam Linder, and Alexandra Bachzetsis on Their Work, Its Institutionalization, and the Art World." *Mousse* 50 (October/November): 76–89.

Huston, Johnny Ray. 2009. "GOLDIES 2009: Monique Jenkinson." *San Francisco*

*Bay Guardian*, April 11. http://www.sfbg.com/2009/11/04/monique-jenkinson.

Ichikawa, Miyabi. 1983. "A Preface to Buto." In *Ankoku Buto: The Premodern and Postmodern Influences of the Dance of Utter Darkness* by Susan Blakely Klein. Ithaca, NY: East Asia Program, Cornell University (1988), 69–70.

Ickes, Bob. 1998. "Martha after Dark." *Vogue*, December, 156.

Isaac, Dan, Brooks Riley, Charles Ludlam, Norma Desmond, and Laurette Bedlam. 1968. "Charles Ludlam/Norma Desmond/Laurette Bedlam: An Interview." *Drama Review* 13, no. 1: 116.

Jae, Hwan Jung. 2012. "Dancing Ambivalence: A Critical Analysis of Mark Morris' Choreography in *Dido and Aeneas* (1989), *The Hard Nut* (1991), and *Romeo and Juliet, On Motifs of Shakespeare* (2008)." PhD diss., Temple University, Philadelphia.

Jamison, Judith. N.d. "Defining an Ailey Dancer: Conversation with Judith Jamison." *Dance Consortium*. http://www.danceconsortium.com/features/article/defining-an-ailey-dancer-conversation-with-judith-jamison.

Jansen, Sara. N.d. "Activating the Archive: On Trajal Harrell's *The Return of La Argentina*." Edited by Ana Janevski, Martha Joseph, and Jason Persse. "Trajal Harrell: In one step are a thousand animals." *MoMA*, 1–6. https://www.moma.org/calendar/performance/1451?locale=en.

Janevski, Ana, and Trajal Harrell. N.d. "Trajal Harrell in Conversation with Ana Janevski." "Trajal Harrell: In one step are a thousand animals." *MoMA*, 1–5. https://www.moma.org/calendar/performance/1451?locale=en.

Jenkinson, Monique. N.d. "Fauxnique: About." http://www.fauxnique.net/about.

Jenkinson, Monique. 2013. Personal interview. July 10.

Jhung, Finis. N.d. "Barre Side Chats: Interview with Robert Carter." *Dance Art*. http://www.danceart.com/BarreSide/Robert_Carter.htm.

Johnson, E. Patrick. 2003. *Appropriating Blackness: Performance and the Politics of Authenticity*. Durham, NC: Duke University Press.

Johnson, Mark. 2007. *The Meaning of the Body: Aesthetics of Human Understanding*. Chicago: University of Chicago Press.

Johnson, Virginia. 2014. "Building Diversity in Ballet: Black Swans Are Still Too Rare." *From the Green Room* (Dance/USA), November 13. https://www.danceusa.org/ejournal/2014/11/13/building-diversity-in-ballet-black-swans-are-still-too-rare.

Jordan, Stephanie. 2011. "Mark Morris Marks Purcell: *Dido and Aeneas* as Danced Opera." *Dance Research* 29, no. 2: 167–213.

Jordan, Stephanie. 2015. *Mark Morris: Musician-Choreographer*. Binstead, Hampshire, UK: Dance Books.

Jordan, Stephanie, and Helen Thomas. 1994. "Dance and Gender: Formalism and Semiotics Reconsidered." *Dance Research* 12, no. 2: 3–14.

Jowitt, Deborah. 2001. "Identities on the Move." *Village Voice*, January 30. http://www.villagevoice.com/2001-01-30/dance/identities-on-the-move.

Jowitt, Deborah. 2006. "Swan Diva: Drag Ballerinas Assault the Classics, Claws Sheathed." *Village Voice*, December 26. http://www.villagevoice.com/2006-12-26/dance/swan-diva.

Jowitt, Deborah. 2010. "Dancing Masculinity: Defining the Male Image Onstage in Twentieth-Century America and Beyond." *Southwest Review* 95, nos. 1/2: 228–42.

Kaufman, David. 2002a. "The Man Born to Play the Heroine Camille." *New York Times*, November 3, 11.

Kaufman, David. 2002b. *Ridiculous! The Theatrical Life and Times of Charles Ludlam.* New York: Applause.

Kawaguchi, Takao. 2013. *About Kazuo Ohno—Reliving the Butoh Diva's Masterpieces.* Kawaguchitakao.com. http://www.kawaguchitakao.com/ohnokazuo/index_en.html.

Kazuo Ohno Dance Studio. N.d. "Kazuo Ohno." CANTA Ltd. http://www.kazuoohnodancestudio.com/english/kazuo.

Kelly, John. 2001. *John Kelly.* New York: 2wice Arts Foundation in Association with Aperture.

Khubchandani, Kareem. 2015. "Lessons in Drag: An Interview with LaWhore Vagistan." *Theatre Topics* 25, no. 3: 285–94.

Khubchandani, Kareem. 2017. "Aunty Fever: A Queer Impression." In Croft, *Queer Dance*, 199–204.

Kirby, Vicky. 1997. *Telling Flesh: The Substance of the Corporeal.* New York: Routledge.

Kirkland, Gelsey. 1998. *Dancing on My Grave: An Autobiography.* Harmondsworth, UK: Penguin.

Kisselgoff, Anna. 1989. "Purcell's 'Dido and Aeneas' as Mark Morris Sees It." *New York Times*, June 9, 3.

Kisselgoff, Anna. 2001. "Camp Finds a Target in Martha Graham." *New York Times*, January 23, E5.

Klein, Susan Blakely. 1988. *Ankoku Buto: The Premodern and Postmodern Influences of the Dance of Utter Darkness.* Ithaca, NY: East Asia Program, Cornell University.

Koestenbaum, Wayne. 1993. *The Queen's Throat: Opera, Homosexuality, and the Mystery of Desire.* Boston: Da Capo Press.

Kourlas, Gia. 2004a. "The Biggest Toe Shoes in Town." *New York Times*, December 19.

Kourlas, Gia. 2004b. "Martha Graham Like You've Never Seen Him." *New York Times*, June 13, AR30.

Kourlas, Gia. "2006. Teetering in Modernism's Temple, Minus a Goddess." *New York Times*, April 16, A21.

Kourlas, Gia. 2007. "Where Are All the Black Swans?" *New York Times*, May 6, AR1.

Kourlas, Gia. 2008. "Heroines of Ballet, Heroically Funny." *New York Times*, December 21, C9.

Kourlas, Gia. 2011. "He's the Shade of Martha Graham." *New York Times*, March 25, AR3.

Kourlas, Gia, and Amber Star Merkens. 2012. "Amber Star Merkens Talks about the Mark Morris Dance Group." *Time Out New York*, August 12. https://www.time-out.com/newyork/dance/amber-star-merkens-talks-about-the-mark-morris-dance-group.

Kourlas, Gia, and Trajal Harrell. 2013. "Trajal Harrell Talks about Bringing Butoh to MoMA." *Time Out New York*, February 11. https://www.timeout.com/newyork/dance/trajal-harrell-talks-about-bringing-butoh-to-moma.

Kraut, Anthea. 2015. *Choreographing Copyright: Race, Gender, and Intellectual Property Rights in American Dance*. Oxford: Oxford University Press.

Labong, Leilani. 2007. "Hot 20 2009: Monique Jenkinson, Performance Artist." *7x7 Magazine*, July 10. http://www.7x7.com/hot-20-2009-monique-jenkinson-performance-artist-1779463951.html.

Landini, Joe. 2007. "Channeling Martha Graham." *Bay Area Reporter*, March 29, 31.

Langlois, Michael. 2007. "A Conversation with Raven Wilkinson." *Ballet Review* (Fall): 22–32.

Lawrence, Tim. 2016. *Life and Death on the New York Dance Floor, 1980–1983*. Durham, NC: Duke University Press.

Leibman, Robert Henry. 1992. "Dancing Bears and Purple Transformations: The Structure of Dance in the Balkans." PhD diss., University of Pennsylvania.

Lepecki, André. 2004. "Introduction: Presence and Body in Dance and Performance Theory." In *Of the Presence of the Body: Essays on Dance and Performance Theory*, edited by André Lepecki. Middletown, CT: Wesleyan University Press, 1–12.

Lepecki, André. 2006. *Exhausting Dance: Performance and the Politics of Movement*. New York: Routledge.

Lepecki, André. 2010. "The Body as Archive: Will to Re-Enact and the Afterlives of Dances." *Dance Research Journal* 42, no. 2: 28–48.

Lepecki, André. 2012. "*Dance Discourses: Keywords in Dance Research* (review)." *Dance Research Journal* 44, no. 1: 93–99.

Lepecki, André. 2017. "On the Way Ongoing Going (Senselessly with an Aim): A Fever." In Harrell, *Not Vogue*, 96–97.

Les Ballets Trockadero de Monte Carlo. N.d. www.trockadero.org.

Levine, Abigail. 2014. "Richard Move in Conversation with Abigail Levine." *Critical Correspondence*, February 5. http://www.movementresearch.org/criticalcorrespondence/blog/?p=8521.

Levine, Debra. 2016. "Trajal Harrell and the Art of Conscientious Hosting." *Fourth Wall*. Walker Arts Center. March 8. https://walkerart.org/magazine/trajal-harrell-bagouet-hijikata.

Livingston, Jennie, dir. 1990. *Paris Is Burning*. Miramax. DVD.

Love, Heather. 2007. *Feeling Backward: Loss and the Politics of Queer History*. Cambridge, MA: Harvard University Press.

Lovemonster, Kelly, and Monique Jenkinson. 2018. "Backstage: Monique Jenkinson and Kelly Lovemonster in Conversation." *Open Space*, January 10. https://openspace.sfmoma.org/2018/01/kelly-lovemonster-and-monique-jenkinson-in-conversation.

Ludlam, Charles, and Gautam Dasgupta. 1978. "Interview: Charles Ludlam." *Performing Arts Journal* 3, no. 1: 69–80.

Macaulay, Alastair. 2000. "Dido's Wounds." *Dancing Times* 90, no. 1077: 815–17.

Macaulay, Alastair. 2011. "Lauding a Great Artist with No Example of Her Greatness." *New York Times*, March 16, C5.

Mackrell, Judith. 1999. "Martha's Divine Seed." *The Guardian*, October 26, 23.

Mackrell, Judith. 2015. "Philip Martin-Nielson: An Autistic Life Transformed by Dance." *The Guardian*, September 7.

Mallarmé, Stéphane. 1983. "Ballet." In *What Is Dance? Readings in Theory and Criticism*, edited by Roger Copeland and Marshall Cohen. New York: Oxford University Press, 111–15.

Manning, Susan. 2004. "Danced Spirituals." In Lepecki, *Of the Presence of the Body*, 82–96.

Markula, Pirkko. 2006. "The Dancing Body without Organs: Deleuze, Femininity, and Performing Research." *Qualitative Inquiry* 12, no. 1: 3–27.

Martin, Carol. 1999. "Mark Morris's *Dido and Aeneas*." In *Dancing Texts: Intertextuality in Interpretation*, edited by Janet Adshead-Lansdale. London: Dance Books, 130–47.

Martin, Randy. 1995. "Agency and History: The Demands of Dance Ethnography." In Foster, *Choreographing History*, 105–118.

Mauk, Norbert. 1994. "Body Sculptures in Space: Butoh Retains its Esthetic Relevance." *Ballet International/Ballet Tanz Aktuell* 8/9: 56–59.

McDonagh, Don. 1972. "Larry Ree Puts on the Grand Manner in Role of Ballerina." *New York Times*, September 3, 28.

Mezur, Katherine. 2005. *Beautiful Boys/Outlaw Bodies: Devising Kabuki Female-Likeness*. New York: Palgrave Macmillan.

Midgelow, Vida. 2007. *Reworking the Ballet: Counter-Narratives and Alternative Bodies*. London: Routledge.

MMDG [Mark Morris Dance Group]. 2016a. "*Dido and Aeneas* Dancer Interviews—The Dance." March 3. https://www.youtube.com/watch?v=zR9LfzNXHaE.

MMDG [Mark Morris Dance Group]. 2016b. "*Dido and Aeneas* Dancer Interviews—The Story." March 3. https://www.youtube.com/watch?v=cau4XieJvVs.

Montgomery, Paul L. 1989. "Mark Morris vs. Brussels Press." *New York Times*, April 29, AR11.

Moore, Madison. 2012a. "Tina Theory: Notes on Fierceness." *Journal of Popular Music Studies* 24, no. 1: 71–86.

Moore, Madison. 2012b. "Fierce: Performance, Creativity, and the Theory of the Fabulous Class." PhD diss., Yale University.

Moore, Madison. 2013. "On Fierceness." Lecture. Center for Lesbian and Gay Studies. CUNY Graduate Center, New York. April 26.

Moore, Madison. 2014. "Walk for Me: Postmodern Dance at the House of Harrell." *Theater* 44, no. 1: 5–23.

Morris, Gay. 1996. "Styles of the Flesh: Gender in the Dances of Mark Morris." In *Moving Words: Re-writing Dance*, edited by Gay Morris. New York: Routledge: 141–58.

Morris, Gay. 2001. "Bourdieu, the Body, and Graham's Post-War Dance." *Dance Research* 19, no. 2: 52–82.

Morris, Mark. 2003. "Mark Morris." In *Grace under Pressure: Passing Dance through Time*, edited by Barbara Newman. New York: Proscenium Publishers, 233–46.

Morris, Mark, and Joan Acocella. 2009. "A Conversation with Mark Morris and Joan Acocella." International Festival of Arts and Ideas in New Haven, Connecticut. https://youtu/iOS4dbx8F2c.

Mouzelis, Nicos. 2007. "Habitus and Reflexivity: Restructuring Bourdieu's Theory of Practice." *Sociological Research Online* 12, no. 6. http://www.socresonline.org.uk/12/6/9.html.

Move It Productions. N.d. http://www.move-itproductions.com/martha/press.html. Richard Move.

Move, Richard. 2003. *Bourne to Dance*. Interview by Matthew Bourne. BBC Television/Channel 4.

Move, Richard. 2007. Personal interview (telephone). April 4.

Move, Richard. 2011. "Where Is Ana Mendieta?" *Women and Performance* 21, no. 2: 167–70.

Move, Richard. 2018. "*Martha @ . . . The 1963 Interview*: Sonic Bodies, Seizures, and Spells." In *The Oxford Handbook of Dance and Reenactment*, edited by Mark Franko. New York: Oxford University Press, 57–76.

Munk, Erika. 1985. "Cross left—drag: 1. Men." *Village Voice*, February 5, 89–90.

Muñoz, José Esteban. 1997. "'The White to Be Angry': Vaginal Davis's Terrorist Drag." *Social Text* 52/53: 80–103.

Muñoz, José Esteban. 1999. *Disidentifications: Queers of Color and the Performance of Politics*. Minneapolis: University of Minnesota Press.

Muñoz, José Esteban. 2001. "Gesture, Ephemera, and Queer Feeling: Approaching Kevin Aviance." In Desmond, *Dancing Desires*, 423–42.

Muñoz, José Esteban. 2008 (1996). "Ephemera as Evidence: Introductory Notes to Queer Acts." *Women and Performance* 8, no. 2: 5–16.

Muñoz, José Esteban. 2009. *Cruising Utopia: The Then and There of Queer Futurity*. New York: New York University Press Press.

Nagy, Evie. 2008. "The Feminine Mystique." *Bust*, April/May, 62–67. http://www.oovy.net/FauxQueens_page.htm.

Nakajima, Nanako. 2017. "The Archiving Body in Dance." In *Moving (Across) Borders: Performing Translation, Intervention, Participation*, edited by Gabriele Brandstetter and Holger Hartung. Bielefeld, Germany: Transcript Verlag, 191–218.

NCAVP [National Coalition of Anti-Violence Programs]. 2013. "Lesbian Gay, Bisexual, Transgender, Queer, and HIV-Affected Hate Violence in 2012." http://www.cuav.org/wp-content/uploads/2013/06/NCAVP-2012-HV-Report-final.pdf.

Nero, Charles. 2000. "Fixing *Ceremonies*: An Introduction." In *Ceremonies: Prose and Poetry*, by Essex Hemphill. San Francisco: Cleis Press, xi–xxiii.

Ness, Sally. 2008. "The Inscription of Gesture: Inward Migrations in Dance." In *Migrations of Gesture*, edited by Carrie Noland and Sally Ann Ness. Minneapolis: University of Minnesota Press, 1–30.

Newton, Esther. 1979. *Mother Camp: Female Impersonators in America*. Chicago: University of Chicago Press. First published 1972 by Prentice-Hall.

Newton, Esther. 1996. "Dick(less) Tracy and the Homecoming Queen: Lesbian Power and Representation in Gay Male Cherry Grove." In *Inventing Lesbian Cultures*, edited by Ellen Lewin. Boston: Beacon Press, 161–93.

NHK Software. 2001. *Kazuo Ohno: Beauty and Strength*. DVD.

Nijinska, Bronislava. 1981. *Early Memoirs*. Translated and edited by Irina Nijinksa and Jean Rawlinson. New York: Holt, Rinehart, and Winston.

Noë, Alva. 2005. "Real Presence." *Philosophical Topics* 33, no. 1: 235–64.

Noë, Alva. 2012. *Varieties of Presence.* Cambridge, MA: Harvard University Press.

Noland, Carrie. 2009. *Agency and Embodiment: Performing Gestures/Producing Culture.* Cambridge, MA: Harvard University Press.

Noy, Kinneret. 2009. "Transcending Bodies: Dancing Gender(s) in *Butoh.*" In *Post-Gender: Gender, Sexuality, Performativity in Japanese Culture*, edited by Ayelet Zohar, 184–203. Newcastle-upon-Tyne: Cambridge Scholars Publishing.

Nyong'o, Tavia. N.d. "Mother Would Like a Cash Award: Trajal Harrell at MoMA." Edited by Ana Janevski, Martha Joseph, and Jason Persse. "Trajal Harrell: In one step are a thousand animals." *MoMA*, 1–4. https://www.moma.org/calendar/performance/1451?locale=en.

Nyong'o, Tavia. 2017. "Dancing in the Subjunctive: On Trajal Harrell's *Twenty Looks.*" In Harrell, *Not Vogue*, 254–57.

Ohno, Kazuo, and Noriko Maehata. 1986. "Selections from the Prose of Kazuo Ohno." *Drama Review* 30, no. 2: 156–62.

Ohno, Kazuo, and Yoshito Ohno. 2004. *Kazuo Ohno's World from Within and Without.* Translated by John Barrett. Middletown, CT: Wesleyan University Press.

Oliver, Wendy. 2005. "Reading the Ballerina's Body: Susan Bordo Sheds Light on Anastasia Volochkova and Heidi Guenther." *Dance Research Journal* 37, no. 2: 38–54.

Orellana, Javier L. 2007. "A Dancer's Life." *New York Post*, February 28.

Ormand, Kirk. 2003. "Oedipus the Queen: Cross-Gendering without Drag." *Theatre Journal* 55: 1–28.

Osterweis, Ariel, and Trajal Harrell. 2017. "Trajal Harrell's (email) Journey from Judson to Harlem." In Harrell, *Not Vogue*, 118–21.

Ostlere, Hilary. 2006. Review of Les Ballets Trockadero de Monte Carlo at the Joyce Theater, New York. *Financial Times*, December 20. http://www.ft.com/cms/s/2/27f807aa-9048-11db-a4b9-0000779e2340.html#axzz1ocwy6tna.

Palmer, Caroline. 2016. "Mark Morris Returns to the Work That Helped Anoint Him the 'Wild Child' of Dance." *Brooklyn Star Tribune*, March 30. http://www.startribune.com/brooklyn-choreographer-mark-morris-takes-on-love-betrayal-and-death-in-dido-and-aeneas/373411981.

Parry, Jann. 2011. "Paul Ghiselin, aka Ida Nevasayneva." *Ballet.co.uk*, April/May. http://www.ballet.co.uk/magazines/yr_11/apr11/interview-paul-ghiselin.htm.

Pasulka, Nicole. 2015. "The Girl King of Boylesque." *Hazlitt*, September 24. http://hazlitt.net/longreads/girl-king-boylesque.

Perel, Marissa. 2013. "Marissa Perel in Conversation with Katy Pyle, Jules Skloot, Cassie Mey, Francis Weisse Rabkin, Sam Greenleaf Miller, Effie Bowen, and

Lindsay Reuter." *Critical Correspondence*, May 20. http://www.movemen-tresearch.org/criticalcorrespondence/blog/?p=7164.

Perron, Wendy. 2000. "Merce at Martha @ Mother." *Dance Magazine* 74, no. 5: 76–77.

Perron, Wendy. 2001. "Move-ing to Town Hall: Dance Concert Makes Loving Fun of Martha Graham." *Dance Magazine* 75, no. 4: 77–78.

Phelan, Peggy. 1993. *Unmarked: The Politics of Performance*. New York: Routledge.

Phillips, Victoria. 2013. "Martha Graham's Gilded Cage: *Blood Memory—An Autobiography* (1991)." *Dance Research Journal* 45, no. 2: 63–84.

Post, Henry. 1975. "Prima Donalds: The Trockadero Transvestite Ballet Is No Drag." *In the Know* 1, no. 4: n.p.

Prest, Julia. 2006. *Theatre under Louis XIV: Cross-Casting and the Performance of Gender in Drama, Ballet, and Opera*. New York: Palgrave Macmillan.

Preston, Sophia. 1998. "Iconography and Intertextuality: The Discreet Charm of Meaning." *Proceedings of Society of Dance History Scholars 21st Annual Conference*. Riverside: University of California Press, 241–52.

Preston, Sophia. 2000. "Echoes and Pre-Echoes: The Displacement of Time in Mark Morris's *Dido and Aeneas*." *Proceedings of Dancing in the Millennium: An International Conference* (Riverside, CA: Society of Dance History Scholars, et al., 2000), 344–48.

Preston, Sophia. 2014. "Mark Morris and the American Avant-Garde: From Ultra-Modernism to Postmodernism." *Dance Chronicle* 37, no. 1: 6–46.

Pyle, Katie. N.d. Description of *The Firebird, A Ballez*. http://cargocollective.com/katypyle/THE-FIREBIRD-a-Ballez.

Pyle, Katie. 2016. Personal interview. September 20.

Reardon, Christopher. 2001. "Errand into the Maze." *Village Voice*, January 9. http://www.villagevoice.com/2001-01-09/news/errand-into-the-maze.

Riding, Alan. 1996. "A Russian Legend Carries on without Russia." *New York Times*, May 5, 11.

Riggs-Leyva, Rachael. 2013. "Reading Music, Gesture, and Dualism in Mark Morris' *Dido and Aeneas*." In *Dance on Its Own Terms: Histories and Methodologies*, ed. Melanie Bales and Karen Eliot. Oxford: Oxford University Press, 389–410.

Ritenburg, Heather Margaret. 2010. "Frozen Landscapes: A Foucauldian Genealogy of the Ideal Ballet Dancer's Body." *Research in Dance Education* 11, no. 1: 71–85.

Roach, Joseph R. 1996. *Cities of the Dead: Circum-Atlantic Performance*. New York: Columbia University Press.

Rodríguez, Juana María. 2014. *Sexual Futures, Queer Gestures, and Other Latina Longings*. New York: New York University Press.

Román, David. 1992. "It's My Party and I'll Die if I Want To!': Gay Men, AIDS, and the Circulation of Camp in U.S. Theatre." *Theatre Journal* 44, no. 3: 305–327.

Román, David. 1998. *Acts of Intervention: Performance, Gay Culture, and AIDS.* Bloomington: Indiana University Press.

Román, David. 2005. *Performance in America: Contemporary U.S. Culture and the Performing Arts.* Durham, NC: Duke University Press.

Román, David. 2006. "Remembering AIDS: A Reconsideration of the Film *Longtime Companion*." *GLQ* 12, no. 2: 281–301.

Salamon, Gayle. 2010. *Assuming a Body: Transgender and Rhetorics of Materiality.* New York: Columbia University Press.

Salamon, Gayle. 2014. "Rethinking Gender: Judith Butler and Feminist Philosophy." In *Emerging Trends in Continental Philosophy*, edited by Todd May. New York: Routledge, 13–30.

Salamon, Gayle. 2015. "Passing Period: Gender, Aggression, and the Phenomenology of Walking." In *Phenomenology and Performance*, edited by Jon Foley Sherman, Eirini Nedelkopoulou, and Maaike Bleeker. New York: Routledge, 186–203.

Samuels, Steven, ed. 1992. *Ridiculous Theatre: Scourge of Human Folly.* New York: Theatre Communications Group.

Sas, Miryam. 1999. *Fault Lines: Cultural Memory and Japanese Surrealism.* Stanford, CA: Stanford University Press.

Sas, Miryam. 2011. *Experimental Arts in Postwar Japan: Moments of Encounter, Engagement, and Imagined Return.* Cambridge, MA: Harvard University Asia Center.

Sayers, Leslie-Anne. 1993. "'She might pirouette on a daisy and it would not bend': Images of Femininity and Dance Appreciation." In *Dance, Gender, and Culture*, edited by Helen Thomas. London: Macmillan, 164–83.

Schacht, Steven P. 2002. "Turnabout: Gay Drag Queens and the Masculine Embodiment of the Feminine." In *Revealing Male Bodies*, edited by Nancy Tuana et al. Bloomington: Indiana University Press, 155–77.

Schechner, Richard. 1986. "Kazuo Ohno Doesn't Commute: An Interview." *Drama Review* 30, no. 2: 163–69.

Schechner, Richard. 1989. "Race Free, Gender Free, Body-Type Free, Age Free Casting." *Drama Review* 33, no. 1: 4–12.

Schewe, Elizabeth. 2009. "Serious Play: Drag, Transgender, and the Relationship between Performance and Identity in the Life Writing of RuPaul and Kate Bornstein." *Biography* 32, no. 4: 670–95.

Shnayerson, Michael. 2013. "One by One." *Vanity Fair*, http://www.vanityfair.com/culture/1987/03/devastation-of-aids-1980s. Originally published March 1987.

Scholz-Cionca, Stanca. 2010. "The Void Embodied: An Encounter of *Butō* and *Nō* in Okamoto Akira's *Mu.*" In *Avant-gardes in Japan. Anniversary of Futurism and Butō: Performing Arts and Cultural Practices between Contemporariness and Tradition*, edited by Katja Centonze. Venice: Libreria Editrice Cafoscarina, 161–71.

Scolieri, Paul A. 2013. "'An Interesting Experiment in Eugenics'": Ted Shawn, American Dance, and the Discourses of Sex, Race, and Ethnicity." In *The Oxford Handbook of Dance and Ethnicity*, edited by Anthony Shay and Barbara Sellers-Young. Oxford: Oxford University Press, 186–209.

Sedgwick, Eve Kosofsky. 2003. *Touching Feeling: Affect, Pedagogy, Performativity.* Durham, NC: Duke University Press.

Senelick, Laurence. 2000. *The Changing Room: Sex, Drag, and Theatre.* London: Routledge.

Senior, Jennifer. 2002. "Mark Morris." *New York Magazine*, December 16. http://nymag.com/nymetro/arts/dance/n_8102/index1.html.

Serano, Julia. 2012. "Reclaiming Femininity." In *Transfeminist Perspectives In and Beyond Transgender and Gender Studies*, edited by A. Finn Enke. Philadelphia: Temple University Press, 170–83.

Shapiro, Peter. 2005. *Turn the Beat Around: The Secret History of Disco.* New York: Faber and Faber.

Shaw, Mary Lewis. 1993. *Performance in the Texts of Mallarmé: The Passage from Art to Ritual.* University Park: Pennsylvania State University Press.

Shay, Anthony. 2008. *Dancing across Borders: The American Fascination with Exotic Dance Forms.* Jefferson, NC: McFarland.

Sheena, Tara. 2013. "A Day in the Life with Katy Pyle." *The Dance Enthusiast*, May 12. http://www.dance-enthusiast.com/features/view/A-Day-in-the-Life-with-Katy-Pyle-2013-05-12.

Shewey, Don. 1978. "Charles Ludlam and the Ridiculous Theatrical Company." *Boston Phoenix*, June. http://www.donshewey.com/theater_articles/charles_ludlam.html.

Shewey, Don. 1987. *Caught in the Act: New York Actors Face to Face.* New York: Plume.

Shewey, Don. 2002. "'Be True to Yearning': Notes on the Pioneers of Queer Theater." In *The Queerest Art: Essays on Lesbian and Gay Theater*, edited by Alisa Solomon and Framji Minwalla. New York: New York University Press, 124–34.

Shulgold, Marc. 2008. "Parody Points at Ballet." *Rocky Mountain News*, September 10. http://m.rockymountainnews.com/news/2008/Sep/10/parody-points-at-ballet.

Shulman, Sarah. 2012. *The Gentrification of the Mind: Witness to a Lost Imagination.* Berkeley: University of California Press.

Siegel, Marcia. 1968. *At the Vanishing Point: A Critic Looks at Dance*. New York: Saturday Review Press.

Siegel, Marcia. 1987. "Brat Ballerina and the Forces of Evil: A Romance." Review of *Dancing on My Grave*, by Gelsey Kirkland. *Hudson Review* 40, no. 1: 131–35.

Siegel, Marcia. 2003. "One-Man Martha: Richard Move Does It All for You." *Boston Phoenix*, February13–20. http://www.bostonphoenix.com/boston/arts/dance/documents/02692376.htm.

Siegel, Marcia. 2008. "Dido's Fate." *Boston Phoenix*, June 3. http://thephoenix.com/Boston/Arts/62515-MARK-MORRISS-DIDO-AND-AENEAS.

Sigourney, Mica, and Monique Jenkinson. 2013. "Designing Women." TYPO International Design Talks, San Francisco, Contrast session. April 11. Yerba Buena Center for the Arts. http://typotalks.com/video/designingwomen.

Singer, Thea. 2008. "Reimagining 'Dido and Aeneas.'" *Boston Globe*, May 30. http://www.boston.com/ae/theater_arts/articles/2008/05/30/reimagining_dido_and_aeneas.

Singer, Toba. 2007. "Martha @ the JCCSF." *Ballet-Dance Magazine*, March 31. http://www.ballet-dance.com/200705/articles/Martha20070331.html.

"Sisters of Perpetual Indulgence." N.d. www.thesisters.org. The Sisters of Perpetual Indulgence Inc.

Smart, Mary Ann. 2004. *Mimomania: Music and Gesture in Nineteenth-Century Opera*. Berkeley: University of California Press.

Smiley, Lauren. 2012. "True and Faux." *San Francisco Magazine*, April 18. http://www.modernluxury.com/san-francisco/story/true-faux.

Smith, Kristin. 2011. "Faux Real—The Bold Italic—San Francisco." *The Bold Italic*, June 23. https://thebolditalic.com/faux-real-the-bold-italic-san-francisco-65bae0a814e.

Smith, Sid. 2012. "Trockaderos Revel in Paradox." *Chicago Tribune*, January 12.

Snorton, C. Riley. 2009. "'A New Hope': The Psychic Life of Passing." *Hypatia* 24, no. 3: 77–92.

Soehnlein, K. M. 2013. "Juanita MORE!: More Than Meets the Eye." *7x7*, August 7. http://www.7x7.com/arts-culture/juanita-more-0.

Sontag, Susan. 1999 (1964). "Notes on 'Camp.'" In Cleto, *Camp: Queer Aesthetics*, 53–65.

Straus, Rachel. 2008. "Men on Pointe." *Dance Spirit*, April, 84–87.

Stein, Bonnie Sue. 1986. "Butoh: Twenty Years Ago We Were Crazy, Dirty, and Mad." *Drama Review* 30, no. 2: 107–26.

Stoneley, Peter. 2007. *A Queer History of the Ballet*. London: Routledge.

Strings, Sabrina, and Long T. Bui. 2014. "She Is Not Acting, She Is." *Feminist Media Studies* 14, no. 5: 822–36.

Sulcas, Rosyln. 2010. "Radical Turn for the Trocks' Youngest Sylph." *New York Times*, December 9, C3.

Sweete, Barbara Willis. 1995. *Mark Morris Dance Group in Dido and Aeneas*. DVD. Canada: Rhombus Media.

Taylor, Diana. 2003. *The Archive and the Repertoire: Performing Culture Memory in the Americas*. Durham, NC: Duke University Press.

Taylor, Verta, and Leila J. Rupp. 2004. "Chicks with Dicks, Men in Dresses: What It Means to Be a Drag Queen." In *The Drag Queen Anthology: The Absolutely Fabulous but Flawlessly Customary World of Female Impersonators*, edited by Steven P. Schacht and Lisa Underwood. Binghamton, NY: The Haworth Press: 113–33.

Thomas, Helen. 2003. *The Body, Dance, and Cultural Theory*. New York: Palgrave Macmillan.

Thoms, Victoria. 2008. "Martha Graham's Haunting Body: Autobiography at the Intersection of Writing and Dancing." *Dance Research Journal* 40, no. 1: 3–16.

Thoms, Victoria. 2013. *Martha Graham: Gender and the Haunting of a Dance Pioneer*. Bristol: Intellect. Distributed by University of Chicago Press.

*Time Out New York*. 2000. "Martha, My Dear," October 19–26.

Tomkins, Calvin. 1976. "Ridiculous." *New Yorker*, November 15, 55–98.

Torr, Diane. 2010. "Q&A with Diane Torr, Co-author of *Sex, Drag, and Male Roles: Investigating Gender as Performance*." University of Michigan Press blog. http://blog.press.umich.edu/2010/10/qa-with-diane-torr-co-author-of-sex-drag-and-male-roles-investigating-gender-as-performance.

Torr, Diane, and Stephen Bottoms. 2010. *Sex, Drag, and Male Roles: Investigating Gender as Performance*. Ann Arbor: University of Michigan Press.

Tracy, Robert. 1996. *Goddess: Martha Graham's Dancers Remember*. New York: Limelight Editions.

Tracy, Robert, and Sharon DeLano. 1983. *Balanchine's Ballerinas: Conversations with the Muses*. New York: Linden Press.

Trebay, Guy. 1996. "Mother Knows Best: The Cloning of Jackie 60." *Village Voice*, September 17, 20.

Trebay, Guy. 2010. "History Moves in Tutus and Greasepaint." *New York Times*, December 29, E5.

Ulrich, Allan. 2010. "Marching to a Different Drummer." *Dance Magazine* 84, no. 11: 26–28.

Upper, Nancy. 2004. *Ballet Dancers in Career Transition: Sixteen Success Stories*. Jefferson, NC: McFarland.

Vaccaro, Jeanne. 2010. "Felt Matters." *Women and Performance* 20, no. 3: 253–66.

Valenti, Chi Chi. 2016. Personal interview. September 21.

Velez, Edin, and Ethel Velez. 1990. *Butoh: A Dance of Darkness*. DVD. Alive from Off Center. St. Paul/Minneapolis, MN: KTCA and Walker Arts Center.

Volcano, Del LaGrace, and Jack [Judith] Halberstam. 1999. *The Drag King Book*. London: Serpent's Tail.

Wainwright, Steven P., and Bryan S. Turner. 2004. "Narratives of Embodiment: Body, Aging, and Career in Royal Ballet Dancers." In *Cultural Bodies: Ethnography and Theory*, edited by Helen Thomas and Jamilah Ahmed. Malden, MA: Blackwell Publishing, 98–120.

Ward, Jane. 2010. "Gender Labor: Transmen, Femmes, and Collective Work of Transgression." *Sexualities* 13, no. 2: 236–54.

Warner, Sara. 2012. *Acts of Gaiety: LGBT Performance and the Politics of Pleasure*. Ann Arbor: University of Michigan Press.

Wenzel, Ryan. 2012. "Playing Her Own Worst Enemy: 12 Questions for Mark Morris Dance Group's Amber Star Merkens." *Bodies Never Lie: A Blog about Dance in New York*. August 15. https://mmdg.dms-secure.com/documents/8-15-12_Playing_Her_Own_Worst_Enemy_Dido_ASM.pdf.

Wolf, Marina. 2000. "Men in Tights: Les Ballets Trockadero Are More Than Fluffy Skirts and Nice Legs." *Sonoma County Independent*, February 24–March 1. http://www.metroactive.com/papers/sonoma/02.24.00/lesballets-0008.html.

Zeitlin, Froma I. 1985. "Playing the Other: Theater, Theatricality, and the Feminine in Greek Drama." *Representations* 11: 63–94.

Zimmer, Elizabeth. 1994. "Comfort Zone: Anita Hill Revenged with Tenderness." *Village Voice*, December, 33–35.

# Index